Upper End of Waterfall, Hagavatn Lake, Central Iceland, 1972. Eliot Porter (1901–1990). © 1990
Amon Carter Museum of American Art. Image copyright © The Metropolitan Museum of Art.
AR6158257. Image source: Art Resource, NY 1979.625.36.

Where Cloud Is Ground

Where Cloud Is Ground

PLACING DATA AND MAKING
PLACE IN ICELAND

Alix Johnson

UNIVERSITY OF CALIFORNIA PRESS

University of California Press
Oakland, California

© 2023 by Alix Johnson

Library of Congress Cataloging-in-Publication Data

Names: Johnson, Alix (Anthropologist), author.
Title: Where cloud is ground : placing data and making place in Iceland /
    Alix Johnson.
Other titles: Atelier (Oakland, Calif.) ; 11.
Description: Oakland, California : University of California Press, [2023] |
    Series: Atelier : ethnographic inquiry in the twenty-first century ; 11 |
    Includes bibliographical references and index.
Identifiers: LCCN 2023005931 (print) | LCCN 2023005932 (ebook) |
    ISBN 9780520396357 (cloth) | ISBN 9780520396364 (paperback) |
    ISBN 9780520396371 (ebook)
Subjects: LCSH: Data centers—Iceland. | Data centers--Location. |
    Information retrieval—Iceland.
Classification: LCC HD9696.67.I22 J646 2023 (print) |
    LCC HD9696.67.I22 (ebook) | DDC 004.068094912—dc23
    /eng/20230621
LC record available at https://lccn.loc.gov/2023005931
LC ebook record available at https://lccn.loc.gov/2023005932

32 31 30 29 28 27 26 25 24 23
10 9 8 7 6 5 4 3 2 1

Contents

Figures

Acknowledgments

In the twelve years it took me to research and write this book, I moved no fewer than ten times. I dragged books, field notes, hiking boots, and hard drives from Berkeley to Oakland, to Montreal, to Kingston, to Gainesville, to Minneapolis, and back and forth from each of these places to Reykjavík at least once a year. This kind of trajectory is common, even relatively comfortable, by the standards of an early-career academic—still, the continual uprooting demanded by this profession is hard. That this work grew and eventually got done amidst all of it is thanks entirely to the people who supported my thinking and being in every place along the way.

I am grateful to Oscar Westesson for being the first person to tell me that you can get paid to go to grad school and suggesting I might be able to get in. With exactly that much information, I applied to UC Santa Cruz because it was close to Oakland and the ocean, and somehow that decision was one of the best I have made. I am so lucky to have worked there with Lisa Rofel, Andrew Mathews, and Don Brenneis, who always modeled incisive critique informed by care, and to have learned from Anna Tsing, Mayanthi Fernando, Danilyn Rutherford, Megan Moodie, and Jerry Zee. The friendship of Suraiya Jetha, S. A. Smythe, Sarah Kelman, and Stephanie McCallum made all the hard parts possible. Soreh Ruffman,

Tara Ramanathan, Savannah O'Neill, Jen Kateri Teschler, and Linda Tran were a home for me in those years.

That I got to start my career at the Ethnography Lab at Concordia University was an enormous gift offered, unnecessarily, by Kregg Hetherington, whose vision made that space so welcoming, weird, and full of life. The Surveillance Studies Centre at Queen's University was no less so, and I am grateful to have spent a postdoctoral year there buoyed by the boundless energies of David Murakami Wood. The University of Florida was the first place I landed long term, and where I finally gathered the courage, and was given the writing time, to return to my dissertation research and draft this book. Thanks go to Marit Østebø, Adrienne Strong, Rae Yan, and Richard Kernaghan for their camaraderie in that process, as well as Andrew Lanser for his research assistance. Today, I am so happy to finish the job at Macalester College, where I could not imagine a more committed department, supportive cohort of faculty, or brilliant class of undergraduates. I am continually bowled over by the privilege of having found such a deeply livable intellectual home.

My debts in Iceland are many and indelible. Thanks first and foremost to all my interlocutors, named and unnamed in this book. Thank you to Gísli Pálsson for the warm welcome and quick connections to the world of Icelandic anthropology. Thank you to Kristín Loftsdóttir for supporting my research, sponsoring my visits at Háskóli Íslands, and inviting me over so often to your house. Thank you to Verena Höfig, the first person who taught me Icelandic, and to Svala Lind Bernudóttir, the most long-suffering one. And thank you to Julia Brenner, Noam Orr, Gunnhildur Helga Katrínardóttir, Elfar Smári Sverrison, Baldur Brynjarson, Brynja Bjarnadóttir, Birkir Brynjarson, and Ragnheiður Harpa Leifsdóttir for making Reykjavík the place it is to me. All my travel to, research in, and writing about Iceland has been made possible by grants and fellowships from the National Science Foundation, the Wenner-Gren Foundation, the American Council of Learned Societies, the American-Scandinavian Foundation, the Leifur Eiríksson Foundation, and the University of Florida Humanities Scholarship Enhancement Fund.

The text that follows has been made so much better by the attentions of Stephanie McCallum, Zahirah Suhaimi-Broder, Nishita Trisal, Kali Rubaii, Norma Möllers, Katie Pace, Alison Cool, Vijayanka Nair, Nafis

Hasan, Nicole Starosielski, Dominic Boyer, Jenna Burrell, Roberto González, and Ashley Carse. My Atelier cohort—Sahana Ghosh, Kaya Williams, and Keisha-Khan Perry—have been a refuge and a big reason anything got written at all. Colin Hoag has not yet read any of this, and still somehow offered vital insights on multiple occasions. The collective spaces I've held with Jen Hughes, Chloe Ahmann, Ali Feser, Amy Leia MacLachlan, and Erin McFee have vitally offset the loneliness of academic writing, and the friendship/group chat of Eda Pepi, Vivian Chenxue Lu, Megan Steffen, Mingwei Huang, and Susan MacDougall has been one of the best things forged in the trauma bonds of grad school. Kelsey Johnson, thank you for everything—we really have come a long way.

At the University of California Press and in the Atelier Series, Kate Marshall, Francisco Reinking, and Kevin O'Neill go above and beyond. I so appreciate the truly wild amount of material, intellectual, and personal support they have shown me. Thank you to Chad Attenborough for administrative heavy lifting, Linda Gorman for copyediting, and Bill Nelson for cartographic work.

Thank you to my parents, Alan and Lily Johnson, for loving me and always letting me do my own thing. Finally, thank you to Bragi Brynjarsson, my favorite person, for the impossibly good life we make wherever we go.

Excerpts and ideas from chapters 1, 3, and 4 have appeared in *Culture Machine*, *American Ethnologist*, *American Anthropologist*, and the *Journal of Environmental Media*. Thank you to the editors for allowing me to republish this material.

Note on Language and Naming

Rather than transliterating Icelandic words into English, I have left untranslated words in their original form. While most of the Icelandic alphabet will be familiar to English readers, a handful of letters lack direct equivalents. I offer the following pronunciation guide for readers to follow along:

Ð / ð: "th," as in "weather"

Þ / þ: "th," as in "think"

Á / á: "ow," as in a response to an injury

Æ / æ: "aye," as in the antiquated assent

Ö / ö: between the stalling words "eh" and "uh"

É / é: "yeh," as in "yep"

LL / ll: "tl," as in "atlas," but pronounced with a voiceless l

Icelandic names will also likely look familiar, and yet distinctive to non-Icelandic readers. What is important to know is that Icelanders' first names are given, but their last names are patronymics: Björk Guðmundsdóttir means "Björk, Guðmund's daughter" and Darri Ingólfsson is "Darri, Ingólf's son." Accordingly, when referencing people in

Iceland—even famous or unfamiliar ones—first names, rather than last names, are used. For example, Iceland's current president is referred to as "Guðni" and never "President Jóhannesson." One exception to this convention, however, is when Icelandic academics are published in international scholarly works. In this case, authors are typically cited by their patronym. For example, works citing Guðni Jóhannesson (a historian in addition to Iceland's president) would follow the format "Jóhannesson 2015." In the following writing, I use first names to reference Icelandic interlocutors, pseudonymized except in the case of public figures speaking in their official capacity, and patronymics in reference to Icelandic authors of published works.

Introduction

PUTTING DATA IN ITS PLACE

Where Cloud Is Ground is a story about data and place, told from one especially unsettled nexus of technological, geopolitical, and environmental change. It sets out to show how digital data—often imagined as diffuse, ephemeral, immaterial—emerges from particular social and material landscapes, is shaped by them, and reshapes them, in turn. It contends that this data is both a product of place and an essential instrument in the making and claiming of place, today. It makes this case through ethnographic attention to the development of a data storage industry in Iceland: the construction, in industrial parks, across countrysides, and along coastlines, of data centers, or facilities where large quantities of data are processed and stored.

Centering place in a story about data may seem anachronistic, even irrelevant. After all, the language we tend to use to talk about data is resolutely placeless. *The cloud*, our current term for the way in which we access computing products and services over the internet, conjures the feeling that our data is "everywhere and nowhere in particular" (Carruth 2014, 340). As it has become more possible to store and process data at a distance, the vast majority of computation has shifted from servers stored inside our homes and offices to data centers sited around the world. And as

1

the infrastructures supporting our digital experience get more distributed, it is easier than ever to conceive of the internet as abstract, while harder to consider the question of where our data comes from, and where it goes.

But our data does not condense from nothing and nowhere, nor does it hover benignly in the sky. Fiber-optic cables traverse seabeds to connect continents; internet exchange points physically append multiple networks; and data centers, described by Jen Holt and Patrick Vonderau as "the heart of the cloud and much of its physical infrastructure" (2015, 75), house the servers that store the data on which our online lives depend.

In recent years, Iceland has emerged as a growing hot spot for the international data storage industry. A range of actors here (Icelanders and others) have set about making the case that the island is an especially good place for data to be. This book traces this process of attracting data to Iceland, of making it fit and making it stick here. That work has included activism and engineering, earth moving, parliamentary debates, and professional nation branding. It has also involved displacements, exclusions, and extractions.

We can appreciate as much by considering one landscape that readers are likely to recognize: Iceland's famous interplay of "fire and ice." From seventeenth-century travelogues to today's highly successful tourism campaigns, the island has been associated in outsiders' imaginations with, on the one hand, its sweeping glacial vistas, and, on the other hand, with the thirty active volcano systems that routinely churn red-hot magma up from the earth. Together, these two forces produce an inimitable landscape, in which massive waterfalls cascade over chiseled basalt columns, windswept desert opens up onto lush pastureland, and waves crash onto craggy beaches with sand in striking black and red. In and around the data center, however, fire and ice produce new meanings and new material consequences. Take the perspectives of three of my interlocutors: Mateo, Egill, and Natan.[1]

Mateo is an American data center developer who splits his time between Iceland and the United States. As part of the management team of a data center I'll call Arctera,[2] and a seasoned public speaker on behalf of the industry, he graciously offered to give me the grand tour of his facility in Southwest Iceland. As he led me into a data hall filled with neatly stacked computer servers, Mateo told me that "the abiding principle of a data center is managing hot and cold air." This is because computational processing generates heat—the same warmth you feel building at the back of your computer if you leave it running too long on your lap—and when servers get hot they run inefficiently, even risk burning themselves out. So for data centers, which house hundreds or even thousands of servers, managing temperature (as well as humidity) is key. At Arctera, this careful balance is established by organizing servers in a series of back-to-back pairs. This staggered system creates what are called "hot aisles" and "cold aisles," or microclimates we could feel on the surface of our skin: cool air was blown up through the floor below us, while the hot air emitted at the back of each server was trapped and efficiently filtered away.

In a warmer climate, like Mateo's native Florida, this cooling process would be very costly, requiring intensive air conditioning. "But in Iceland," Mateo said, smiling, "you just open the windows." What's more, Iceland's glacial rivers and geothermal fields (a product of the island's tectonic activity) produce an annual excess of inexpensive energy, which data centers use to keep their servers running twenty-four hours a day. It was precisely this combination of climate and energy that convinced Arctera to site its data center here. For Mateo, then, Iceland's fire and ice are natural assets that make the island inherently well suited to the industry; they are resources that, with a little engineering, support the basic mission of the data center seamlessly.

·   ·   ·   ·   ·

Egill is an Icelander with a background in business, who works at a state-backed but privately partnered agency whose mandate is to attract foreign direct investment. About a decade ago, he was tapped to head up a fledgling effort to build a data center industry in Iceland. So he set about learning how to pitch to people like Mateo—developers looking for a new place to build—and he has carried out that mission with impressive success. Egill's agency often uses natural imagery in its promotional material. Over the years I have collected, from his downtown Reykjavík office, brochures that feature rushing rivers, snow-capped mountains, and almost impossibly blue glacial lagoons. These photos are meant to evoke the connotations Mateo spoke to—the cool climate and abundant energy that can be harnessed for the data center sector. But Egill, who keeps his finger on the pulse of industry trends and investor attitudes, also knows he has to be careful in communicating this idea of Iceland to the outside.

Consider the Eyjafjallajökull eruption of 2010. Egill and his team had been active for a few years then, making contacts and making the rounds at trade shows, starting to gin up international interest in Iceland as a data center locale. And then, the volcano Eyjafjallajökull erupted, creating an ash cloud that rode the jet stream to Europe and grounded flights across the continent for a week. "You know, not a single light bulb in Iceland went out in that eruption," Egill told me wearily. There was vanishingly little property damage and virtually no injuries. But investors were spooked by the volcano all the same. "People would see our table at the conferences and walk right past us," Egill said. "It was like they thought the whole island was on fire." So after years of focusing their promotional efforts on Iceland's wild and powerful nature, Egill and his team turned to damage control. For the first time, they featured an image of the Reykjavík cityscape on the home page of their investor website. Fire and ice, then, for Egill are symbolic resources to be managed strategically—part of a carefully crafted image of Iceland that walks a fine line between abundance and excess.

.   .   .   .   .

Natan is an environmental activist. Though still young, he has invested much of his life and career in conversations about how Icelanders should relate to the landscape they are, in his view, lucky enough to live amidst. In the past years, Natan has turned his attention to the environmental impact of the data storage industry. Natan told me he isn't against data centers on principle—he understands they serve a function and need energy to run. What he takes issue with is the staging of Iceland as an enclave for them, and more specifically of Iceland's energy potential as endless and without impact. Geothermal energy, he reminds me, comes from drilling boreholes; hydropower comes from damming rivers. As the data center industry continues to expand in Iceland, more energy will be required to meet its needs.

When I asked Natan what motivates his activism on this subject, he told me that his answer to this question had changed: "Five years ago, I probably would have said we should save nature so people could go and appreciate it. I would have said we should preserve nature for the next generations." But more recently, he has come to understand that position as "too human-centered," and thus not really in line with his values. "Now I say nature should be protected for its own sake, because we have no right to destroy it." By way of example, he turned our conversation toward the ongoing volcanic eruption at Geldingadalir Valley that had started about a month before. As the lava from it had started to slowly flow in the direction of a roadway, construction crews were busily erecting land barriers to reroute its path. "Of course," Natan said, "many people are in favor. But there are also those who say we should let nature take its course, we should appreciate seeing what the lava does on its own. Almost like the lava has its own rights." For Natan, Iceland's fire and ice operate by their own logics, belonging only and fundamentally to themselves. To channel them toward the digital demands of a human population would be shortsighted and unjustifiable.

.   .   .   .   .

These brief snapshots each provide a different entry point into the process of placing data in Iceland: Mateo builds and operates data centers, Egill paves the way for them to come, and Natan endeavors to shift public opinion toward reckoning with their broader impacts. From their different vantage points, they are all deeply and divergently engaged in negotiating the relationship between data and the Icelandic landscape. The chapters that come follow their, and various others', efforts. They also look beyond Iceland's geophysical features to consider how data is equally situated amidst national identities, historical narratives, and postcolonial politics on the North Atlantic's Arctic edge.

In this, the following work has three aims: first, to shed empirical light on data storage infrastructure and industry, in particular how the rapidly proliferating facilities that house our digital data are sited, sold, and run. Tracing these often invisibilized constellations of land, labor, affect, and capital is a vital aspect of understanding our increasingly online lives. The book's second aim is to theorize the broader relationship between place and data, interrogating the ways that data depends on place, and place depends on data in turn. It does so by taking data storage as a window into still-open questions of spatial politics, sovereignty, and imperial power in Iceland. Finally, its third aim is to offer one model for engaging with the so-called cloud ethnographically, a project in which anthropologists are increasingly enrolled (Douglas-Jones, Walford, and Seaver 2021). Today, even those of us who don't set out to study these systems will nevertheless find them mediating our field experiences, and our interlocutors' lives; in the process, we are faced with new questions—and old ones—about our objects, ethics, and epistemologies. This book offers one example of what it might look like to inquire into what this data is, what it does, and why it matters where it lives.

WHERE DATA LIVES

Attending to the site of data's physical storage, the particular patches of ground that data centers occupy, is only one way of understanding data's relationship to place. One might just as well ask how data constitutes urban spaces (Mattern 2017, 2021), or how data is mobilized in drawing borders and defending them (Chaar-López 2020; Möllers 2020). One might equally trace the ways that data produces space as racialized and is marshalled in the deployment of policing and state violence (Benjamin 2019; Brayne 2020). Or, one might consider the potential of data, collected and directed with care, to foster dynamic and decolonial relationships to locality (Duarte 2017; Hunt and Stevenson 2016). Data storage, then, opens just one window among others onto the project of placing data in the world. But it is, I hope to show, an illuminating vantage point.

A data center, also known colloquially as a "server farm," is simply a facility where data is processed or stored. These are sites where multiple—and often many—servers are run at the same time, sharing space and pooling resources like air conditioning and electricity. Conceptually, data centers are heirs to the "computer rooms" of the 1940s and 1950s, when sprawling mainframes required their own dedicated spaces and technical teams. Computation then took place within a centralized architecture, a single engine at the heart of a corporation or government agency. With the development, however, of microchips and personal computers in the

1980s, computational power was redistributed. While data centers were still needed to accommodate the operations of large-scale organizations, most individuals had all the power and storage they needed built into their own PCs.

This dynamic shifted again, however, at the turn of the twenty-first century, with the advent of cloud computing. As our digital demands exponentially expanded, the means to store and manage all this data moved from the confines of our own computers to the ever-expanding online. For example, rather than downloading music or video files, most consumers today stream media from third-party service providers, to which they pay subscription fees. They access applications ("software as a service") through web browsers as often as they download them. And rather than cull proliferating photos and documents to fit within the limitations of their own hard drives, they purchase real estate for all that data in the cloud. Tom Boellstorff aptly describes this recentralization of computational resources as a "return to the mainframe in virtual form" (2010, 5). Data centers are essential architecture in this new arrangement.

Today, data storage is a $50 billion industry.[3] At the time of my research it was estimated that there were over three million data centers in operation (Carruth 2014), and more were being constructed around the world at a rate increasing by 15 percent every year (Hogan 2018). The utility of these numbers is limited, however, by the expansive variety of operations and facilities. A server room in a corporate office counts as a data center. So, too, does the China Mobile facility in Hong Kong, the world's largest data center at the time of this writing, clocking in at 7.7 million square feet. Another way, then, of understanding the scale of data storage is attending to what those data centers store. The International Data Corporation, a market research firm, estimated the collective sum of global data at thirty-three zettabytes (ZB; one zettabyte is equal to one sextillion bytes) in 2018. It also predicted this number would grow to 175 ZB by 2025, with the majority of this data stored in data centers.[4] Yet another metric for measuring data centers is by the electricity they consume. A moderately sized ten-megawatt data center uses about as much energy as 5,000 homes. Meanwhile, the world's most power-hungry data center currently uses 150 megawatts a year. Taken together, data centers accounted at the time of my research for 416 terawatt hours, or roughly 3 percent of all power generated worldwide.[5] Or, as the environmental organization Greenpeace put it, if the cloud were a country, its energy consumption would be the fifth largest in the world.[6]

These figures—and the way they feed into a growing network of international infrastructures and industries[7]—position data storage as an increasingly urgent object of inquiry. They also lead me to propose two analytic shifts: first, from an emphasis on data flow to data *fixity*, and second, from a focus on data's contents to data's *forms*.

Contemporary imaginaries of data are defined by motion: from the idea that communicative connection "compresses space-time" to the oft-quoted adage that "information wants to be free." Speed is our primary metric for understanding internet access, and much of data's transformative potential is understood in terms of its ability to travel across traditional borders and boundaries. In Iceland, telecommunications are often described as "arteries" or "life veins" (*lífæð*) of society, calling up a ceaseless, circulatory churn (Bjarnason 2010). Meanwhile, the English-language metaphor of "streaming" suggests the "continuous, uninterrupted processuality of data transmission" (Denecke 2020) and imbues this transmission with a bucolic, riverine quality. Tapping into Enlightenment-era ideals of a world in motion (Mattelart 2000), data is most often understood as mobile, meaningful not in its mere existence but for the fact of its unhindered flow.

Data centers, however, complicate this common sense. As facilities where data stops and tends to stay awhile, data centers instantiate a kind of stasis as essential as the cloud's many mobilities. While immobility in relation to infrastructure often signals its failure or breakdown, in the case of distributed computing it is a feature rather than a bug. In fact, storage is integral to the way our informational lives are organized, and it has been for quite some time. Media theorist Friedrich Kittler, for example, conceptualized the paper book's innovation as harnessing "unstorable data flows," and that of the gramophone as its disruption of "writing's storage monopoly" (1999 [1986], 9, 70). Storage emerged as a central concern for the cyberneticians of the 1950s and '60s, who dreamed of a total database of information but worried over the practicalities of access (Halpern 2015). And disk storage, located in the hard drive since the 1980s, has since been read as a key metric for advances in computational technology (Kirschenbaum 2012).

But today, a computer's hard drive is just the tip of the iceberg; the majority of its users' data will come to rest somewhere else. And if storage has always been linked to location,[8] implying a putting of things in their place, today the physical footprint of data storage is both bigger than ever, and less evident. Turning, then, from considerations of data flow to data *fixity*, I suggest that as much as we need to understand data's movements, we also need to understand how data is made to stay in place. Such a project makes clear how the ordering of data also entails particular orderings of space, stuff, and sociality—that is to say, it conditions and arranges particular forms.

When social scientists address ourselves to digital data, as we increasingly have in recent years, we tend to focus on its contents. By data's contents, I mean the specific information that gets encoded into ones and zeroes, bits and bytes. Scholars have asked how particular leaks and viral videos, selfies and datasets, hashtags, and search terms are coming to shape cultures, economies, and politics. In doing so, some have illustrated the ways that our data, far from being an objective reflection of reality, is shaped by social and cultural values (Gitelman and Jackson 2013; D'Ignazio and Klein 2020; Thylstrup et al. 2021); others have shown how data is collected and deployed toward deeply inequitable ends (Noble 2018; O'Neil 2016; Couldry and Mejías 2019; Eubanks 2011). This important and expanding body of research helps us understand what gets encoded within data, as well as what data can conceal, distort, and exclude. My own work is indebted to and aligned with these efforts, insofar as it seeks to understand and expose the function of power in relation to data, often obfuscated by claims to technological neutrality. It proceeds, however, from a different starting point: in this book, rather than data's contents, I am interested in taking seriously data's *forms*.[9]

By data's forms, I refer to the ways in which digital data as a worldly, often unwieldy, object exerts weight, directs force, and produces concentrations and displacements. Here I am thinking less of data's representational aesthetics or materialities (Dourish 2017; Manovich 2001; Walford 2020), and more of form as literary critic Caroline Levine has capaciously defined it: "an arrangement of elements—an ordering, patterning, or shaping" (2015, 3). I am thinking of the ways that data reorganizes the world. Data, to be saved, gets recorded on metal through the manipulation of magnetic fields by read-write heads. As it accumulates there, it fills hard drives and servers. Those servers stack up and fill data halls. Those data halls, linked and networked into a data center, might take the place of a farm or a factory; it might bend local tax law in its favor; it might draw technicians, construction crews, or even thieves. As one data center developer put it to me: "Running a data center is not like running a regular technology company. It's more like a real estate company with technology mixed in." Conceptualizing data in this register leads us toward different ways of reckoning with its impact.

A focus on data's forms shares much with recent reminders of the internet's irrepressible materiality. Academic and journalistic observers, upturning early ideas of digital ephemerality, have shown how our online lives are undergirded by wires, chips, routers, and screens, themselves composed of minerals mined from the earth.[10] Attending to the materiality of data centers, then—from their component parts to their power consumption—is one important piece of the following investigation into digital data's forms. But it is not the extent of it. A mere insistence on, or accounting of, the physical stuff involved in storing and processing data gives limited insight into why data centers have found a niche in Iceland, or the contours of the debates surrounding it now that it has. This kind of analysis requires sustained attention to the ways that meaning and materiality intertwine.

Consider, again, the question of "fire and ice." For Mateo, the American data center developer, these two dramatic features of the Icelandic landscape are resources his facility can consume. But Mateo was only introduced to their potential through Egill and his team, who perform the narrative labor of selling fire and ice as productive forces, fundamentally compatible with the information technology (IT) industry. This is no small feat since, as chapter 1 will detail, not long ago those same features signaled exactly the opposite: for centuries, the extremes of Icelandic climate and landscape were invoked by European observers to frame the island as hostile and "primitive." Furthermore, the elemental affordances of fire and ice need to be channeled in order to be made available: cold air is filtered in through data center windows, the flow of glacial melt directed through hydroelectric dams, the steam produced by tectonic instability harnessed through turbines and generators. The sheer physical presence of fire and ice, then, is just one part of the equation that has drawn data to Iceland in recent years; that process also relies on their deliberate arrangement, the marshalling of these distinct materialities into narrative as well as infrastructural forms.

As we will see, data's forms and fixities are inseparable from the histories, imaginaries, inequities, and aspirations that bring them into the world. They are shaped by colonial teleologies of technological "progress," gendered and racialized notions of digital deserving and competence, and national anxieties about sovereignty and national standing. They are also imbricated with landforms and earth processes that lend the construction of data centers particular traction and appeal. The question, then, is not only where data centers are located, a matter of compiling an exhaustive "cloud atlas" for our times.[11] Instead, I am interested in the project of *placing data*: how it articulates with already-existing discursive, social, and material orders, and how it enables or forecloses others yet to come. This is not just a call for attention to local particularity for its own sake (the anthropologist's too-easy answer to everything); it is a necessary effort if we want to understand the often invisible but nevertheless formidable world of data we are creating with our every click, swipe, and save.

ISLAND IN THE NET

Perhaps unsurprisingly for a small island in the North Atlantic, over seven hundred miles away from nearest land, information technology has played a prominent role in Icelandic national narrative. The first telegraph line, dragged ashore in 1906, is often told as a turning point in Icelandic history:[12] as Sigurveig Jónsdóttir and Helga Guðrún Johnson describe it in their official history of Icelandic telecommunications, "centuries of isolation had been broken and the [Icelandic] worldview changed" (2006). Later developments have slid rather seamlessly into this framework: for example, a 2003 statement from the Prime Minister's Office declares that "Over and above the way it affects other nations, IT has in a sense broken the barriers of Iceland's isolation. After all, Iceland is an island in the mid-Atlantic, which inevitably made it more difficult for residents to communicate and carry on business with the rest of the world."[13]

My own research in Iceland was often met with recitations of the same progress narrative, affirmations that the once-isolated island was becoming ever more connected. Take, for example, a story first told to me by Benedikt, a veteran engineer at Iceland's national telecommunications company, but then repeated so many times over the course of my fieldwork that I lost count. I was visiting Benedikt at his office in Reykjavík, asking after Iceland's fiber-optic cables, when he told me that understanding the contemporary network would require a bit of history he was happy to provide. In December of 1839, Benedikt told me, while Iceland was still a dependency of Denmark, the Danish King Frederick VI died. But back then, he said, "Iceland didn't just get news from abroad like it does now—we had to wait until the ship came in the spring. So that year," he said with the smirk of the twenty-first century citizen, "Icelanders celebrated Fridrik's birthday as usual, not even knowing our king was dead." Benedikt would go on that day to detail the development of telecommunications in Iceland—but the story he started with underlined the long way that the island, through its connections, has come.

The story of King Frederick, and the telegraph that ultimately looped the isolated Icelanders in, are classic examples of what media theorist Nicole Starosielski has termed "connection narratives": stories that herald the arrival of new technology as total, "a binary change of state from international separation to connection" (2015, 67). Connection narratives may rightfully highlight the profound and widespread changes associated with information technology. At the same time, Starosielski warns, these stories have important limitations, tending to shepherd our expectations down predictable paths. We might draw a very different line through Icelandic history, for example, if we focus less on information exchanged with its outside, and more on the information that has stayed in place—if we turn, that is, to Iceland's famous manuscript archive.

In a 1996 report titled "Vision of the Information Society," then–Prime Minister Davíð Oddsson wrote: "It so happens that Iceland's cultural heritage consists, for the most part, of information."[14] By this, Oddsson meant that material monuments are few and far between in Iceland. Since turf was the primary building material used before the 1900s, few such structures survived the centuries. What *has* persisted, however, thanks to the care and cultivation of Icelanders, is the written word: a unique collection of manuscripts dating back as far as the twelfth century. Texts ranging from family histories to land records to legal codes chronicle the period following the arrival of Norse settlers and their captives from the Irish and British Isles to the island around 870 CE.[15] Meanwhile, volumes of prose and poetic verse set down the skaldic tradition of Old Norse literature. The earliest of these texts were imprinted on calf skin, some of which persist in climate-controlled archives; others were copied and recopied over the centuries, their paper and colored illustrations marking innovations in information technology. A rich trove of data for historians, genealogists, and literary scholars,[16] more than three thousand manuscripts remain today, recognized by UNESCO as world cultural heritage. But the manuscripts, as both object and concept, have also played a vital role in Icelandic national history.

In 1262, following a period of protracted internal conflict, the settlers of Iceland (who by this time identified as Icelanders, their own distinctive group) submitted to the Kingdom of Norway, becoming a *skattland* ("tax land") or tributary of the crown. In 1397, Norway joined Sweden and Denmark in the Kalmar Union, and when the Union disbanded in the early 1500s, Iceland emerged as a dependency[17] of Denmark; it would remain one until 1944. These six centuries of foreign rule profoundly shaped Iceland, carving out for it a familiar place in colonial cartographies. The island was long perceived, and portrayed by outsiders, as an exotic and decidedly out-of-the-way place. The cartographer Ortelius's 1570 map, for example, depicted Iceland as a lonely land mass spewing magma, surrounded by a rich variety of sea monsters. Early European travelers emphasized the otherness of its inhabitants and struggled to sort them into familiar racial and cultural categories.[18] But where aspects of Iceland's landscape and material culture suggested distance or difference from an emergent European core, its collection of manuscripts created a connection.

In 1609 the Icelandic scholar and clergyman Arngrímur Jónsson published a treatise called *Crymogæa* (a Greek neologism for "Ice Land"). In it, he painted a proud picture of Iceland's early "golden age," describing the distinctive society, system of governance, and literary culture established in the Icelandic manuscripts. His Danish readers may have been put off by the text's patriotism, but they were nevertheless intrigued by the sources from which he drew—which included not only records of Icelandic settlement, but also a set of works known as the Kings' Sagas (*Konungasögur*), which chronicled the history of the Nordic kingdoms. Shortly thereafter, the Danish king commissioned Arngrímur to write a history of the Danish nation, based on the medieval Icelandic accounts; the Swedish crown would soon follow suit. Through these exchanges, in which what we might call Icelandic data was deployed in the service of the Scandinavian kingdoms, Iceland took on a new role as the cradle of Nordic civilization; the island came to be seen as a kind of archive where the past had been uniquely preserved.[19] As Danish politician Orla Lehman put it, the old Norse customs appeared to live on in Iceland, "as if frozen between the distant icy mountains, where the storms of time never reached."[20]

Such a designation, of course, cut both ways—being seen as someone else's history is, at best, a backhanded compliment. But Icelanders would strategically claim this association in their independence struggle, starting in the nineteenth century. As early nationalists agitated for Icelandic autonomy, they cited the manuscripts as national history and cultural heritage: proof of a distinctive and continuous society, eminently capable of governing itself. At the same time, Icelanders referenced their literary tradition in claiming racial and cultural proximity to Denmark in a way its other colonies never could.[21] For example, upon learning that Iceland was slated to be included in the 1905 Colonial Exhibition—a degrading display of the people, architecture, and artifacts of Denmark's colonial holdings—Icelanders expressed their outrage by declaring themselves a "culture nation" rather than a "nature nation," a distinction drawn from colonized people in Greenland, Africa, and the Caribbean (Loftsdóttir 2012). Rather than contesting the colonial order of things, then, nationalists used the manuscripts to make the argument that Iceland had been misclassified within it.

In the end, the Icelandic nationalists' strategy was successful: the island achieved a "peaceful secession" (Hálfdanarson 2000) from Denmark, attaining home rule in 1904, followed by formal sovereignty in 1918, and full status as an independent republic in 1944. But even as Iceland steadily extricated itself from colonial relations, the medieval manuscripts remained a point of contention. Over the course of the eighteenth century— during which Iceland was beset by famines and natural disasters—a large number of Icelandic manuscripts were shipped to Denmark, to be preserved and studied at the University of Copenhagen. Icelanders first called for their repatriation in 1907, were met with silence, and reiterated the request in 1930. This time, the demand provoked a substantial debate in the Scandinavian nations, turning on whether the manuscripts were properly Icelandic, or rather part of a broader Nordic patrimony. Ultimately, the Danish Parliament refused to acknowledge that Iceland had any legal claim to the manuscripts—but agreed nevertheless to return the majority as a "gift." The first texts returned, with great fanfare, to Reykjavík in 1971.

Through this very brief consideration of the Icelandic manuscripts—their preservation, mobilization, and ownership—my aim is not simply to echo (past and present) nationalists' assertions that Iceland's relationship to information is unique. Instead, I offer up this history to illustrate the kind of approach I propose in this book, one that goes beyond questions of information technology's "impacts" to ask how place gets made in relation to data, and how data gets made in relation to place.

To say that place is "made" entails an understanding of place as something more than a fixed and static backdrop against which the action of sociality occurs. In this view, developed across a number of disciplinary histories, place is understood instead as a process and project, always emergent and thus always open to change. Setha Low describes one such formulation, her framework of "spatializing culture," as "a dialogic process that links the social production of space and nature and the social development of the built environment with the social construction of space and place meanings" (2017, 7). In other words, place is (re)produced as people move through and make claims upon it; as skylines and sewage systems are pieced together; as narratives (factual and fictional) cohere. In Iceland, where the question of *what kind of place is this*—colonized or colonizer, core or periphery, isolated island or connected hub—has been puzzled over for centuries,[22] place-making is an explicit, and at times contested process. I do not seek to resolve but rather join in this puzzling as data gets enrolled in this ongoing work.

To return to the manuscripts: the emergence of Iceland as a continuously inhabited territory was recorded, and recopied, on those fragile vellum leaves. At the same time, as Icelandic nationalists suggested, the

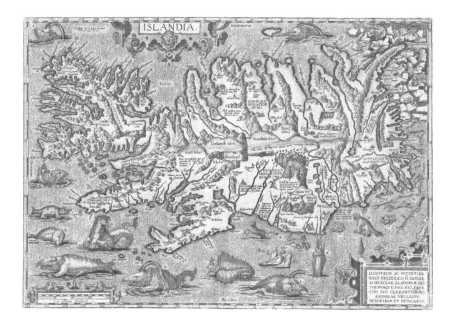

Figure 1. Map of Iceland published by Ortelius in 1570, exemplifying a historical view of Iceland as remote, exotic, and hostile.

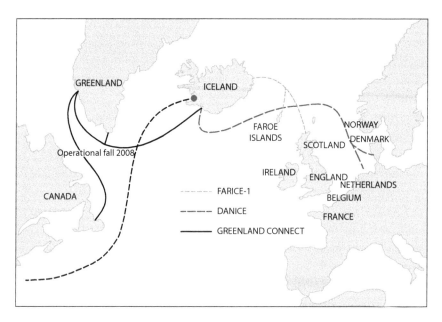

Figure 2. Map of Iceland's fiber-optic cable connections as of 2014, including a planned (since canceled) line to the United States.

very fact of keeping these records marked the emergence of an Icelandic people, distinctive from the societies from whence they came. Lastly, over the years, the right to maintain and access the manuscripts proved a salient site where colonial rule and postcolonial sovereignty were negotiated. Taking the manuscripts, then, as a starting point, we can see that identities and political claims in Iceland were being staked on the capacity to store and process information, long before computers ever could. What's more, we see how Iceland's ambiguous status as a "Northern borderlands" (Oslund 2011) troubling traditional boundaries mediates the role that information has played in Iceland, as well as the ways it has been strategically deployed. In *this* history, Iceland is not a given, stable entity, which straightforwardly benefits from access to IT; instead, particularly placed information is a key player in the making and claiming of Iceland. As Shannon Mattern writes, "Clay and code, dirt and data intermingle" (2017, xii). In taking up the question of data storage in Iceland, these are the dynamics—more than the transformations of new technology—I am most interested in accounting for.

When he invoked Iceland's "heritage of information," Prime Minister Davíð Oddsson set out to link Iceland's history to its then-imagined future in IT. The rest of his report, like many others issued in the 1990s, is saturated with tropes of digital connectivity, and its potential to usher in prosperity, development, and exchange. But as we have already seen, these are not the only things data can do. In keeping close to Iceland's specific—if notoriously unsteady—ground, then, this book asks what happens when data emerges not just as a fleeting, ephemeral presence, but as an enduring inhabitant of this particular place.

THE CLOUD AS GROUND

Large-scale data centers have the look and feel of warehouses, built for something awkwardly inhuman in nature and scale. Servers are stacked in towering rows, port lights flickering on one side and power cables trailing off on the other. The temperature inside is on the cool side of comfortable, actively managed, as Mateo showed me, through the constant exchange of hot and cold air. A low hum, the sound of hundreds of machines whirring in unison, sets off reverberations in your skin, teeth, and throat. This sheer and irrepressible physicality is what has led many observers to describe data centers as a place, sometimes *the* place, where the cloud meets or touches the ground. And yet, as the title of this ethnography intimates, I am making the case that something more happens here.

In Iceland I suggest that increasingly *the cloud is ground*, a provocation I intend to be taken in two ways. First, as we have already seen, the structures and infrastructures that support cloud computing are densely entangled with particular social and natural landscapes. Iceland's glacial rivers and geothermal wells fuel data centers, while its cold climate keeps their servers running comfortably. But connecting to these sources of sustenance, and ensuring their ongoing availability, entails signing contracts; breaking ground at construction sites; lobbying for tax incentives; and tapping into municipal politics. It means strategically invoking national stories and stereotypes, pulling forward particular historical threads. These are not merely ephemeral "touches," or moments where the cloud and ground incidentally "meet"; instead they signal the deliberate and consequential reorganization of space, politics, and earth processes. The cloud is ground where these transformations are taking place.

Second, I invoke the ground's conceptual meaning—as in the "grounds of an argument" or the "grounds for belief." In this sense, the ground refers to facts already established, a point of departure that can be taken as given, and thus taken for granted. The cloud and all that it makes possible—instantaneous access, continuous updates, infinite-seeming data storage—is quickly shifting into this territory. Most of us move confidently forward on the foundation that our data production and consumption are well supported and can continue to expand. Rarely do we stop to ask: What are the costs of this arrangement? Who bears them and who benefits? How is this distribution decided upon? The cloud is ground insofar as its planet-spanning infrastructures remain poorly understood and largely unremarked upon.

It was Geoffrey Bowker who introduced (1994), and with Susan Leigh Star developed (2000), the framework of figure and ground for the study of infrastructure. Shifting attention from the celebrated inventors and watershed moments typically imagined as the drivers of change, Bowker and Star focused instead on the technical standards, classification systems, protocols, and normative practices that enable the development and operation of technology, terming their method "infrastructural inversion." In claiming that the cloud is ground, I set up such an analysis, widely influential in anthropology—much of what follows traces the typically backgrounded infrastructure that undergirds our digital experience. But at the same time, I also draw attention to the difficulty of making such conceptual cuts. Is the cloud the innovation or is it the infrastructure? Is it the evident or the obscured? Where does the cloud end and its "social context," or its "surrounding environment" (see Ballestero 2019; Carse 2014), begin? Where cloud is ground, these questions are not easily answered, but they inform my long-term, multisited, and somewhat itinerant approach to this research.

This book draws on eight years[23] of fieldwork in Iceland (2012–2020), following four main groups of actors: state representatives marketing Iceland as a site for data center development; digital activists advocating for change in Icelandic law; data center executives and engineers operating facilities in Iceland; and residents of the Reykjanes Peninsula, where the data center industry is currently concentrated. The substance of these various lines of inquiry differed (sometimes drinking coffees, sometimes attending trade conferences, sometimes shadowing technicians in their work), while the boundaries between these groups often blurred. "Iceland is small," I was told, at least weekly—for example, one friend I made early in fieldwork turned out to be the sister of one key interlocutor *and* the ex-partner of another one. But working across them, I ask how data gets made "Icelandic" and how Iceland gets figured as a good place for data to live. Alongside participant observation (and where it was not possible), I conducted over eighty interviews, and also traced the work of placing data within Icelandic media.

The reader will note that this ethnography of data storage is only sometimes sited at data centers. This is a split focus that first felt like a limitation, but quickly became a deliberate choice. As I learned in the early days of preliminary fieldwork, my time at data centers would be circumscribed by security strictures (discussed in detail in chapter 5) that made sustained ethnography inside difficult. Concerns about theft, tampering, and corporate espionage mean that most data centers are closely guarded spaces, with only authorized (and supervised) visitors allowed inside. Over the years, I took advantage of the access available to me, arranging multiple visits inside multiple data centers. But the majority of my ethnographic project wound up unfolding outside these facilities, as I worked to untangle the broader relationship between data and place. That question took me further afield in Iceland: to Parliament and political party meetings in Reykjavík; to a fiber-optic cable landing station on the southeast coast; to the mouth of a glacial river in the West Fjords; and to various kitchen tables in Reykjanes where the drone of the nearest data center could be just faintly heard. I have found these sites to be just as constitutive of data storage in Iceland as the server farms, themselves. These, too, are places where cloud and ground comingle, and are reciprocally remade.

Digital data, of course, was stored, discussed, and dealt with in Iceland long before I arrived. But over the course of my ethnographic research, commercial data centers surfaced in Iceland and shifted from the niche of a select set of technicians to a topic of public commentary and concern. At the start of my fieldwork, two large-scale data centers operated in Iceland; two more were built during the time that I lived there, and several more have been erected since. By 2016, just four years after the industry arguably came into existence, data storage accounted for 1 percent of the island's GDP.[24] By the time I left my last extended period of fieldwork, real concerns were being raised about whether the island could support continued industry growth. This intensification, described variously as a "boom," "frontier," and "gold rush," is what first drew, then held my attention around these often-opaque infrastructures.

It is important, however, not to overstate the public presence of the data storage industry—data centers are by no means the primary issue most Icelanders feel they are faced with today. In this regard, a conversation I had while writing this book is telling: I was spending a long weekend in Hornstrandir, a secluded nature reserve in Iceland's West Fjords, when I struck up a conversation at the guest house with a young couple who had also come to stay. They asked what I did for a living and I told them, at which point one partner started peppering me with questions that revealed a keen attention to the industry's development. The other partner asked, "Wait, we have data centers here?" During the period I describe, then, data storage was not a determining influence on everyday life in Iceland; rather, it got braided into the fabric of that living, such that for many people it remained in the background, while for others it emerged as an undeniable event. The cloud, that is, flickered between figure and ground here as it does for so many of us elsewhere. These selective and contingent visibilities comprise, then, another line of inquiry in this account.

One last piece of my research process I want to surface at the outset is that the time period traversed in the following pages coincides with my own extended (and ongoing) process of making a place for *myself* in Iceland—first as an ethnographer, and eventually as a person who married and made a family here. That story is not foregrounded in the ethnography, but my shifting status as a person invested in this place, yet not of it, undoubtedly shaped the research I did. As my ties have deepened, I have gained some kinds of access as a fully vetted member of an Icelandic family; at the same time, I have felt the stakes of my engagement heighten as someone who is not entirely an outsider, and yet will never belong here effortlessly. As much, then, as I emphasize in these pages the particularity of the interface between data storage and Iceland, I also wish to underline the particularity of my own entry point: a situated position of being claimed, of making commitments, and of striving for the accountable kind of exchange Icelandic anthropologist Gísli Pálsson has called "democratic communion" (1995).

My own investments in Iceland, then, are multiple. But I hope to make the case over the following pages that you have reason to be invested, too. For one thing, through the cloud's complex distributions, you may be bound to this place through your data, whether or not you have ever set foot on its windswept soil. But even if your own data has not yet wound up here, the ongoing effort to accommodate digital infrastructure in Iceland raises questions that implicate and demand attention from all of us. The problems and possibilities of placing data are essential to contend with, wherever it is we call home.

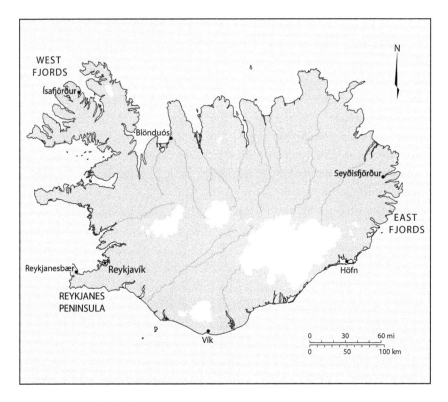

Figure 3. Map of Iceland.

THE CHAPTERS

The chapters in this book follow the decade-long development of an international data storage industry in Iceland. Tracing the efforts of selling, siting, building, and operating data centers, it takes each of these projects of placing data as, simultaneously, practices of making place.

Part 1 is concerned with *articulations* between Iceland and the data storage industry. These chapters interrogate the construction of Iceland as an especially good place for data to live—including efforts on the part of Icelanders to represent the island, engagement by outsiders drawn in by their own interests, and strategic coproductions between them. Both tack between historical imaginaries and contemporary configurations, paying attention to the ways the past is felt in the present, and the present makes its own claims upon the past.

Chapter 1 traces the tactics of state representatives pitching Iceland as a viable site for data center development. Unpacking their conference presentations and promotional materials, I examine their primary strategy of establishing a "natural fit" between Iceland and industry. Emphasizing appealing images of the Icelandic landscape, and tapping into long-standing ideas of Icelandic wilderness, these professionals make the case that Iceland is a unique place where data storage can be environmentally sustainable. But while some aspects of Iceland's environment are easily appropriated by the industry, others—for example, the island's tectonic volatility—need to be obscured or overcome. This chapter, then, shows how data is sustained by particular landscapes *and* is attracted by the (discursive and material) labor of mobilizing and modulating them.

Chapter 2 takes up the Icelandic Modern Media Initiative (IMMI), a 2010 parliamentary resolution with the stated intention of making Iceland an international "data haven." After Iceland's national standing was called into question following the 2008 financial crash, I suggest that IMMI attempted to restore the island's credibility by creating an exceptional data space—an effort that speaks to the centrality of data politics in the performance of liberal Western modernity. Tacking between the perspectives of information activists who inspired IMMI and functionaries tasked with implementing its ideals, this chapter tracks how data storage emerged as a salient political object, at the nexus of a universalizing discourse of "information freedom" and a specifically Icelandic catastrophe. While IMMI never achieved the legal intervention it aimed for, this chapter charts its aspirations, obstacles, and afterlife to examine the ideological commitments underpinning data's emplacement today.

Part 2 shifts to consider the work of constructing and operating data centers, as well as the experience of living in their vicinity. It asks how data gets practically *anchored* in Iceland—and to what effect—through close consideration of two locations chosen, cultivated, and changed by the data center industry.

Chapter 3 takes up the construction of data centers on Iceland's Reykjanes Peninsula, the primary site of industry development today. While data storage has been pitched here as a transformative development, this chapter shows how data centers fit into the footprint left by the last foreign presence on Reykjanes: the Naval Air Station Keflavík (NASKEF), a Cold War American military base active from 1953 to 2006. As data centers inherit the infrastructures of occupation, including its facilities, fences, and powerlines, I argue that they also reprise some of its social and spatial arrangements. Drawing primarily on ethnography with longtime Reykjanes residents, this chapter shows how lasting patterns of everyday exclusion, themselves indexing geopolitical inequalities, affix data in Reykjanes, today.

Chapter 4 interrogates emerging efforts to develop data centers in Iceland's countryside. Small towns, isolated by geography, infrastructure, and economics, are increasingly seeking out the IT industry in a bid for "connectivity," broadly conceived. But analyzing such efforts from the perspective of developers, I argue that the data storage industry is actually attracted to out-of-the-way places, and in many ways makes them more marginalized. Developing the concept of the *on-the-way* place, a figure that unsettles both techno-optimistic assumptions and anthropological understandings of marginality, this chapter disentangles digital integration from the promise of social and material gain. Doing so, it clears ground for a spatial critique of digital infrastructure and industry.

Finally, part 3 addresses itself to *excess*, or all that which fails to fit neatly in the nesting-doll equation of data contained in data centers, and data centers contained in Iceland. Chapter 5 tells the story of a high-profile data center break-in, known as "The Big Bitcoin Heist," alongside my own efforts to gain access to the industry. Considering questions of industry obscurity, I argue that while data center security protocols claim to protect the data inside, what they really shield are data centers' inequitable and extractive relations. This chapter, then, reframes the data center's "secret" as something not hidden away on the inside, but distributed, like the cloud itself, across the Icelandic landscape. Doing so, it makes a case for analyzing the data center inside out, that is to say, focusing less on its shielded insides, and more on its many and varied entanglements with the world outside its walls.

Where Cloud Is Ground thus sheds light on the complex life of digital data by specifying the distributions of distributed computing. It contends that where our data lives matters—not only because digital infrastructure and industry have local impacts, but also because place is made in relation to data and data is made in relation to place. Ultimately, this book shows how the uneven and unequal arrangement of digital data is not natural, automatic, or the inevitable outcome of a rational economic calculus. Instead, this always-emerging geography is densely entangled with land-forms and earth processes, and suffused with cultural histories, practices, and politics. In other words, it is impossible to take the place out of data. I turn next to the process of putting data in its place.

PART I Articulation

1   A Natural Fit

On a sunny spring day in 2015, I sit on the patio of a picturesque *kaffihús*, nursing my coffee with a view of the harbor below. The coffee shop behind me is built in the old Danish style, with ornate wooden features and a richly green patinaed roof. It sits at the end of a small street boasting a quaint boutique called *Fallegur* ("beautiful"), a small museum that emphasizes Iceland's volcanic history, and an ice cream shop—all of which draw a steady but unhurried stream of foot traffic past my comfortable perch. The harbor itself is quiet that day, save for occasional birdsong. A couple of trawlers bob lazily in the water, while fish nets draped across the dock sway in the light breeze. And then, above my head, comes the sudden scream of wheels on rails, followed by the sound of actual screaming, as the roller coaster Blue Fire hurtles by.

Hulking over the quiet town of Rust in western Germany, Europa Park is a massive theme park where attractions are grouped by region of the world. Golden domes and a simulated space station signal "Russia"; tiled fountains and flamenco shows evoke "Spain"; and a safari boat shuttles visitors down a dark river past an "African village," surrounded by animatronic jungle animals. "Iceland" is surprisingly well represented at the theme park, boasting a full town complete with its own lighthouse, whaling station, and the charming street front where I passed an uncanny afternoon. I had made my way there, from the actual Iceland, in order to attend that year's World Hosting Days conference—the self-described "world's most important event for the hosting and cloud services industry." That year, I was one of four thousand attendees who spent breaks from busy days of conference programming wandering around this surreally off-season world.

Given that the cloud is often imagined as nowhere and everywhere, the choice of location for this conference felt apt: the dizzying sense of dislocation celebrated inside was echoed outside in the way we shuttled between events on a monorail, looking down at miniature replicas of regions, stylized and simplified. From that vantage point, it was easy to feel that place was a plaything; a relic; a special effect. This notion was reinforced by the oft-repeated claim that attendees had come from "all over the world" to be here (in reality, the vast majority came from Europe and North America), and the winking reminders that what we did at World Hosting Days— particularly at its nightly parties—would stay there. Conference-goers seemed to feel and feed off of this giddy freedom; after dining in the Colosseum-themed restaurant, they sipped from sodas and left them half- empty, mid-stride and mid-sentence, dropping trash on the ground. And yet, despite the sense of escape from location cultivated deliberately at World Hosting Days, place mattered—and profoundly—to the cloud architects and investors gathered at the conference.

Its importance was driven home to me the next morning in the buzzy exhibitor hall where sales representatives in corporate polos jostled to demonstrate their wares. Software, servers, and cooling systems were up and running; each table that comprised the hall's complex labyrinth was bedecked with pens, lighters, key chains, and other swag. More than a few vendors had hired models to showcase their merchandise, which helped only slightly to balance the deeply skewed ratio of women to men. Amidst all this, though, I had no trouble finding what I had come to see. From across the melee, I quickly spotted aurora borealis blue and green. As I came closer, the "Iceland booth" came into full view: a vendor cubicle wallpapered by high-resolution images of stunning waterfalls, snowy mountains, and intricate ice fields. A pastiche of Iceland's most photogenic features, the booth was already making its presence felt—heads swiveled toward it, drawn in, like I was, by this audacious insinuation of the Icelandic landscape into an otherwise anodyne conference room. At the helm of it stood Egill, a formidable man in his forties, with salt-and-pepper hair and a painful handshake. As project manager for the Icelandic state's data center development initiative, he had generously invited me to be his guest at the conference. Grinning, he now offered me a shot of vodka at 11:00 a.m. "I tried to bring *Brennivín*"—an infamously awful Icelandic spirit—he told me, "but ran into a bit of trouble at customs."

The Iceland booth, which travels the world through cloud industry conferences like this one, is the result of a joint effort between the state-backed foreign direct investment agency, the national telecommunications operator, the national power company, and several municipal representatives. Their common goal is to attract foreign direct investment to Iceland in the form of data center construction and clientele, and they have chosen to do so by leaning into Iceland's natural assets. In the process, Egill and his team distill the essence of Iceland down into a strategic and appealing image that rivals the "Icelandic village" on display in the nearby park.

In this chapter, by following the project of attracting data centers to Iceland—of pitching Iceland as a viable place for information to live—I examine the ways in which Icelanders and others articulate a "natural" fit between Iceland and industry. This link is made on the basis of Iceland's environment, which offers abundant renewable energy and a consistently cool climate. But making this case is more than a simple calculation of costs and benefits: it is a matter of conjuring, telling (and selling) convincing stories about place. In the data storage industry, well-worn imaginaries of the Icelandic wilderness are strategically recuperated, to profitable—albeit sometimes unpredictable—effect. At the same time, while some of Iceland's landforms and earth processes lend themselves readily to this promotional project, others raise problems for articulating a kinship between Iceland and the data storage industry. Data, then, is drawn to Iceland not only by the plain availability of natural resources, but also by the narrative work of mobilizing cultural histories alongside material landscapes.

DATA'S ENVIRONMENTS

The Iceland booth is far from alone at World Hosting Days in its strategic deployment of location. Over the course of the three-day conference, I sought out place-based pitches and found them, particularly across the European hubs: Germany, Ireland, the Netherlands, Luxembourg. Each reflected a national strategy for data center development that proclaimed a particular relationship between data and place. At "the Luxembourg Lounge," for example, another national oasis carved out in a cubicle at the exhibitor hall, a representative named Thierry told me that Luxembourg intended to become a "trust center" in the industry. Briefly indulging me in reprising the pitch he makes to developers, Thierry emphasized Luxembourg's tech-savvy workforce and its reputation for security. In contrast to the Iceland booth's maximalist leanings, the "Luxembourg Lounge" was decorated with a sparse aesthetic, its walls primarily occupied by charts on clean white backgrounds.

This struggle for regional distinction in data center development was unsurprising given the industry's rapid and growing expansion, described by Jean-François Blanchette as "the defining infrastructural work of our times" (2011, 1043). There was money to be made in specialized hardware like servers, network equipment, and cooling systems; software for data center management and automation; and services ranging from analytics to security—all of which were on the program and in the exhibitor hall that year at World Hosting Days. But there was also money to be made in data centers themselves, both for developers and key players in the places where they were built. Data centers sign contracts for bandwidth and electricity, they buy or lease large tracts of land, and they hire—at least in the early phases—a large number of construction workers, and sometimes engineering firms. Data center development, then, can be a significant site of economic activity, and source of foreign direct investment. At the time of my research, the business was booming. As one World Hosting Days speaker that year put it:

> There's one topic that I promise you won't hear anyone talk about over the next couple days at this conference: that is *to compute less*. Cisco is not going to talk to you about their *slower* networks, or HP about *reducing* their capacity in compute, right? Data is growing, it's growing exponentially.

Competition over this still-growing market was constant, explicit, and occasionally fierce.

One advertisement run in the World Hosting Days conference program by the Luxembourg-based European Business Reliance Centre (EBRC) depicts a bright blue EBRC data center, surrounded by cartoons that poke fun at lesser ones: the "wholesale data center" is patched and barely stitched together; the "red hot data center" is smoking, apparently about to overheat; the "cheesy data center," a reference to Switzerland, is full of holes and thus presumably vulnerable. The "fairy data center," an obvious dig at Iceland, sparkles, calling up the island's association with supernatural beliefs and beings, in order to suggest unserious business.

Helgi, an energetic Reykjavík municipal representative, and another regular presence around the Iceland booth, rolled his eyes at the EBRC brochure and recalled to me a similar scuffle with Sweden: "Around the conferences, Sweden had started closing their presentations by saying 'And we don't even have any ice!' Now, hey, I know what that means, that's not fair!" Here Helgi grinned and spread his hands wide in a let's-just-be-reasonable gesture: "So, you know, at the end of my last presentation, I threw in 'And we don't even have any nuclear reactors!'" Daníel, a municipal representative from Reykjanesbær and another member of the Iceland booth team, evoked a different kind of threat when he added, "It's funny, people who have been meeting with the Swedes always come back very enlightened about all the problems in Iceland. But one could always say, 'Well, we don't share borders with Russia . . .'" as he gave a suggestive shrug.

The state agencies, then, tasked with attracting the international data center industry, do what it takes to distinguish the benefits of *their* place. This means offering up competitive numbers on power pricing, bandwidth, latency, and land—as well as, occasionally, disparaging their competitors'. But it also means crafting a convincing narrative about the relationship between data and a particular locale. In Iceland, this has meant situating data in relation to the natural environment.

In order to understand how data storage gets aligned with Icelandic nature, we need to say a bit more about what a data center is and does. A data center is, at its core, a place where multiple computer servers are run at once. A data center can be an in-house operation (for example, those owned by Google or an agency of the government), or a colocation center, where multiple clients lease space and infrastructure. While most data centers look like nondescript warehouses, innovative designs range from experiments with underwater storage, to speculation over shooting data centers into space. The technology inside data centers also varies widely, as different outfits devise proprietary power sources, backup systems, sensors, and security features to meet their own particular needs. "Data center," then, is a flexible category that encompasses a wide range of places and processes. But across the many tours, interviews, and shadowing sessions that have comprised my long-term fieldwork, the developers and engineers I met all agreed on one point: data centers are places that consume enormous amounts of energy and produce enormous amounts of heat.

In the conference room of his sleek Reykjavík office, before we both traveled to World Hosting Days, Egill had described the issue in this way: "Building a data center is easy: you just build a steel frame and throw in the cables. But then you need to keep those machines running. This means you need to keep them from overheating." All computational processing generates heat as a by-product—heat that can slow and eventually shut down a server's functioning. Preventing thermal disaster is a nontrivial issue in a data hall containing hundreds or thousands of servers, snugly arranged on dozens of racks. Power, then, used both to fuel servers directly, and to keep them sufficiently cool, is essential for data centers to function. "Power," as Egill put it, "is the driver in the data center game." In recent years, power is also becoming a significant source of industry consternation.

Despite early IT industry rhetoric of "greening" (framing computation as an alternative to paper waste), data centers' massive power consumption has raised concerns. Primarily reliant on unsustainable sources, data centers' carbon emissions matched the commercial airlines' in 2015.[1] The environmental NGO Greenpeace has released reports on the industry since 2012, asking of various industry giants "How clean is your cloud?"[2] and encouraging consumers to choose to "Click Clean."[3] Also in 2012, *New York Times* journalist James Glanz published a damning series on data centers called "The Cloud Factories," in which he argued that "this foundation of the information industry is sharply at odds with its image of sleek efficiency and environmental friendliness."[4]

As computation has emerged as a significant contributor to anthropogenic climate change, energy consumption has become a pressing issue for the data storage industry, not only as an outsized operational expenditure, but also an increasingly urgent public image problem. Effectively shamed by environmental reporting, many of the major tech companies have declared their commitment to reducing their carbon footprint, fast.[5] In the search for a way forward, more and more are turning north. As it turns out, if the ambient temperature around a data center is colder, the energy required to cool servers there is reduced. This realization has resulted in emerging concentrations of data storage in cold places: in 2013, Facebook built a data center in Luleå, Sweden; Google runs a facility in Hamina, Finland; and Microsoft announced its plans to build two data centers in Norway in 2018. In addition to the server farms, bad puns have proliferated: the Arctic region is now described in the industry as "the node pole."[6]

Iceland, with its coastal winds and long winters, seems ideally situated to get into the game. On top of its temperate cold, which cuts down air conditioning requirements, Iceland's abundant hydroelectric and geothermal energy (which comprise 73% and 27%, respectively, of electricity on the national grid) make the island an especially appealing locale. Iceland is one of few countries that produces more renewable energy than is, or could ever be, consumed domestically. Historically, this surplus has been directed toward power-intensive industry—most notably, aluminum smelting. But where smelters have been critiqued as environmentally damaging, data centers are positioned as a cleaner, less controversial use of Icelandic energy. As one data center developer told me, "It's not so expensive to move data from one place to another. But it *is* expensive to move heat and cold. So you're using nature more effectively if you put your data in Iceland." And, as Egill likes to put it, "Data storage is a *cents*—not a dollars—industry."

Egill's agency started looking into data centers in the early 2000s. In the following years, the Icelandic government commissioned a series of research reports on the potential of the industry; the consulting firms BroadGroup and Price Waterhouse Coopers[7] differed on some details, but agreed that Iceland was well positioned to attract and host data center development, emphasizing in particular Iceland's climate and energy. Another study, commissioned by members of the European Parliament,[8] evaluated Iceland as a case study for "realizing European ICT possibilities" based on three metrics: energy, jurisdiction, and connectivity. While jurisdiction and connectivity, the authors concluded, are complicated questions of political will, energy emerges as a plain matter of place: naturally abundant, readily available, and reliably distributed in Iceland.

The authors of these commissioned reports are tactful: sustainability in the data storage industry should be an incentive in and of itself. But each also makes clear that Iceland's natural assets could certainly make for some powerful PR. Iceland's cool climate and abundant energy make possible not only cheap data centers but "green" ones,[9] a boon for an industry struggling with its image as an energy hog. Thus while industry critics pit data centers against the environment, situating the two as separate and incompatible things, Icelandic advocates have started suggesting the possibility of a "natural" fit. Turning next to the promotional materials deployed by Egill's team and their associates, I trace the specific stories being told about the Icelandic environment. I suggest that by tapping into well-established imaginaries of Icelandic wilderness, they situate computation within the landscape—not as an interloper, but as an integral part.

WILD GREEN YONDER

The camera sweeps slowly, then faster, over an ice field. From a drone's-eye-view, the glacial formations look like marble, intricately veined and dramatically cleaved. The shot pulls backward, producing a dizzying sense of immensity as the striations multiply. Then, the frame shifts from glacier to verdant green mountains, and as the beat drops on a synth-heavy instrumental background, the words *Iceland: The Coolest Location for Data Centers* enter the frame.

The promotional video produced by Egill's office is a two-minute case-maker for would-be developers, meant to offer an enticing visual introduction to Iceland, while communicating some of its unique selling points. In so doing, it sketches a narrative arc that is instructive in understanding data's emerging place here. After the title shot, we find ourselves briefly inside a data center, indexed by a row of black servers, blinking green. But then, we depart over a series of iconically Icelandic landscapes. The camera soars over black lava fields, churning waterfalls, lush pastureland—even through a tunnel carved into a glacier—over which statistics on

Iceland's renewable energy are superimposed. Then finally, from atop a snow-capped and windswept mountain, the camera travels back down, until a convincing CGI rendering of a data center comes back into view. We seem to slip down, in between the fan blades in the ceiling, and settle back into the rows of server racks inside. The closing shot reads: "From pure power of nature to your clients."

This video pitch for Iceland as a data center location offers a tantalizing survey of the island's striking and varied terrains. But the short film does more than simply show off Iceland's impressive landscapes: it also situates digital data within them. The sparse storyline traced by the camera's movement connects the hypothetical data center to a series of sites linked by their productive potential. In this presentation, nature is not merely a decorative backdrop; it is the engine that implicitly fuels your enterprise. That is to say, the waterfall and lava field are not just emblematic of Iceland's energy; they are quite literally where it comes from, in the form of hydroelectric and geothermal power. The ice and snow, likewise, are both proof and product of the same cold that will maximize server uptime while keeping operational costs down. As such, the images in the video are not only iconic, but indexical in the Peircean semiotic sense: they communicate logical relationships that are projected to hold should you, the viewer, build your data center here. The associations being leveraged suggest that as developers are invited to traverse these spectacular landscapes, it is not their own bodies they are meant to imagine into them; the salient point is that their data will be right at home.

The emphasis on natural imagery in this video is reproduced across the industry. As we have already seen, it saturates the Icelandic presence at trade shows, setting the Iceland booth ostentatiously apart. It also shapes the visual communication of other businesses invested in attracting data centers to Iceland. Landsvirkjun, for example, Iceland's national power company, is one of the key players poised to benefit from this development, selling long-term contracts to the energy-intensive industry. The company, in addition to sending representatives along to conferences like World Hosting Days (where they can speak directly to the pricing agreements potential clients are likely to secure), has also produced a website and a series of brochures that make a case for why "the future of data centers is in Iceland." Across these materials, photographs of the Icelandic landscape

Figure 4. Still image from promotional video marketing Iceland as an ideal site for data center development.

are graphically merged with images of server farms. Grassy fields transition seamlessly into data center white space (the industry term for the areas where IT equipment is placed); craggy waterfalls scaffold a set of server racks. Such images, like the *Invest in Iceland* video, suggest a kind of movement, even in their single frames. What is less clear in these photos is whether we are meant to read a mere coexistence between green space and white space, or the active conversion of one into the other.

It is worth noting that none of the sites featured in these promotional images are actual regions where data centers are being developed: the latter include Reykjavík, the Reykjanes Peninsula, Blönduós to the north, and Hornafjördur to the southeast. Instead, data is insinuated into a broader "Icelandic environment," whose dramatic productive capacities make data storage a perfect fit. Through a visual convergence of the natural and technological sublime[10] here, the landscape is narratively wrapped around digital data, not forcibly bent but easily accommodating. At the same time, human labor is notably elided, such that it is not the power company that services the data center; it appears to be the glacial river itself. Iceland, then, emerges not just as site or service provider, but as digital data's *natural home.* As one British developer, clearly sold on the strategy, put it: "Iceland is where evolution would put a data center."

Icelandic data center enthusiasts, though they do so effectively, are far from the first to suggest a symbiotic relationship between data and nature.

While technology is often figured in contradistinction to the natural world—whether as means to subdue, overcome, or escape it—it is also thoroughly entangled in ecological imaginaries, digital data perhaps especially so. Critics have noted, for example, that the evocative language of online "streaming," data "flow," and "cloud" computing are clearly modeled on environmental equivalents.[11] According to technological historian Fred Turner, these are not accidental metaphors.

Tracing a history of American cyber-utopianism, Turner has argued that a specific strand of counterculture significantly shaped lasting understandings of information technology (2006). This influential group Turner calls "the new communalists" developed a vision of IT, beginning in the 1970s, as a vital conduit for enabling a back-to-the-land lifestyle. Centered around Stuart Brand's *Whole Earth Catalog*, which later transitioned online into the "Whole Earth 'Lectronic Link" (WELL), they dedicated themselves to exploring its communal and consciousness-shifting potential. A key piece of this vision, inspired by Norbert Wiener's cybernetics, was the resonance of IT with ecological processes. The opening lines of Richard Brautigan's 1967 poem *All Watched Over by Machines of Loving Grace* are illustrative:

> I like to think (and
> the sooner the better!)
> of a cybernetic meadow
> where mammals and computers
> live together in mutually
> programming harmony
> like pure water
> touching clear sky.

Versions of this vision were carried forward by WELL members, including Howard Rheingold, author of *The Virtual Community,* who described "homesteading in cyberspace" (1993, 21), and Kevin Kelly, cofounder of *Wired* magazine, who wrote that the internet would "lead humanity back toward a reintegration with nature" by echoing its "distributed, decentralized, collaborative, and adaptive" elements (Turner 2006, 202). From the very early days, then, of the internet, a prominent discourse with widespread resonance situated data processing in explicit relation to the land.

Placing data within an Icelandic environment recalls some of these influential associations. But it is also a distinctive project. Because rather than bucolic backdrop or model of ecological harmony, in Iceland nature has been figured as *wilderness*.[12] Such ideas, which have long circulated about the island, shape the way that data lands in this specific landscape (Johnson 2019b).

Throughout antiquity, Iceland was viewed as part of Ultima Thule, the conceptual endpoint of the knowable world. Ancient Greeks and Romans suspected the "hyperborean" region was a dystopia, since they reasoned no "civilized" culture could cope with such overwhelming whiteness, quiet, and cold (Davidson 2005). In the Middle Ages and early modern eras, visitors memorialized the singularity of Iceland's environment, coining the still-active clichés of "fire and ice" (Durrenberger and Pálsson 1989). At times, these accounts openly linked Iceland's landscape to the mystical, magical, and diabolical—for example, suggesting that its volcanos contained passageways directly to hell (Ísleifsson 2011); later on, the novelist Jules Verne would pick up on these associations, choosing the glacier Snæfellsjökull to serve as the threshold of his journey to the center of the earth (1871). Clearly, these exoticizing characterizations are projects of imagination more than empirical description. But beginning in the seventeenth century, Danish colonial agents would come to know the Icelandic environment up close.

While Iceland became a formal dependency of Norway in 1262, with its chieftains' acceptance of the Old Covenant, foreign rule in Iceland was, for a long period, extremely indirect.[13] This would start to change when Iceland's administration shifted from Norway to Denmark with the breakup of the Nordic Kalmar Union. Under King Christian IV, who ruled from 1588 to 1648, the Danish state embarked for the first time on a program of centralizing colonial control on the island. While it cited material hardship as cause for benevolent intervention, another incentive was likely the effort to coax a profit from the as-yet disappointing dependency. Between 1602 and 1787, Iceland was placed under a Danish trade monopoly with regular quotas for imports and exports. During that period, colonial officials conducted land surveys and experimented with development efforts, technology transfers, and new regulations like land enclosure laws (Hálfdanarson 2006; Oslund 2011). Such actions, the first of their kind on the island, suggest a cautiously optimistic understanding of the Icelandic environment as one that could be rendered productive and predictable. And yet, these colonial development initiatives quickly grew complicated.

For example: In 1771, in response to a famine, the Danish government began importing reindeer from Norway, hoping they might encourage Icelanders to herd. Thirteen reindeer were sent to the Westman Islands, most of which died there within their first year. Another shipment of around thirty animals was sent to the Reykjanes Peninsula, and while this fledgling herd survived a bit longer, these too eventually died off (Thórisson 1984). But the next round of reindeer, this time sent to Iceland's northeastern region, finally thrived there—though Icelanders, unsurprisingly, never took to herding them. In fact, they multiplied so prolifically that before long, farmers were complaining of reindeer competing with sheep for pastureland. In 1810 a sheriff in the Northeast argued that the reindeer had become "more of a plague than a benefit" and requested permission to start hunting them down (Oslund 2011, 73).

As the failure of development efforts like this one accumulated, it seemed to confirm for Danish colonial agents that Iceland was wild and could not be tamed. Following the Laki volcanic eruption in 1783 and the devastating famine that followed it, some officials went so far as to suggest relocating all Icelanders to the Danish Jutland Peninsula, as Iceland had clearly proven uninhabitable. While expressed with dismay by would-be Danish administrators, however, this idea of Icelandic environmental excess would go on to be reclaimed by the nationalist movement.

Most historians trace the Icelandic nationalist project back to the early nineteenth century, with the establishment of the Icelandic Literary Society in 1816.[14] Its members, young Icelanders studying in Copenhagen, and drawing on the medieval manuscripts housed there, began drafting a national narrative of the island as a distinctive community defined by its long-standing engagement with a forbidding natural environment. Rather than understanding them as obstacles, these poets, painters, and later on politicians started claiming Iceland's extreme landscape and climatic conditions as a defining source of strength and pride. The poet Jónas Hallgrímsson, for example, one of the founders of the nationalist journal *Fjölnir*, was educated as a naturalist and often drew depictions of the

Icelandic landscape into his tributes. In the words of cultural historian Karen Oslund, nationalists argued that "Icelandic nature is extreme, unpredictable, even wild, but people live within this wilderness, and their character has been formed by the struggle with this nature" (2011, 54).

Thus while Iceland's environment once marked the island with a detrimental kind of difference, in the nineteenth century Icelanders retold this relationship, reframing the island's wildness as powerful and empowering. This intervention, which linked Iceland's national character to its natural environment, continues to resonate and do work today. For example, in the early 2000s, the Prime Minister's Office undertook a nation-branding project that emphasized links between nature and Icelandic ambition, innovation, and success. As the resulting report, *The Image of Iceland* (*Ímynd Íslands*), stated, "The untamed forces of nature are analogues to Icelanders' wild and often bold and unpredictable behavior. Yet, these characteristics should not be intimidating, as they have been central to the life-struggle of the nation; they should be celebrated and used."[15] Plainly taking up tropes from the nationalist movement, the Prime Minister's Office mobilized nature to reassert a distinctive natural/national Icelandic character (Gréttarsdóttir, Ásmundsson, and Lárusson 2015).

At the same time, Iceland's fast-expanding tourism industry has likewise marketed its environment to travelers as "Europe's last wilderness": exotic, otherworldly, and wild.[16] For example, the tremendously popular campaign "Inspired by Iceland" is known for imagery akin to that of the data center video: sweeping pans over richly varied landscapes; evocative tropes of "fire and ice"; an appealingly depopulated environment into which tourists can easily imagine themselves. Increasingly sold as a "stop-over" destination (a connection point for international travelers, strategically positioned between East and West), Iceland is presented as a safe place to play with alterity, to immerse oneself in a startlingly other environment that inspires awe in today's travelers, rather than dread (Lund, Loftsdóttir, and Leonard 2017). As is evident in the proliferation of travel companies, hotel developments, and Gore-Tex–clad tourists on the streets of Reykjavík, these efforts have so far been wildly successful.[17]

In Iceland, then, nature-as-wilderness has been constructed over the centuries with equal parts anxiety and pride. On the one hand, imaginar-

ies of Icelandic wilderness have advanced European projects of self-fash-
ioning and justified colonial rule; on the other hand, they have afforded
Icelanders opportunities to challenge these efforts and stake out their own
claims. Today, the growing data center industry in Iceland constitutes a
new occasion for mobilizing these imaginaries. As we have seen, images of
the environment are used in this context to index power (electrical, rather
than political, this time). Servers are fed by the force of rushing rivers and
cascading waterfalls. At the same time, while wind and snow have been
debilitating for human travelers, data is only sustained by the cold. In
making these associations, Icelanders pitching the island to the industry
actively produce a "natural" fit: not quite the ecological harmony articulated by Turner's "new communalists," but a more active, lively, symbiotic
relationship. In the process, Iceland emerges as a kind of wild green yon-
der, where data and nature coexist without cost. Mateo, the American data
center executive, puts a point on it when he tells potential clients that
cooling servers is as simple as "opening the windows" and letting in the
"raw Icelandic air."

Egill and his associates, then, have been successful in producing a profitable portrait of Icelandic nature. Across efforts like the Iceland booth
and the promotional video, they actively tap into a rich repertoire of
imagery that positions the island's wilderness as generative and desirable.
But the cultural histories that inform this narrative practice—much like
the Icelandic landscape itself—are volatile. They may produce powerful
affective attachments, but they are just as liable to shift under your feet.
This is because the same environment that produces the power to fuel
server farms also produces windstorms, rogue waves, and volcanic ash.
The nature that anchors claims about the Icelandic national character is
the same wilderness that once marked the island as hyperborean dystopia.
When your starting premise is a dynamic and unpredictable landscape,
your pitch rests on inherently unstable ground.

NATURALIZING RISK, NATURALIZING DATA

I didn't set out to write about nature in Iceland. In fact, for much of
my time there, I felt emphatically opposed. My research on the island

coincided precisely with the peak of Iceland's tourism boom, and—perhaps at pains to distinguish myself as a doctoral student from the droves that descended on Reykjavík every year—I set myself firmly against its allure. I felt a stubborn resistance to swooning over the landscape and a satisfaction in surprising Icelanders when I told them I had not come for that. But more broadly, as I saw the same tropes and tones of wonder being deployed repeatedly, across genres and media, the topic of "Icelandic nature" came to feel oversaturated, its affective power exhausted and analytic potential foreclosed.

But "Icelandic nature," as it turned out, would not wait to be appreciated—much less analyzed. Some days, it woke me like a battering ram at my window. It came close to ripping the door clean off my car. The wind in Iceland is known for blowing tour buses off mountain roads, with unnerving regularity. When it is very bad, it can pull the road itself up, tearing sheafs of asphalt away from the ground. Less viscerally, the weather is the reason that Icelanders give for preferring to keep plans short term and flexible; after all, you might get snowed in. Or, against all odds, the weather might be still and sunny—and when that's the case, no one is going to feel beholden to any plan that would have them stuck inside. Environmental happenings, then, distribute agencies in Iceland, in both routine and unpredictable ways. The autumn that I moved to the island, I felt these effects most acutely through the eruption at Holuhraun.

Though the volcanic event is referred to as "Holuhraun," the eruption originated in Bárðarbunga, one of the largest volcanoes on the island, in August of 2014. But instead of spurting upward in an iconic effusion, the magma instead flowed underground through the Vatnajökull glacier. It continued on to a large lava field called Holuhraun, where it bubbled up through surface fissures over the next six months. The path the lava took meant avoiding a destructive eruption, but it also dragged 9.6 million metric tons of sulfur dioxide (SO_2) into the air. Such chemical by-products of volcanic activity can be every bit as deadly as the lava itself: in 1783 the Laki eruption resulted in the death of 20 percent of Iceland's population from fluoride poisoning and the famine that followed, as toxic gases killed off crops and livestock (Karlsson 2000). Holuhraun's effects, however, were not nearly so damaging. During the worst of it, the SO_2 spreading across the island materialized in watery eyes, occasional headaches, and an eerily beautiful golden moon. Those of us in Reykjavík monitored the numbers, which hovered in the range of the technically safe. But as one friend remarked cheerfully during this period, as the two of us debated going out for a run, "We don't have any predators in Iceland. It's just the ground that's trying to kill us!" It quickly became clear to me that confronting "nature"—both viscerally and categorically—would be unavoidable. It certainly was for Icelanders trying to establish a data center industry on the island. For them, too, volcanoes like Holuhraun would prove to be key.

Split down the middle by the mid-Atlantic plate boundary, Iceland is a hot spot for tectonic activity. The island has over thirty active volcano systems and experiences a major eruption about every five years. This churning, incessant turnover of earth is made visible in the large lava fields that cover four thousand square miles, or in the island of Surtsey off the south coast of Iceland, which rose up from the sea and into visible existence during an offshore eruption in 1963. The flip side of the "fire and ice" equation, volcanoes are perhaps the most charismatic characters in Iceland's "wild" environment. But while cold plays an ambient and enabling role for data storage, helping situate Iceland as an ideal site, and glaciers melt productively into rushing rivers that can be tapped for hydroelectric power, volcanoes are a more equivocal element. Iceland's seismic activity, after all, produces geothermal energy. It paints the multicolored mountains that are featured on postcards and keeps the natural hot springs reliably warm. But it also produces disruptive eruptions that could, theoretically, put data at risk.

This potential was illustrated in the infamous Eyjafjallajökull eruption of 2010. While the eruption itself was a relatively small one, Eyjafjallajökull created a massive ash cloud, also known as an eruption plume, that drifted down to the European mainland. For over a week, flights were grounded on the continent. In addition to air travel, economies across and outside[18] Europe were affected as imports and exports were put on hold. That year, Egill and his team had been meeting with an American executive, building a relationship that he hoped would attract "the next big data center"—and emphasizing precisely the kind of wild environment celebrated in their promotional video and Iceland booth. But, he said, drawing a triangle on a piece of paper in front of us, "It was like going up a mountain—or, if you like, a volcano." Tracing a jagged line up its left side, he told me, "We had been climbing up slowly, slowly. Then . . ." Here, he scribbled a spray at the top of his volcano and tossed his pen across the desk. "It started to spew and we just rolled down again."

Egill's was not the only team thwarted by Eyjafjallajökull. Siggi, an Icelandic data center developer, who had been in talks at the time with an American company about pursuing a joint construction project in Iceland, told me their last meeting was the day after the eruption:

> Even though there was absolutely no influence on the area where the data center was planned, when you're sitting in New York you're just looking at a spot on the map. It's all the same place. And when you're on a phone meeting, they don't believe that you're not out there shoveling ash!

According to Siggi, the American company lost interest after that call.

In the project of branding Iceland in relation to its environment, Eyjafjallajökull was a significant setback. Ruefully swiveling in an executive chair, Egill remembered, "You would watch on CNN and every day for a month, it was just volcano." The Eyjafjallajökull eruption appeared, to those outside the island, as a direct threat to infrastructure and industry. Headlines at the time, including "Eruptions and Disruptions," "Ash in the Supply Chain," and "The Cloud that Closed a Continent," emphasized Iceland's outsized—and unwelcome—impact on its surrounding countries. In doing so, they also called up long-standing ideas of Iceland as excessively, irrepressibly wild. Echoing classical and colonial imaginaries of Iceland as unknowable, unpredictable, and dangerous, international news stories framed Eyjafjallajökull as a primordial interruption to modern mobilities.[19]

In the wake of Eyjafjallajökull, Egill's team hired an engineering company to write a risk assessment of seismic activity in Iceland. Their report patiently explained that the tectonic plate boundary that bisects Iceland is a divergent, rather than a convergent, rift: the North American and Eurasian plates are moving apart. This means, as Egill put it, "There is constant release here"; Iceland experiences hundreds of earthquakes weekly, but the vast majority are imperceptibly small. Likewise, volcanic activity is constant but relatively contained. Fissure eruptions like Holuhraun, which percolate up through cracks or "vents," are much more common than explosive eruptions like Eyjafjallajökull. What's more, the sites of these occasional effusions are well known and purposefully distant from population centers (unlike the San Andreas fault that directly threatens Silicon Valley, as Egill likes to remind Americans). Despite its disruptive impact outside Iceland, Eyjafjallajökull caused no injuries and minimal property damage in Iceland itself—as Egill emphasized, no one even lost power. All the same, as discussed in the Introduction, he did add some cityscapes to his data center promotional material, alongside the glaciers and pristine streams—a subtle signaling that the Icelandic landscape was not entirely, or overly, wild. Ultimately, though, by the time I arrived in Iceland, pitches to the data storage industry were again focused squarely on Icelandic nature. Having briefly experimented with a kind of Latourian purification—driving a comfortable wedge between nature and culture (1993)—the Iceland booth, in all its gaudy glory, marked a return to celebrating wilderness, a doubling down on the experience of living on the edge.

Mateo offered an explicit example of this strategy at the previous year's World Hosting Days. As a data center developer running a facility in Iceland, Mateo is both a target audience of Egill's narratives and a partner in coproducing them. While Egill and his team seek to attract data centers to Iceland, convincing new companies to build, or existing operations to expand here, Mateo's success depends on attracting clients to rent the space, power, and connectivity he provides. He is also aware that growing the data center industry in Iceland will ultimately give it more clout and sway. "First we collaborate, then we compete," he once said of his fellow developers. So while Mateo's company has its own presence at World Hosting Days, he also spends time at the Iceland booth and aligns his own messaging with the broader effort of attracting data centers to Iceland.

When Mateo took to the stage in 2014, pacing before a larger than life–sized PowerPoint, he delivered a rousing presentation on data centers as "data factories," emphasizing that—like traditional factories—server farms rely on power in order to produce. Iceland, he argued, was the best place to source it, as the island guaranteed low prices and green appeal. At the end of his talk, when he opened the floor to questions, a Dutch man at the back of the room raised his hand. "What I can remember of Iceland is that big volcano. How do you deal with that?" he asked. Without missing a beat, Mateo responded:

Yes, there are volcanoes in Iceland, I think everybody knows that. *We like volcanoes.* We need volcanoes. You would not have any of that 100 percent renewable if you didn't have that geothermal energy, where you have it, in Iceland. It is all over the island and it's a very powerful resource for us to have. That being said, site location and site preparation is key, whenever you're putting a data center anywhere in the world.

While later chapters will take up this question of "site location and site preparation" in detail, for now what I wish to draw attention to is Mateo's deft reframing of the volatility of Iceland's environment as a necessary and appreciated "resource." In fact, as Mateo emphasized in his answer to another audience question that day, the instability of the landscape actually enables an unusual stability in power pricing. Because the availability of renewable energy is far more predictable than that of fossil fuels, longer contracts are available in Iceland than elsewhere. As Mateo put it:

> When you think about Iceland, the contracts that we have in place guarantee your power. I don't know any other place in the world that you can go to your provider and say, "Can you please print out my power bill five years from now, ten years from now, fifteen years from now?" You can't do that anywhere in the world. In Iceland, because you're talking about renewable resources, they can do that, they can easily accomplish that. That's the key differentiator.

When volatile elements of the environment threaten the "natural fit" being articulated between Iceland and industry, those in favor of developing data centers in Iceland must narrate a convincing workaround. Sometimes, this looks like distracting with cityscapes, or dispelling investors' fears with research. But more often, it looks like strategically reappropriating the unpredictability at Iceland's very core. Egill and Mateo's post-Eyjafjallajökull efforts both argue that data is not kept safe through its distance from the threatening wild. Instead, data thrives where it fits into the landscape—a living entity fueled and fed by the constant activity of the Icelandic earth. Taking this tack, the risk inherent in Iceland's environment is resolved through representations of computation as a lifeway inherently suited to this place.

It is not only Iceland, then, being promoted in data center industry campaigns: a concept of data is being put forward, too. It bears some resemblance to Brautigan's cybernetic meadow, "where animals and computers live together in mutually programming harmony." Its novelty, however, might lie in the "living": data is not passively placed into the landscape; instead, it takes an active part in it. While elsewhere it is figured as a power-hungry interloper, in Iceland data's needs are met as a matter of course. Whereas other national narratives emphasize data's need for protection (for example, the "Luxembourg Lounge's" security-centric pitch), in Icelandic efforts data's fragility is overshadowed by its insatiability. Through pitches like the Iceland booth and promotional video, data is put forward as a ravenous and robust thing that has, in Iceland, met its match.

Such a move echoes, strangely enough, Icelandic nationalists' intervention: the assertion that *the* defining element of Icelanders was their ability to withstand Iceland, itself. Through this maneuver, settlers' descendants defined a distinctive identity and claimed the right to manage their own affairs. This narrative work resonates through today's reclamation of wilderness: by emphasizing data's symbiosis with the Icelandic environment, data center supporters suggest not only that Iceland is an ideal place for data storage, data is also an ideal inhabitant of Iceland. Data is domesticated in this gesture. Data is *naturalized,* not only rendered part of the landscape, but granted official status and standing, a "citizen" despite its origins elsewhere.

Following, over the years, this process of placing data in Iceland, another relatively recent arrival often sprung to my mind: the bright purple Nootka (Alaskan) lupine that carpets broad swaths of the island today. Introduced in the 1940s as groundcover to help restore overgrazed farmland, the lupine spread aggressively across the island and is viewed by environmental scientists as a paradigmatic example of an invasive species out of control. While the lupine has been effective in stemming the tide of erosion, endemic on the island and threatening to its vegetation and soil, it also chokes competing plant life, stamping out biodiversity wherever the flower gains a foothold. Opinions are mixed about lupine in Iceland— most everyone knows that the plant causes problems, that it probably never should have been brought in the first place. And yet, Icelanders also comment on how nice it looks here, how deeply familiar it now feels.

At the baptism of a friend's baby, for example, a group of us gathered in the garden where the hosts passed out lupine petals to throw as confetti.

Figure 5. A data center construction site in Reykjanes, amidst a thatch of invasive Nootka (Alaskan) lupine. Photo by author.

After a sing-along to *Fylgd*, a song that lovingly describes the Icelandic landscape and tells the child it addresses, "this land is yours" (*þetta land átt þú*), some attendees threw their lupine petals enthusiastically, while others looked anxiously to the seeds strewn across the ground—seeds that would undoubtedly establish a stranglehold on the new parents' pristine lawn. Lupine in Iceland is undoubtedly harmful; it is also definitively at home. Not for nothing, an advertisement for one Nordic IT company's Icelandic data storage arm opens with footage of a blond woman spinning contentedly in a lush field of brilliant purple lupine.

Insofar as ideas of Icelandic wilderness tap into a long and ambivalent history of imagining the island from the outside, Iceland's abundance will always threaten excess, will always have the potential to become overpowering. Echoes of otherness threaten to destabilize the operation: if developers and clients are attracted to ideas of Iceland's "untouched" environment, they also have to contend with risk as the other side of the wild. Part of data center supporters' strategy, then, has been absorbing and redirecting that risk—suggesting that here, wilderness does not need taming because data is the thing it is best suited to serve. Doing so, they mobilize foundational logics of Icelandic place-making, carrying forward a long legacy of narratively shaping the island's unruly landscape into a strategic (if somewhat capricious) resource.

CONCLUSION

Data, and therefore data centers, have to go somewhere. As the data storage industry is currently structured, their placement comes with certain perks—most immediately, a shot of foreign direct investment that has proven appealing to a wide range of locales. That place is central to the contemporary project of data storage, then, is not an analytic insight for Egill and his team—it is the premise of their positions and the promotional materials they create. Through the circulation of natural and national imaginaries, they deftly stitch together the demands of data and the capacities of the Icelandic environment, thus situating the industry conceptually in Iceland, in anticipation of its material arrival.

As we have seen, however, some landscape features stretch the "natural" narrative that Egill and others articulate, requiring more aggressively recuperative moves. "Icelandic nature," then, is effectively mobilized in stories that seek to naturalize a connection between data and (this) place, but it is not subsumed by or reducible to them. Icelandic wilderness may be a productive construction,[20] but it also operates outside of human conceptualizations, plans, and priorities. Like the routinely howling winds and less regular volcanic eruptions, some elements of Iceland's physicality are intractable, requiring not only a reframing of Iceland, but also of digital data itself.

Ashley Carse, in his study of the Panama Canal and its many tendrils extending into surrounding ecologies, has argued that environments can be *made into* infrastructure through engineering and organizational work. He shows how, in the case of the canal, this infrastructuring takes place through moving earth and pouring concrete, as well as displacing communities for water reservoirs and instituting new regimes of forestry and agricultural management (2014). The operationalizing of nature as infrastructure is plainly on display in the data center, as energy is channeled in from rivers and tectonic rifts, and "raw Icelandic air" filtered in the windows. The start and end of infrastructure is unclear in a context where climate is conceived as part of the enterprise. But insofar as data storage operates as an industry, with developers attuned to price breaks and public relations boons, strategic storytelling should be understood as a vital part of this project. The "technologies of imagination" (Vonderau 2017) deployed in data center development also sanction and shape the industry's course. As the marketing director of a cloud services firm based in Reykjavík once told me of her company's promotional efforts, "Oh, we're still exploiting nature. We're just doing it in a different way." What we see, then, in the ostentatious Iceland booth, the smooth CGI amalgamation of green space and white space, and other projects courting data center development is not the mere description of a "natural fit" between Iceland and the data storage industry; it is one careful co-constitution of place and data, and the effortful tending to this lucrative link.

In later chapters, we will interrogate the claims embedded in this proposition, that Iceland's environment can accommodate data centers without cost; we will examine the more expansive and ambivalent territorial shifts associated with rendering nature infrastructure here. But for now, I want to linger a bit longer on the project of putting Iceland forward as a good place for data to live. This argument has been made not only on the basis of Iceland's environment, but also with reference to the people and politics of this place. Shifting definitively, then, from the international sales space of the data storage industry to the island where we will analyze its development, the next chapter takes up a legislative effort that framed Iceland as a "data haven" for the world. In claiming this unique niche, another set of Icelanders (again in collaboration and competition with outsiders) carved out a place for data in Iceland, while offering an answer to a then-urgent question: *What kind of place is Iceland, anyway?*

2 The Switzerland of Bits

What does it mean to be a place that stores data? We might come at this question in any number of ways. By now we have a sense for why data storage can be profitable, especially so in particular parts of the world. We have seen how some seismic and climatic properties lend themselves to the operations of the industry. And we have traced the narrative work that situates certain landscapes in symbiotic relation to digital processes. But these considerations do not speak directly to the question of storage's significance, the question of what storage enables, implies, and inspires (Shyrock and Smail 2018). This much was made clear to me in one conversation I spent trying to explain my research to a couple of Icelandic friends, unaffiliated with the industry. "So," one concluded, "Iceland is becoming something like a bank vault for the world's data?" "Or," the other one promptly chimed in, "something more like a trash can." While neither of these interpretations may be exactly accurate, both speak to the stakes of the enterprise. In this chapter I take up one especially audacious imagination of what data storage could do for Iceland, and what it might be made to mean.

On June 16 of 2010, a parliamentary resolution called the Icelandic Modern Media Initiative was unanimously passed in the Icelandic *Alþingi,* voted through by all five parties in Parliament. These included the center-left Social Democratic Party (*Samfylkingin*), the conservative-leaning Independence Party (*Sjálfstæðisflokkurinn*), the environmentally minded Left-Green Party (*Vinstri Grænir*), the historically agrarian and increasingly populist Progressive Party (*Framsóknarflokkurinn*), and the insurgent upstart Citizens' Movement (*Borgarahreyfingin*), voted into Parliament for the first time the year before.[1] What this diverse and divided Parliament agreed upon was the proposition that Iceland would make itself a "safe haven" for digital data internationally.

The Icelandic Modern Media Initiative (often glossed affectionately as IMMI) committed to passing a comprehensive package of legislation, assembled by mixing and matching the most "information friendly" laws from around the world. The result was to be a unique jurisdiction—a so-called data haven—where information could be safely stored and freely spread. Deliberately invoking the idea of the tax haven, but twisting its logics toward transparency, IMMI aimed to make Iceland a new kind of political exception, capable of catalyzing international change. Over ten years later, IMMI has not yet succeeded in that purpose and seems unlikely to do so anytime soon. But the effort, as it unfolded over the course of my fieldwork, nevertheless offers up important insight into shifting relationships between data and place.

This chapter, then, takes a short detour through recent history to ask how and why data became such a salient object, capable of cutting across Icelandic politics. Tracing the project's aspirations, successes, and stall-out, I argue that while IMMI was framed in the universalizing terms of transparency and information freedom, it was in fact a uniquely Icelandic experiment which emerged from the country's immediate experience of financial crisis, as well as its more protracted imperial history. As the island's status and standing were called into question following the financial crash of 2008, IMMI performed a recuperative maneuver: it addressed immediate anxieties within Iceland while also working to restore its national image by filling the position of "data haven." Thus while all states actively address themselves to controlling information (Bernal 2014), elevating and emphasizing this capacity as IMMI does clarifies the particular values—and value—encoded in data management today. I suggest that administering information correctly is becoming a measure for alliance and compliance with a normative mode of liberal Western modernity. IMMI leveraged these associations, drawing data to Iceland as it secured the island's status on the right side of what Bill Maurer has called "hierarchies of rank" (2008, 172).[2] In doing so, it made a different kind of case for placing data in Iceland, situating the island geopolitically in terms of its ability to store.

A HAVEN FOR INFORMATION

The ambition, and the innovation, of the Icelandic Modern Media Initiative lay in its meticulous attention to the pathway by which information makes its way to the public, and its commitment to preventing abuses of power along the way. We might think of that pathway, as one chart on the IMMI website invites us to, as proceeding from a source (a person who has information), to their device (which transmits and stores that information), to a journalist (who courts and curates that information), to a publisher (who releases that information), to the rest of us, who ultimately receive that information when we click or flip our way through the news. The premise of IMMI is that each link in that chain needs to be protected, and few places in the world currently protect them all.

For example, some countries (such as South Korea and New Zealand) have established legal protections for whistleblowers, shielding citizens who expose corruption or illicit activity from prosecution. Some countries (like Belgium) explicitly protect the electronic devices of journalists from search and seizure. Some countries (like the United States and Argentina) forbid the practice of "prior restraint," or government intervention that would stop the news from being published. Some countries (like Norway and Estonia) enshrine in law the presumption of public access to government documents. IMMI identified each of these (and several other) protections as vital to a free and well-informed public, and set out to bring them together under a single legal regime. In all, IMMI sought interventions across ten sectors of Icelandic legislation: judicial process; prior restraint; communications; source protection; whistleblower protection; intermediary (third party service provider) liability; the statute of limitations on publishing liabilities; "libel tourism" (the practice of selectively filing a lawsuit from a country where libel laws are more lax); the creation of virtual limited liability corporations (the significance of which we will get to shortly); and freedom of information law. Finally, IMMI established an Icelandic Prize for Freedom of Expression, to be administered annually.

IMMI, then, proposed an overhaul of Icelandic information law in the interest of creating a unique jurisdiction that unambiguously favored—a formulation I heard often in those years—"transparency for government and privacy for citizens." But IMMI's ambitions were not limited to Iceland: not only were its laws culled from international sources, they were meant to be accessible outside of Iceland, too. As the resolution text states: "The flow of information has no borders and most of the media is moving to the internet. That is why the time has come for a modern legislative regime that can promote and defend global freedom of expression, in principle and in practice."[3] IMMI proposed to create that regime, and by making Iceland "an attractive environment for the registration and operation of international press organisations, new media start-ups, human rights groups and internet data centers," extend its protections to those who needed them most.

In passing its suite of laws, IMMI aimed to spark a migration: international media outlets, hosting companies, and others would flock to Iceland and, in so doing, move their data there. With a corporation registered and its data stored in Iceland (and this is where the provision for virtual limited liability companies kicks in), both would be subject to Icelandic law. Under IMMI, this meant their data would be free from government meddling, and thus able to make it out into the wider world. In this way, by creating international points of access, IMMI invited potential users outside of Iceland to benefit from its protective legislative environment, while neatly circumventing their nations' own. As Birgitta Jónsdóttir, one of IMMI's key sponsors in Parliament, put it:

> Iceland will become the inverse of a tax haven; by offering journalists and publishers some of the most powerful protections for free speech and investigative journalism in the world. Tax havens' aim is to make everything opaque. Our aim is to make everything transparent.[4]

IMMI's intervention, then, while ostensibly global, was also meaningfully place-bound. Flying in the face of earlier rhetoric that emphasized the deterritorializing nature of the internet—its projected potential to blur national borders and make state power less relevant—IMMI in fact relied on Iceland's very territory and stateness to extend protections outside its shores (von Bargen and Fish 2020). If IMMI was to succeed in making Iceland an "information haven," it would do this work by moving computer servers, the incorporation of companies, and employment contracts onto the island, within the borders of physical space where Icelandic law held sway. In other words, to make information "free" IMMI would fix it, giving that data a legally advantageous home address.

This is the principle of data sovereignty in practice, the idea that data is subject to the laws of the place where it is stored. Historically, this has meant that a company that handles people's data needs to comply with the regulations of the country in which that company, and those people, are based. The advent of cloud computing, however, has complicated this equation: What happens if the company is headquartered in another country than its users? And if that company's data is hosted someplace else? In 2010, at the time of IMMI's proposal, these questions were the subject of debate and litigation (see Jaeger, Lin, and Grimes 2008); they are still far from decisively resolved.[5] Some had already found ways to exploit inconsistencies between jurisdictions, gray zones in international law. For example, the media organization WikiLeaks, known for anonymously releasing classified documents, made a practice of strategic jurisdiction-shopping in its publication process. As founder Julian Assange put it in an address at the 2010 Oslo Freedom Forum:

> We, in the past three years, have been attacked over 100 times legally, and have succeeded against all those defenses by building an international, multi-jurisdictional network, by using every trick in the book that multinational companies use to route money through tax havens. Instead, we route information through different countries to take advantage of their laws, both for publishing and for the protection of sources. And that endeavor has been successful in putting over a million restricted documents into the historical record that weren't there before. (Assange 2010)

Where WikiLeaks built a distributed network, IMMI aimed to offer all these benefits in one place. In doing so, it carved out an informational state of exception, conceived as a "haven" of a new kind. But like

WikiLeaks', IMMI's proponents often invoked the comparison to tax havens, jurisdictions that offer low tax rates for foreign investors and high levels of financial secrecy. Again, as spokesperson Birgitta Jónsdóttir quipped, "Tax havens' aim is to make everything opaque. Our aim is to make everything transparent."

At first blush, this distinction—transparency versus opacity—would seem to make all the difference. Tax havens are the undisputed global bad guys, while IMMI deploys their tactics in the interest of the public good. And yet, as Bill Maurer has convincingly argued, tax havens do not spring up of their own autonomous volition; instead, these legal spaces have emerged as the result of long-standing colonial relationships, processes of place-making in the service of someone else's needs (1997). In the rest of this chapter, I frame IMMI's intervention as a similar place-making process—a project of carving out not just a unique jurisdiction, but a distinctive claim to national status and standing. Like the tax havens to which it is favorably contrasted, IMMI is also the product of ongoing, unequal encounters, through which the island has been at some moments marginalized and at others decisively aligned with power. Understanding IMMI, then, requires digging into the particular conditions of its making, and the making of its relatively widespread appeal.

HACKING POLITICS

While IMMI made its public debut in 2010, the slow work of consolidating its politics had, at that time, long been underway. This is true of almost any legislation that ultimately graces the floor of the *Alþingi*; ideas are often shuttled between members of Parliament, experts, and advocacy groups before a piece of legislation is finalized. But IMMI was not developed by Parliamentarians, academics, or the journalists poised to benefit from its passage: IMMI was built by Icelandic hackers, deploying the tools and tricks of their trade.

A small group of hacker-activists had been organizing in Iceland around issues of free software and open standards—concerns they shared with a growing group of Free and Open Source Software (F/OSS) enthusiasts around the world (Kelty 2008; Chan 2013)—since the early 2000s.

In 2008, they formed the Icelandic Digital Freedoms Society (*Félags um Stafraent Frelsi á Íslandi,* abbreviated as the FSFÍ), and it was at that society's first conference in Reykjavík where the vision for IMMI was initially named. John Perry Barlow, American libertarian and founder of the Electronic Frontier Foundation, had been invited to deliver a keynote at the conference. Toward the end of his talk on the decline of digital freedoms globally, titled "On the Right to Know," he made the apparently offhand comment that "My dream for this country is that it could become like the Switzerland of Bits."[6] Smári McCarthy, one of those early activists, later recalled to me that "Some people just forgot about that—everyone agreed that he had given a really good speech. But some of us, especially the people at the core of this organization [the FSFÍ], we thought, well, we need to figure out what to do about this."[7]

Smári recounted those early efforts to me over a series of coffees, beers, and milkshakes in the first weeks and months of my fieldwork. It was largely through his invitations and introductions that I first got to know the small city of Reykjavík, especially its green spaces and side streets still free from the tourist-oriented "puffin shops" (or *lundabúðir,* so named for their most popular souvenirs) increasingly clogging its main drags. Joining his cadre of programmers turned political activists, I passed afternoons and evenings that first summer shuttling around the central square of Ingólfstorg, from cozy coffee shops to even more compact bars, laptops always in tow.

That he indulged me in this way is a sign of Smári's passion for the project and enthusiasm for bringing others on board. That he could detail the origins of IMMI for me so cogently, in quippy sound bites or exacting detail, is a sign of the attention that it, and he, were getting at the time. As a graduate student interested in IMMI, I was, by no means, alone; my early research proceeded amidst a steady stream of international media on the initiative.[8] Tellingly, some of Smári's friends and fellow activists would routinely confuse me with another academic (a political scientist on a Fulbright scholarship) and a reporter on assignment from AP. IMMI had an energy and urgency about it that many were eager to understand.

Following the Barlow keynote, Smári told me, a small group within the FSFÍ started meeting and broaching exploratory talks with members of government. And then, the financial crisis of 2008 hit. "We were totally waylaid," Smári said. "Everybody had bigger things to worry about." But also, he said, "Some of us became much more explicitly political. We saw that the form of democracy we'd been running wasn't actually sufficient. That there had been a lack of information flow that prevented those who needed to make decisions from having the information they needed to make those decisions." At the following year's FSFÍ conference, they invited Julian Assange and Daniel Domscheitt-Berg, the founding figures of WikiLeaks, to offer the keynote.

WikiLeaks today is known for publishing, among other things, the "Afghan War Diary," the "Iraq War Logs," a cache of US State Department diplomatic cables, and the emails of the Democratic National Committee during the 2016 Hillary Clinton campaign; it is also known for the espionage and sexual assault allegations that led to its founder Julian Assange's seven-year hideout in an Ecuadorian embassy, followed by his arrest in London in 2019. But in 2009, in Reykjavík, Iceland, WikiLeaks was known for releasing the loan books of Kaupthing, the largest bank in the country before the financial collapse. Documenting excessive risk-taking and dubious lending practices, including loans issued to borrowers with a significant stake in the bank itself,[9] the Kaupthing leak was a bombshell in the wake of the financial crash, exposing a blend of corruption, hubris, and incompetence that complicated the government's ongoing insistence that Iceland had fallen victim to international forces beyond its control. Assange and Domscheitt-Berg spoke at the FSFÍ conference (as well as on the popular TV talk show *Silfrið*) and they stayed on after the conference ended, joining FSFÍ members in their discussions of what making Iceland a "Switzerland of Bits" could mean.

Smári described the work that followed as "hacking." Because the activists involved in the FSFÍ all came from a computer programming background (Smári himself started tinkering at the age of twelve), it was this skill set they brought to bear on legislative change. As Smári recalled one afternoon over onion rings, when the group started seriously pursuing legislation, he got in touch with a Swedish politician friend who taught him how to read what he called "legal code." Over two long days, his friend introduced him to law's "internal reference system" and then set him loose to set up a wiki and start poking around. "That's a very typical hacker thing," Smári told me. "You get something complicated and you tinker with it until you kind of understand. There's this inherent playfulness, you know, enjoying understanding how systems function, and fiddling with them—seeing if you can make them do weird things."

Smári plainly delights in this kind of process; to converse with him is to wander down winding garden paths of esoterica he has accumulated through extensive travels and a wildly varied career. In 2009, however, Smári directed his formidable attention to probing for weaknesses in Icelandic information law and combing the international landscape for fixes that Iceland might add. Ultimately, these wound up including details from American, British, and Norwegian Freedom of Information Acts; Belgian source protection law; and Swedish telecommunications regulation.

Smári was not the only one who situated the origins of IMMI in hacker practice. Birgitta Jónsdóttir, IMMI's chief sponsor in Parliament, frequently makes the connection, too. In 2009, Birgitta was a longtime activist, an MP for the renegade postcrisis political party The Citizen's Movement (*Borgarahreyfingin*), and proud claimant to the title "the only geek in Parliament." She also became an ardent supporter of WikiLeaks and helped produce the infamous "Collateral Murder" video from footage leaked by Chelsea Manning in 2010. Birgitta would spearhead the IMMI resolution and help secure the votes it needed to pass in Parliament.

I only spoke with Birgitta one time. The most public face of IMMI internationally, and an active member of Icelandic Parliament, Birgitta was more difficult to get ahold of than the programmer types I would reliably run into at neighborhood haunts. For months, I showed up at events where she was speaking and read her (many and varied) public writings before I summoned the confidence and the contacts to set up an interview. I met her on the unseasonably sunny balcony of her Reykjavík office, where Birgitta proceeded to hold court for over an hour like the seasoned speaking professional she is. She, too, did so in the idiom of computation.

Where Smári described the process of building IMMI as akin to hacking, Birgitta (who got her start as a web developer in the 1990s) tended to describe the IMMI resolution *itself* as a kind of hack. By this, I mean that she routinely figured IMMI as a creative work-around that unsettled the existing system, as a clever and elegant solution to a problem, executed with a touch of subversive pleasure and pride. For example, at one point Birgitta explained to me, "In IMMI the most important bit, I think, for the global context, is to find a hack so that we can protect intermediaries from being in the role of randomly taking down stuff because of copyright holders." In this formulation, IMMI enacts a "hack" by skirting the pitfalls of copyright law, cutting off a route by which, as she put it, "mega corporations feed off people's imaginary assets." Later on, Birgitta summarized the resolution differently: "WikiLeaks had already hacked the system by storing different bits of information in different countries. . . . What Iceland aimed for was creating the conditions that could hold it all here. IMMI," she went on, "isn't about Iceland only—Iceland is the platform you can build it on." By calling Iceland the "platform," Birgitta framed the island (and its legislation) as a kind of base layer, akin to an operating system on which computer programs run; Iceland, in this case, may set the conditions, but can be deployed toward any number of ends. In changing the rules of the game, then, IMMI would act not only on Icelandic legislation, it would "hack" the whole global media environment.

Birgitta, a self-described "poetician" (her term for being a poet and a politician at once), clearly enjoys eloquently riffing on a theme. That day, she also described Iceland's current constitution as "virus infected," and the new one—written in the wake of the financial crisis, but not yet adopted at the time of this writing[10]—as much-needed "new hardware." She said of IMMI, "I always say, when I meet other lawmakers, 'This is C-V—copy-paste at will!'" But the language Birgitta uses is not only a metaphor: it references a shared set of experiences central to the formation of a shared worldview. Smári and Birgitta's overlapping assessments signal that IMMI originated in the practices, understandings, and ideals of computer programming, hacking more specifically. The two share with each other, and many of their IMMI coconspirators, a lived experience of encountering unfreedom in computational contexts (for example, in the form of restrictive copyright licenses), *and* the experience of crafting alternatives, workarounds, and countermeasures. Such experience produces a particular orientation that is widely if inexactly shared (Coleman 2004). It is this common practice, and overlapping context, that make both the process and product of IMMI legible as "a very typical hacker thing." It was, indeed, such a "hacker thing" that one Icelandic journalist I spoke to (one of the people who could, arguably, benefit from IMMI the most) said definitively, "Journalists would never have come up with this."

If IMMI, then, emerged from such a particular context, was shaped by such a specific worldview, how did it find such widespread appeal in Iceland? How did work started by the highly specialized FSFí obtain not only an audience in Parliament, but its unanimous approval? Understanding IMMI's influence requires tacking back to the financial crisis that first derailed the FSFÍ's work—the crisis that first propelled Birgitta into Parliament. The financial crash of 2008, I argue, created the conditions in which IMMI's aspirations were not only legible, but also desperately wanted. If the crisis fundamentally destabilized many Icelanders' sense of their place in the world, crafting a new relationship to digital data has helped some of them carve it out again.

A CRISIS OF IDENTITY

When I first started visiting, then living in, Iceland, the financial crisis of 2008 was still a touchstone. People referred to the crisis repeatedly, habitually, even compulsively, in order to situate themselves and mark their lives. Before the crisis, things were one way; after the crisis, they were another. One entrepreneur I met, when asked how he decided to start his own company, answered quickly, "It happened in the crash. Watching everything crumble down, all systems, technical and human . . . it did a reset on society." Another friend described the crash as a wake-up call: "I always thought Iceland was different from other places, that its size meant we took responsibility for each other. But what the bankers had done—it was like, what the hell is going on here?" She credits the crisis with opening her eyes, if darkening her outlook. One couple I met decided to have a child together, another decided to separate, and both pointed back to a hinge that swung open in the backdraft of Iceland's economic collapse.

Among Icelanders, I heard the crash (*hrunið*) mentioned matter-of-factly, glossed as a well-trodden steppingstone. To me, though, it was often first referenced with a held gaze, one that lingered one beat past the pace of conversation, until my nod signaled I knew just what that meant here. The financial crash of 2008, of course, was "global" in the sense that its ripple effects spread across borders easily. But it also signified something particular wherever its losses were acutely felt. In Iceland, its fallout was still visible not only in the ways that people wrapped their life stories around it, but also in half-finished construction projects around the Reykjavík harbor, in still-constricting capital controls, and in the way our first lesson in Icelandic class for foreigners was focused on accurately expressing our unemployment—many among us were *í vinnuleit*, or looking for work.

Between 2002 and 2007, the period now referred to as "the miracle years" (or, alternately, "the manic millennium" [Mixa 2009]), Iceland burst explosively onto the international banking scene. Such an arrival was unexpected, as it would have been unthinkable just a decade before; until the 1980s, foreign currency restrictions were standard and access to capital was limited, distributed politically. On the initiative, however, of Prime Minister Davíð Oddsson (who would go on to become Chair of the Central Bank), a series of neoliberal reforms rapidly liberalized banking practices, cutting regulations and lifting capital movement restrictions.[11] Meanwhile, the privatization of previously national fishing resources created and concentrated new wealth.[12] Icelandic banks and firms responded to this mix of means and motive with a concerted push toward global acquisitions, fast expanding Iceland's international profile, alongside its national debt portfolio. Quickly dubbed the "Business" or "Venture Vikings" (*útrásarvíkingar*),[13] the cohort of young, male bankers at the forefront of these investments were held up as national heroes (Loftsdóttir 2015). By 2008 the market value of Icelandic stocks had increased 700 percent, while its three major banks were steeply leveraged at eight times the national GDP (Aliber and Zoega 2011).

By October of the same year, following the fall of Lehman Brothers, and many other firms around the world in its wake, crisis arrived in Iceland with a speed and scale that mirrored the island's preceding success. This moment is memorialized in a still-referenced television announcement by then–Prime Minister Geir Haarde, who ended his message with the solemn and unsettling invocation, "God bless Iceland." Almost immediately, the government was forced to shut down the stock market, its three major banks fell into receivership, and its currency was devalued by 66 percent. This meant the price of (mostly imported) consumer products—as well as the debts of Icelanders who had borrowed during the "miracle years"—effectively doubled overnight. In November, the Icelandic government accepted a $2.1 billion "stabilization package" from the International Monetary Fund.[14] Each of these developments was painfully impactful for Icelanders, resulting in loan defaults, lost savings, and cutbacks in social services.

As is now the stuff of leftist legend, the economic crisis in Iceland quickly precipitated a political one (Bernburg 2015). As the dust cleared, a consensus emerged that the crisis had resulted from corruption within the financial sector, left unchecked and even encouraged by government. Popular outrage sparked the largest protests in Icelandic history, which met every Saturday from October into January in the square across from the *Alþingishús*. Protesters, sometimes numbering in the thousands, implicated Geir Haarde's conservative government in both the ill-gotten gains of the previous decade and the preceding neoliberal projects of privatization and deregulation that enabled Iceland's banking risks in the first place. Although the movement, dubbed "The Pots and Pans Revolution" (*Búsáhaldabyltingin*), was largely peaceful, on January 20, 2009, police used batons and tear gas to disperse the restless crowd. Six days later, the ruling coalition ceded to public pressure and finally stepped down. Snap elections delivered a majority to a left-leaning coalition of the Social Democratic and Left-Green parties.

Understandably, the period following the crisis was characterized by a hunger for political reform. IMMI, then, emerged amidst a wide range of efforts designed to redirect and restore faith in Icelandic governance—from a slate of new political parties, to e-governance initiatives, to a council elected, then appointed, to rewrite the Icelandic constitution. But accounting for IMMI's particular appeal in this moment requires understanding another dimension of the Icelandic financial crisis, its widespread resonance as a crisis of identity, too.[15]

A common refrain that followed the financial crash in Iceland was the lament "We look like a Third World country now." To me, these words were often bracketed with air quotes, signaling that their author felt the stretch of the analogy, and yet still found it the best available fit. With it, they suggested, albeit somewhat sheepishly, that the recent revelations of corruption, the forced resignation of the government, and the acceptance of a multibillion-dollar IMF loan all added up to the kind of predicament in which fellow "First World" countries do not tend to find themselves. They seemed to raise a specter of coloniality supposedly long since put to bed.

Comparisons made at this juncture between Iceland and others confirmed a shift in company. For example, Michael Lewis's much-anticipated book *Boomerang: Travels in the New Third World* opened by explaining the Icelandic financial crisis, placing a premium on what the author diagnoses (in about a week-long visit) as a distinctive strain of masculinity, comparing "the Icelandic male" to "moose, rams, and other horned mammals" (2011, 26). Or, "Think of Iceland as Grand Sicily," Birgitta Jónsdóttir wrote in an article titled "Democracy in the Digital Era." Later in the same piece, she likened the country's corruption to that of "some African countries which declared independence a decade after Iceland."[16] Tapping into a well-trodden teleology of political "development," it is the surprise of Iceland's peers here that is meant to pack a punch; maybe, Icelanders and others seemed to wonder, Iceland was not as Nordic-model modern as it was made out to be.

The question *What kind of place is Iceland really?* has long been an anxious and animating one. With its six-hundred-year colonial history, its long-standing associations with isolation and alterity, *and* its relatively wealthy and white-dominant population, the island has occupied a kind of "Northern borderlands" (Oslund 2011), straddling conceptions of the European self and other, core and periphery, colonizer and colonized. Such shifting identifications can be read from the European record, in which travelers often described Icelanders as "uncivilized"—sometimes in the register of the noble savage, and other times that of the barbaric primitive (Ísleifsson 2011). They can equally be seen in Icelandic attempts to correct that record; for example, Árngrímur Jónsson's 1609 treatise *Crymogæa* states that its primary aim was to "defend the fatherland," to show that "even though Iceland is 'neither Italy nor Greece', it belongs to the society of Christians and not that of 'pagan barbarians'" (Durrenberger and Pálsson 1989, xv).

The question of Iceland's place in relation to Western imperial formations is still resonant, still decidedly unresolved. Where Iceland has been defined in relation to others, notions of centrality and marginality, difference and sameness, belonging and exclusion play off one another—powerfully, strategically, unpredictably. As anthropologist Kristín Loftsdóttir has argued,

Icelanders now occupy a place "within the category of 'white', 'masculine' and 'civilized', but their positioning within that category can in no way be seen as secure" (2011, 18). And if Iceland's imprecise and unstable coordinates in lasting schemes of global classification mean that questions of status and standing come up with regularity, the financial crisis of 2008 posed these questions with particular force.

Loftsdóttir drives this point home in her analysis of the infamous IceSave banking fiasco (2012, 2019). In 2006, as part of its international expansion, the Icelandic bank Landsbanki established an online savings bank called IceSave, operating in the Netherlands and United Kingdom. As such, Landsbanki's sudden bankruptcy in 2008, and the depletion of the Icelandic Depositors' and Investors' Guarantee Fund, did not only threaten the finances of Icelanders, it also put more than three hundred thousand foreign depositors' savings at risk. In line with the European Union's deposit guarantee program, the United Kingdom demanded that Iceland cover the losses; when they found no compensation forthcoming, the British government invoked the Anti-Terrorism, Crime, and Security Act to freeze Landsbanki's assets in London.

Icelanders, unsurprisingly, bristled at the invocation of crime and terror in their national time of need. One group of the particularly aggrieved, adopting the name InDefence,[17] took it upon themselves to organize a response: they encouraged Icelanders to send postcards to the British prime minister, with the caption "Do I look like a terrorist to you, Mr. Brown?" As Loftsdóttir argues, these postcards, featuring smiling images of largely blond and blue-eyed Icelanders, were designed to invoke a contrast with a familiar Other—the more "likely" Muslim and Middle Eastern terrorist—in order to distance and differentiate Icelanders.[18] In her assessment, the IceSave debacle and its aftermath illustrate both the instability of Iceland's national standing *and* the tools it has at its disposal, nevertheless. IceSave showed how easily Icelanders could wind up within the category of alterity, and also how effectively whiteness and a sense of "civilization" could be mobilized to pull them out again.

The financial crisis, then, destabilized not only Iceland's economy but also its status and self-conception—prompting a range of efforts to decisively reestablish Iceland's place in the world. I want to suggest here that IMMI worked as one of these. On a political level, IMMI's emphasis on accountability responded to Iceland's crisis in governance. If the financial crash had resulted from secret deals, insider trading, and inappropriately personal relationships, then IMMI promised to restore political order by enacting clear and cutting-edge procedural rules. In these aims, IMMI aligned with other concurrent reform initiatives, such as the effort to redraft the constitution, setting term limits for the president and prime minister, and instantiating a referendum mechanism by which citizens could put issues to vote. IMMI's self-described "ultra-modern" freedom of information provisions—for example, its stipulations around public access to government documents—suggested that going forward officials could and would be held in check.

Meanwhile, proponents of IMMI also touted the economic benefits that Iceland stood to reap. As one member of Parliament told me, waggling his fingers in exaggerated air quotes, "IMMI is not just 'human rights'. This is about huge economic opportunity. It will support a growing sector in the economy." This MP, registering a different take on IMMI than Smári and Birgitta's more insurgent accounts, was not alone in this assessment. By creating an appealing legislative environment, many argued that IMMI would attract and promote economic development. IMMI's potential to attract not just media but other data-driven industries (through strengthened protections for internet "intermediaries" and loosened restrictions on "virtual" limited liability companies) made it appealing as a business proposition, too. As the resolution itself states, "It is hard to imagine a better resurrection for a country that has been devastated by financial corruption than to turn facilitating transparency and justice into a business model."[19]

Lastly, however, and perhaps most importantly, IMMI addressed that less neatly defined need evoked in the crash as crisis of identity. It addressed itself to the vexing question *What kind of place is Iceland really?*, its feared fall from grace from Nordic-model nation to as-yet-defined something else. This resonance was just as important as its political and economic incentives. IMMI responded to the anxieties piqued by the financial crisis by declaring a niche in data storage. Staking such claims, I argue, helped place Iceland squarely within a steadily sedimenting geography of data management that maps onto familiar civilizational divides.

INFORMATION'S ORDERS AND OTHERS

In its early days, techno-optimistic accounts cast the internet as inherently democratic and *democratizing*.[20] Unfettered access to information, analysts prophesied, could not help but expose corruption, increase government transparency, and uplift the voices of the systematically oppressed. For these reasons, information technology (IT) quickly emerged as a prominent centerpiece for international development programs (Donner 2008). Nicholas Negroponte, cofounder of the MIT Media Lab and the One Laptop Per Child (OLPC) initiative, went so far as to crown the internet as "the way to world peace."[21] Free information, in other words, was meant to make for a freer world. And yet, things have not quite shaken out that way.

As it turned out, it didn't matter much that you had access to the internet if you could still be arrested for publishing critical material—or have your data seized before you even got the chance. Gag orders and defamation suits worked just as well in the age of the internet, as did intimidation tactics targeting journalists. As Jo Glanville, editor of the Index on Censorship put it, "The Internet has been a revolution for censorship as well as free speech."[22] What's more, as the aftermath of the "Arab Spring" uprisings illustrated, the internet itself—if used in ways that threatened leadership—could easily be locally, literally, shut down. In other words (specifically, the words of several IMMI enthusiasts), we *had the technology* to transmit information extensively and efficiently, but social, political, and legal systems were selectively slowing it down.

IMMI, then, conceived as a project of creating an information "haven," offered not only a progressive vision of data management, but an actual outlet for the same; the resolution, were it implemented, would offer the services of both lock box and launch pad for people living in places where information remained unfree. But exactly who were those people and where were those places? If IMMI posited the need to carve out an exception, what was the alternative it allowed its users to escape? This, the resolution suggests, is poor data management: practices of holding data too tightly, or not tightly enough. If IMMI intervenes as an activist corrective, it does so by framing the rest of the world as dangerously out of sync; it does so by tapping into familiar characterizations of order, and its outsiders, on the internet.

Consider, for example, "The Great Firewall of China." First coined in 1997 by *Wired* reporters Geremie Barmé and Sang Ye, the "Great Firewall" describes the assemblage of policies and technologies that regulate internet use in the People's Republic of China (PRC), the range of filtering, surveillance, and censorship mechanisms that limit what people can see, and share, online.[23] The "Great Firewall" has been much discussed since Barmé and Ye's article, but their seminal account largely sets the tone: it situates the Chinese state as backward-facing and archaic, the relic of a prior era that has not yet caught up.[24] If anything has changed in the twenty-plus years since their reporting, it is that Western journalists are now forced to grapple with the Chinese system's undeniable endurance.

Framing China as an isolationist, out-of-sync relic, is, of course, nothing new. The same observations are routinely made with reference to the culture, politics, and economics of the PRC (Rofel 1999). But it is worth noting that China is now also viewed, and represented in Western media, as excessively closed *informationally.* This new site of scrutiny signals a larger shift: data management, that is, how a state facilitates (or forecloses) the transmission of information to and between its citizens, has become a new yardstick for countries' compliance with geopolitical norms. China's excessive hold on data is viewed as an aberration, in a resonant simplification of political difference that Maximilian Mayer has described as "digital orientalism" (2019). China, then, with its too-tight grasp on information, represents one far edge of digital unfreedom. Russia has come to embody another.

If the Russian hacker has become a household figure since the 2016 American presidential election, it is worth remembering that he was active in Western imaginations well before. Russian hackers, assumed to be backed by Putin's government, were implicated in the Wall Street hack of 2013 and were early suspects in the Sony hack of 2014 (which was later concluded to be an inside job). As sociologist Norma Möllers writes, "'Russian trolls are framed as taking advantage of the 'uncivilized' nature of cyberspace, either by disseminating pro-Russian propaganda or by intentionally exacerbating existing conflicts" (2020, 14). Put differently, if the internet is the new "Wild West," Russian hackers are its bandits, exploiting weak systems and unregulated space. Or, as a 2020 *New York Times* article detailing the threat of cyberattacks on the presidential election put it,

"Chaos is the point."[25] As cybersecurity, then, becomes a key site for the production of state power and nationalist sentiment, Russia is figured as informationally invasive—insinuating itself into other states' affairs online and deliberately muddying their data sets. Where China is critiqued for its informational closure, Russia appears as an avatar of informational excess.

The "African scammer" is yet another figure that haunts Western internet imaginaries: the hopeless romantic, the long-lost relative, the temporarily illiquid prince. These savvy actors are seen as weaponizing global connectivity, procuring ill-gotten international gains. In fact, as Jenna Burrell has argued, it is precisely Western stereotypes of Africa that some Ghanaian scammers use to their advantage, conjuring vague visions of poverty and violence in order to play predictable roles in their appeals (2008). Though online scams are far from exclusively African in origin, the continent has nevertheless come to be associated with this aberrant practice (Hu 2015) and Africans are aggressively pursued by vigilante "scambaiters" who frame their pursuit in racist and civilizational terms (Nakamura 2014). It is a sense of informational anarchy that shades these relations, unchecked by presumably absent or dysfunctional government, and coming to occupy a third pole of perceived online threat.

My goal here is not to defend practices we might classify as citizen surveillance, cyberwarfare, and fraud.[26] Instead, I want to draw attention to the ways that these behaviors are read according to already-existing rubrics, which position the West as orderly and appropriately "open," and the rest of the world as insufficiently so. My point is precisely how possible, even intuitive, it is to draw these lines and achieve some consensus about who belongs on either side. "Bad" states mismanage information, hoarding, leaking, meddling, locking down. Conversely, "good" states practice— or at least know to publicly celebrate—some combination of information freedom and security, an ongoing commitment to transparency discourse coupled with appropriately scaled and directed data management.[27]

These are, I emphasize, *discourses* rather than assessments of actual fact. This much is evident in the glaring contradiction, for example, of the United States. Consider the coexistence of then–Secretary of State Hillary Clinton's full-throated condemnation of whistleblower Chelsea Manning and her declaration the very same year that "Those who disrupt the free flow of information in our society or any other pose a threat to our economy, our government, and our civil society."[28] Clinton's two-minded-ness on this subject, I would argue, is less a sign of individual hypocrisy than of the ways that information management has obtained political gravity, has emerged as one of the always-shifting admission criteria to the liberal, modern, "civilized" Western world. Only within such a framework could the United States effectively—in spite of overwhelming evidence to the contrary—represent itself as the kind of state that manages its information in an open, equitable, and democratic way.

In other words, information management practices are coming to stand in as a sign for something else—a something else I will gloss as "rank" here, since so many other terms apply. For example, information management slides easily into association with modernity, a slippery signifier defined less by empirical benchmarks than by a relational sense of what the West has and what others—geographically or culturally outside it—lack (Chakrabarty 2000; Trouillot 2002). The concept of modernity charts a comparative axis, positing a single trajectory through history and marking people and places as either "ahead" or "behind." Today, for example, information management interventions such as the digitization of state bureaucracy are often uncritically described as "modernizing," tapping directly into this teleology (O'Hara 2020). IMMI makes the same move in describing its freedom of information provisions as "ultra-modern." One member of Parliament, speaking in passing, once glossed the resolution's contents to me as "You know, all that good modern stuff." The modern here signals a threshold of technological advancement whose clearing brings Iceland up to date, if not ahead of its time.

Liberalism is another distinction that appropriate information management can confer. Conceived in political terms as a model in which the state is charged with securing the freedom of individuals, liberalism is associated with particular *liberties*—including representative democracy, freedom of speech, and freedom of the press. A specific mode of information management is implied in the very presence of these entitlements and considered essential to their maintenance; meanwhile, state practices of information management can either enhance (e.g., the online availability of government records enshrined by IMMI) or erode them (e.g., the censorship of the internet). Like modernity, the tenets of liberalism are less useful as a kind of concrete checklist and better conceived as "a moving target developed in the European empire and used to secure power in the contemporary world" (Povinelli 2006, 13); liberalism lays down another us-them distinction, another ranking exercise in which the management of information comes to play a pivotal role.

As critical scholars have long argued, both modernity and liberalism are inescapably racialized. Both concepts emerged amidst the vastly unequal encounters of colonization and the extreme unfreedoms of racial slavery (Lowe 2015). As such, these ideals, which set the terms of civilizational progress, reveal their limitations in a stubborn inability to theorize the violence and dispossession at their core (Gilroy 1993). Despite early predictions that "cyberspace" would render race irrelevant (thus naturalizing racism rather than confronting it), media theorists have shown that race remains salient in determining who achieves the status of digitally liberal modern, whose informational practices are read as in line with the internet's foundational freedoms and whose are excessive, aberrant, or anti-.[29] We might draw, then, another near-concentric circle atop this Venn diagram of terms: whiteness is another category of rank with which information management comes to be associated. As Tung-Hui Hu writes, "the shadow of the racialized other still resurfaces in calls for Internet freedom," rendering the idealized internet an inherently white space (2015, 87–88). Reflecting on the boldness of IMMI's intervention, one activist and early supporter of the resolution (who told me her marriage into a mixed-race family had afforded her a fresh perspective) said, "We're really lucky we're white. If we were an island off South America or Africa we would have been treated differently."

Again, in drawing these lines, the point I wish to highlight is information management's increasingly intuitive affiliation with a host of other freighted, comparative terms: modernity, liberalism, and whiteness. Practices of storing and sharing information are conceptualized as elements of these formulations and deployed in order to align people and places with them. This context helps situate IMMI's intervention, as well as its widespread appeal. If the financial crisis raised the question *What kind of place is Iceland really?* and suggested as one answer *Not what we thought*, then the act of casting the island not only as a model for good information management but as its international catalyst had the effect of affirming the island's position within these familiar hierarchies of rank.

Previously, drawing on Smári and Birgitta's analyses, I described IMMI as "hacking politics": the resolution was a clever fix for Iceland's legal environment that also threw a productive wrench into the global media landscape. Here, I want to position it as a hack of another kind, an exquisitely simple operation of moving Iceland from out-group to in-group, from one side to the other side of a salient line. If Iceland emerged from the crisis looking like a poor information manager (what is corruption, after all, if not information inappropriately siloed or shared), IMMI quickly reversed its course to make Iceland "information haven" to the world. It was a move that, through its full-throated enunciation of liberal freedoms and modern modes of governance, performed the same genre of place-making project as a postcard campaign mocking the near-definitional impossibility of an Icelandic terrorist. In this way, then, IMMI was framed as an exception, but its effect was profoundly normative. In a world where appropriate information management draws the dividing line between "us" and "Others," Iceland's becoming a haven for information is an act of nestling into belonging, rather than risking it.

Of course, the bold stance IMMI carved out for Iceland was not entirely without exposure. To be an exception is to risk becoming an outlaw. In fact, one official I spoke with in the Interior Ministry voiced concerns over making Iceland an information haven: "You cannot predict what would come out of it," she told me. "Would it be more likely that we would have criminal people here? Would terrorists have an eye on Iceland? We don't know." Outside Iceland, IMMI's international mission also courted controversy. In 2011, former Bush administration member Marc Thiessen wrote a blog post titled "Shut Down WikiLeaks' Icelandic Safe Haven," arguing that "The IMMI calls into question Iceland's seriousness as a NATO ally, and Iceland needs to realize there will be consequences for its actions." One way of restating this problem might be, was Iceland becoming the *Switzerland* of Bits, or the Caymans, the British Virgin Islands, the Seychelles? But the story that dominated, dismissing practicalities (including the fact that IMMI was passed as a Parliamentary Resolution and did not yet have a clear path toward being made law), was a celebratory one. The *New York Times*, for example, heralded "A Vision of Iceland as a Haven for Journalists";[30] the Italian *La Repubblica* celebrated "The Country Without a Gag."[31] By making the island a haven for information,

IMMI worked to communicate not only Iceland's economic and political recovery, but also the broader idea that Iceland was (*still,* or *again,* or *indisputably*) a modern, Western, First World, working place.

In suggesting IMMI was well timed, that it served this broader function, I do not mean to imply that it was cynical. It is clear to me that IMMI's developers and many of its supporters believed—and still believe—in its ideals. As for those ideals, it is not my aim to debunk them; I, too, see press freedom and public access to government information as eminently worthwhile social goods. What I want to do is highlight the ways in which information activists' pursuit of these improvements, and others' intuitive appreciation of the same, did not emerge from or operate in a vacuum. Our desires (political and otherwise) are always shaped by our environments *and* our imaginations of others and elsewheres. In the case of IMMI, its aspirations connected with a felt need to situate Iceland within the safe terrain of the "civilized." These fixations, as we have seen, are by no means unique to Iceland, but they operated with particular force here following the disruption of the financial crisis, and they formed part of the pull that led every member of Parliament to sign the IMMI resolution on June 16, 2010.

That triumphant signing, however, would be just the start of it. After IMMI was unanimously adopted as a resolution, a long, slow legislative process ensued. Recall that IMMI was not in itself legislation; it was a commitment to enact legislation later on. After IMMI was passed as a parliamentary resolution, it was assigned to a steering committee which would manage the long-term labor of translating IMMI's priorities into legal change. Then, that steering committee's recommendations were left to languish. Then, it was replaced by another one. Over the following years, the full span of my research, this process has trudged along, largely behind closed doors, with few substantive updates to report. While the bulk of this chapter, then, has addressed itself to the bang that IMMI started with, I conclude by turning to its resolving whispers.

THE EXCEPTION AND THE RULE

Following those first summers of preliminary research, during which time I documented the percolating progress of Smári, Birgitta, and their peers,

I moved to Iceland and started my fieldwork in earnest in the fall of 2014. What I found when I got back and asked after IMMI was an experience akin to observing an object in space: it seemed to flicker in and out of existence, maybe just distant, maybe already dead. In 2011, the architects of IMMI had founded an organization, the Icelandic Modern Media Institute, with the aim of continuing to compile best practices in global freedom of information and helping to advance the IMMI resolution through advocacy and participation in ministerial working groups. In 2012, the Icelandic Pirate Party (*Pírataflokkurinn,* or more often simply *Píratar*) was founded on the model of the International Pirate Party movement, taking up its focus on issues of intellectual property, privacy, transparency, and civil rights. Smári and Birgitta were both founding members, and Birgitta was among the first cohort to represent the party in Parliament; Smári would become a Pirate Party MP in 2016. These initiatives and others carried forward the work—and the spirit—of the original IMMI resolution, but had not yet made Iceland the information haven it set out to be.

In the summer of 2015, I met with the then-chair of the IMMI steering committee, Kristján, in a bright fifth floor meeting room of his office downtown. Kristján, unlike the authors and advocates of IMMI, is a lawyer who specializes in data privacy. Trim and clean-cut, he quicky made clear to me that he "wouldn't presume to be called a hacker," himself. "I am a lawyer," he said plainly. "I was hired for this job. I approach it as a practical task." Kristján was asked to take the helm by the minister of education and culture, under which work on IMMI was housed. While the resolution was passed under a Social Democratic government in 2010, it did not make substantial progress during its tenure. Under the Conservative government that had been reelected after it, however, the project had been re-funded and Kristján was cautiously optimistic. "Support won't be pronounced," he told me, "but under the surface it is there." As he walked me through a series of spreadsheets, his complex but clear system of project management, I shared his sense of possibility.

Four years later, however, on a phone call I placed from Florida, Kristján acknowledged that we had entered an aftermath, without ever really having experienced an event. "This is something of an epilogue," Kristján told me wearily. "None of the bills that we presented became law."

Kristján's team had painstakingly developed a series of proposals based on the tenets of the IMMI resolution and these proposals were handed over to the minister, but another parliamentary election took place not long after that. The incoming minister signed off on the IMMI proposals, but then they were not taken up by the government. "It's not so much that they declined them," as Kristján put it, "but they had other things on their plate and they chose to let this go."

Some of IMMI's proposed reforms have, in fact, moved forward. For example, a new Freedom of Information Act was passed in 2013, although it did not meet IMMI's original, "ultra-modern" aims. This law was amended in 2019,[32] and according to the Icelandic Modern Media Institute, "significantly improved." Source protections were also strengthened as part of the 2013 law, preventing journalists from being forced to reveal their sources in the absence of consent, or a judge's order. IMMI's more ambitious whistleblower protections, however, have not yet advanced. Following the appointment of a new steering committee in 2018, two additional laws have since passed: one limiting the liability of third-party hosting services,[33] and another clarifying the responsibilities of government employees to make information available to the public.[34] Meanwhile, efforts to remove data retention policies (which require telecommunications carriers to save users' data for six months in the interest of criminal investigation) seem to have stalled out, as doing so would conflict with EU directives, to which Iceland is subject as a member of the European Economic Area. At the time of this writing, proposals related to prior restraint, or libel and defamation, have not yet been put forward to Parliament.

IMMI, then, has prompted a serious and substantive review of Icelandic information law. A number of laws have been passed or updated, moving Icelandic legislation in the general direction of IMMI's aims. And yet, in any case and by any measure, Iceland is not serving as the "information haven" that IMMI originally set out to create. Despite the initial hype (and upset), Iceland has not become a mecca for insurgent news organizations or a launching pad for liberatory leaks. One network engineer, the first time I met him, started our interview by saying, "When I got your email I thought to myself, I'm going to have to tell the poor girl that Iceland isn't living up to its image!" A journalist I came to know in Reykjavík put a finer point on it:

> When I first heard about IMMI I thought, "beautiful, a great idea." But I was
> a little bit naive. People talk about it in a very simple way, this fairytale idea
> of the world they want to create. But when you look at the reality, Iceland is
> not close to being a haven for journalists, not in any sense.

He himself felt the absence of this status acutely when he was sued for
libel following his reporting on a high-profile incident of government corruption in 2014. After his case was settled out of court, against his wishes,
by the news outlet where he was employed, he described the IMMI resolution to me as a "Christmas decoration"—something that politicians said
they supported because it looked good but did not intend to do anything
about.

There are many reasons for this anticlimactic outcome, ranging from
the political to the pragmatic. For one thing, priorities shift quickly in a
context of crisis recovery. If, in 2010, the news cycle percolated with imag-
inative political initiatives, by 2015 it had returned to more quotidian
concerns. Perhaps, as some people read the situation, the government was
deliberately burying the IMMI resolution; perhaps, as others reasoned, it
had simply been confronted by more pressing issues. Either way, the political urgency that led to its passage as a resolution dissipated when it came
time to make IMMI into law.

The vision of IMMI was also inhibited by the affordances of material
infrastructure. Creating a "data haven" that would function not only sym-
bolically but practically would require robust and redundant connectivity,
which Icelandic engineers conceded they still lacked. At the time, the
island was connected by only three subsea fiber-optic cables: one to
Denmark, one to Greenland, and one to Scotland. This level of connectivity has proven perfectly adequate for sustaining Iceland's domestic traffic
but would not be sufficiently robust or redundant to accommodate the
demands of a global data hub. This meant, as another network engineer
put it—after first making sure he would not be named:

> If someone, say the US, wanted to get at something in Iceland, it would be
> easy to close Iceland down. They could cut off the cables at the entry points!
> You can't make a data haven in a country of 300,000 with a failed economy
> and two fiber-optic cables.[35] People have to understand their place in the
> world.

Of course, Iceland's place in the world is precisely the point. It is easy to read IMMI's outcome as a failure, to dwell on the gulf between exceptional ambition and everyday reality. But my interest in IMMI has focused on the ideological foundations its widespread popularity revealed. If IMMI sought not only to build a haven for information, but also to ambitiously recast Iceland itself, I have argued that it achieved one of these aims. By affiliating the island, through its information management, with meaningful signifiers of rank, Iceland reclaimed national status and standing following a devastating and deeply unsettling financial crash. Tapping into ideological currents that associate particular ideals and practices of data management with the "First World" rather than the "Third World," IMMI helped carve out a fresh place for Iceland on the right side of that obstinate line. As such, while IMMI was framed as an exception (a move that echoes efforts like Icelanders' response to IceSave and the Colonial Exhibition of 1905),[36] it actually draws our attention to an emergent but still effective rule, namely, the extent to which the ability to hold data appropriately—to keep it safe while making it "free"—is becoming a crucial metric for membership within the normative category of the "civilized" Western fold.

CONCLUSION

In a place that has long straddled the line between "core" and "periphery," confused the distinction between "West" and "rest," questions of rank have remained unsettlingly open, subject to shocks and reconfigurations that prompt the question *What kind of place is Iceland really?* It was in such a moment, a post–financial crisis, that the IMMI resolution achieved public purchase and information management became an important proving grounds. Specifically, the idea of Iceland as an information haven, a place that claimed a distinctive capacity to store and manage data well, proved a particularly effective vehicle for rehabilitating Icelandic political identity. As such, IMMI was not simply a reform measure, a targeted effort to change Icelandic information law. In starting a conversation about data sovereignty, it demonstrated that where data lived could matter, could confer benefits (and, perhaps, incur risks). In doing so, it showed how

Iceland's place in the world might be altered or affirmed by placing data, rendered by the cloud at once freshly mobile and yet still meaningfully fixed.

To return to the tax havens against which IMMI initially defined itself, these sites' exceptional status is neither accidental nor autonomously generated; it has been produced with and in the service of others, along predictably inequitable lines. As Bill Maurer writes, "tax havens have historically taken root in jurisdictional anomalies—holdovers of empires, feudal city-states, territories never fully incorporated into the Westphalian system of nation-states" (2008, 171). As such, efforts to shut down tax havens on the basis of financial fairness have only exposed the fiction of equivalence in a so-called "market of equals": tax havens are places whose economies were explicitly crafted in others' interests (Maurer 1997). IMMI, in proclaiming a haven for information, was an indisputably Icelandic project that nevertheless took shape amidst these long-standing and pervasive hierarchies.

At a moment when Iceland, itself a "holdover of empire," risked exposure as an underdeveloped, still-dependent territory, IMMI torqued the "haven" formulation to make the island into another kind of exception—not only a model for good information management, but a "platform" for its spread. Doing so, it aligned Iceland with ideals central to Western self-image, upholding associations between particular kinds of data management and long-standing civilizational divides. Ultimately, the most salient difference between IMMI and the tax havens might not lie in the bright line between "secrecy" and "transparency," but rather in the connotations information management carries that money management does not—the way that IMMI made Iceland not just a vessel for data, but a vehicle for liberty and liberalism, progress and modernity. As Birgitta said, with an impish grin during our interview, "*No one* wants to be against freedom of information."

As we have seen, the aspirations of IMMI have not (at least yet) been realized in Iceland. And yet, over the course of my research, as I watched IMMI languishing, I also watched data centers cropping up steadily in the rural and industrial outskirts of Reykjavík. I heard them humming along, ever louder, and read a growing number of explainers, then exposés, on their accelerating development—this, in spite of the fact that all this data remained unprotected by IMMI's umbrella of legislative reform.[37] IMMI, then, speaks less to the jurisdictional conditions strictly *required* to store data in Iceland and more to the stakes of such a project. The following chapters expand on this theme.

These next chapters shift, then, as my own research did, from the high-minded ideas of marketers and ideals of activists to the practicalities of data storage infrastructure and industry. They trace how data is anchored in Iceland through developers' plans, negotiations with municipalities, and eventually large-scale construction projects. They also ask how these efforts are experienced by the people who live amidst data centers today, including those who work inside them, and those who observe their operations from outside. As we will see, these more localized and everyday efforts are equally projects of Icelandic place-making; they are occasions of mutually transformative encounter between cloud-in-the-making and mutable ground.

PART II Anchoring

3   Something from Nothing

It is by now a trope in the travel writing about Iceland to describe the landscape that meets you at Keflavík International Airport as something akin to the surface of the moon. From the tarmac you can see mountains, but not very tall ones. Instead, the Reykjanes Peninsula is mostly lava on all sides, more dramatic black boulders clustered close to the water, and fields that flatten gradually, further inland. When the weather is wet but not yet freezing, they are blanketed by a near-fluorescent layer of green moss; in the winter the land ripples and dimples under snow. It is a stark sight I've often seen unnerve first-time travelers—it can take a moment to decide whether the vast expanse is barren or beautiful, coldly unnerving or quietly serene.

Hundreds of thousands of people traverse this landscape daily on their way to and from the Keflavík airport. It is the entry point for tourists, eager to make their way out to hikes, hot springs, and the Reykjavík nightlife. It is, apart from ships and ferries, the only way off the island, too. Reykjanes is a place, then, that people tend to pass through. This much was made clear to me quickly in my fieldwork: Icelanders told me that if I wanted "authentic" Iceland I should live on a sheep farm; if I wanted to have fun, I should stay in Reykjavík. But I found myself rooted, nevertheless, on the Reykjanes Peninsula for the majority of my research, because if Reykjanes is a place that many people experience in passing, it is also a place where data stays. Today, the peninsula is a hub for data center construction; Iceland's first large-scale data center was built on Reykjanes in 2012. Over the course of my research, that facility was expanded, and a second was constructed nearby. Since then, a third data center has been built on the peninsula, and more are always said to be on their way. In the time I spent living on Reykjanes, observing these developments, I came to understand that the reason so much data now resides here is the same reason so many people move right through; both are the inheritance of Reykjanes's fifty-year history as an American military base.

From 1953 to 2006, the peninsula was occupied (and *occupation* is indeed the word many Icelanders use to describe it) by the Naval Air Station Keflavík, or NASKEF. The base began as a fueling platform in the early years of World War II, but as that war came to an end with another already on the horizon, the American government identified Iceland as a strategic outpost on the hinge of an increasingly bipolar world. In 1951, the United States and Iceland signed a defense agreement granting the right to station American troops here. Over the following decades, NASKEF was built into a full-scale, functioning community, equipped with the airfields, arsenals, living quarters, backyards, and baseball fields its growing population required. The road to Reykjanes, then, bisected two lived realities. On one side, lower and closer to the water, were the Icelandic towns of Keflavík and Njarðvík, small city centers ringed by residential neighborhoods, modest harbors, and a coastline aggressively patrolled by Arctic terns. On the inland side, atop a slightly elevated plateau, was an American bastion in the North Atlantic: a massive architectural and infrastructural undertaking, a major economic driver and source of employment, and a site of ambivalent socialities stretched across that lonely and windswept highway.

This chapter considers the 2006 decommissioning of NASKEF, and the area's remaking in its wake—in particular, its emergence as a site for data center construction. While the arrival of the data storage industry on Reykjanes has been pitched as a transformative, distinctly future-facing development, I am interested in how neatly data centers have seemed to slide into the footprint left by the American base. As interna-

Figure 6. Map of the Reykjanes Peninsula.

tional data centers inherit the infrastructures of American occupation, they also reprise some of their social and spatial arrangements, tracing over the lines that NASKEF carved into the earth on Reykjanes, as well as into its residents' rhythms and routines. Documenting both infrastructural accretions *and* selective processes of wearing away, I argue that the data storage industry takes traction from the region's fraught military legacy. Digital data, then, is emplaced in Iceland not only by new construction, contracts, and investments; it is also, equally, anchored by persistent histories. Digital development proceeds not only through processes of innovation or "disruption"; on Reykjanes, it is built into, and out of, imperial remains.

WITHDRAWAL

On March 15, 2006, it was announced that the Naval Air Station Keflavík was closing. After a fifty-three-year presence in Iceland, the base would be drawn down over the course of just six months. As was explained first to the Icelandic government, and much later to Icelandic NASKEF employees, American military interests had shifted, and the Pentagon now planned to "adjust accordingly to meet the current global threat."[1] NASKEF would be one of many bases in Western Europe closed down in favor of more temporary installments—at once a response to growing antibase sentiment, financial constraints, and the emerging priorities of the United States' "War on Terror." Pursuant to a negotiated Joint Agreement, the United States would transfer all territory and facilities to the Icelandic authorities, "in the condition existing at the time of their return,"[2] as well as records and plans of the area. Moving forward, this space would be administered by a limited liability company under the prime minister's authority, which would "systematically convert the area for profitable civilian uses without disrupting the community."[3]

In his March announcement, Colonel Phillip Gibbons admitted, "We all realize this is not the ideal way to draw down a military force."[4] Two months later, Captain Mark Laughton put a finer point on his assessment: "It's like trying to cram a pig down a snake's throat."[5] In its last year, NASKEF was home to approximately 1,200 American service people, 100 Department of Defense civilians, and 900 Icelandic jobs. These numbers had already declined since the base's Cold War heyday, but remained significant in relation to the municipality of Reykjanesbær, which was formed in 1994 by consolidating the small towns of Keflavík, Njarðvík, and Hafnir; together, their population was around ten thousand.

By all accounts, six months was a punishing timeline for transition, and uncertainty erupted amidst the ranks. The month of the announcement, the base's weekly radio show was flooded with anxious inquiries: How do we dispose of our vehicles? How long will ATMs be stocked with American cash? Can houseplants be given to Icelanders as gifts? One caller asked, "How will turmoil with Icelanders affect packing out and shipping household goods?" He was told, however, convincingly, "No turmoil expected. They will provide professional service, as always."[6] This sense of intimate entanglement, definitive difference, and unflagging expectation across it, encapsulated in the NASKEF radio host's remark, speaks pointedly to the relationship between the base and the Icelanders around it. As is the case in other places where US military installations have been "hosted," opinions on the base were decidedly mixed.

Iceland's military entanglement began when British forces—after having twice tried and failed to secure basing rights—showed up onshore in May of 1940. Seeing as how Iceland had (and still has) no standing army, diplomats were received graciously enough by the government, and officials made tight-lipped appeals for the Icelandic public to welcome the British soldiers as "guests" (Hálfdanarson 2011). A year later, however, British troops were overextended, so the United States took their place on the island for the remaining duration of the war. By 1943, fifty thousand troops were stationed in Iceland, threatening to outnumber Icelanders in Reykjavík. This arrangement was hastily ratified in a bilateral defense treaty whose stated intention was defending Iceland against an anticipated German advance. If anyone doubted the benefits of such protection—and many, including both Nationalists and Socialists in government did—significant trade incentives were offered to Iceland to sweeten the deal (Ingimundarson 2011).

Occupation was only meant to last as long as the war did, but as the Second World War drew to a close, the United States was already looking east. Iceland, halfway across the Atlantic and at the center of the geopolitically strategic "GIUK" (Greenland-Iceland-United Kingdom) maritime gap, was right on the route it was feared a nuclear bomb could travel, on the path it was worried that Communism could spread. So in line with its Cold War strategy of global base-building,[7] the United States pushed for a new defense treaty that would secure it more permanent rights in Iceland.

This proposal faced significant popular and parliamentary resistance. Iceland, after all, had just declared independence from Denmark in 1944,[8] and few were eager to enter into another allegiance that would tie the nation so tightly to another foreign power. Furthermore, the everyday intimacies of occupation in Reykjavík were becoming cause for popular alarm. For example, relationships between Icelandic women and foreign soldiers (glossed as *ástandið*, or "the situation") were a site of intense and anxious scrutiny, resulting in a program of public health surveillance and the institutionalization of "at-risk" girls.[9] By 1949, however, political winds were shifting, and Parliament voted to join NATO—albeit over popular protests so strenuous that the United States made contingency plans in the case of a Communist coup (Ingimundarson 2011).[10] In 1951, following the North Korean invasion of South Korea, the Icelandic government came back to base negotiations with the United States and the resulting agreement established the Iceland Defense Force, a unit of American and NATO soldiers stationed in Iceland, meant to shield it from (or, depending on one's perspective, use it as a shield against)[11] the Eastern Bloc.

It was at this point that American presence on the island shifted decisively from Reykjavík to Reykjanes, where the Allies had built an airfield on the Miðnesheiði Plateau. This installation was expanded over the course of the Cold War to accommodate a permanent contingent of soldiers. Contractors extended runways and updated facilities; they built commissaries and dormitories, control towers and schools. These efforts transformed the plateau, while enrolling thousands of Reykjanes residents in the extended project of sustaining American occupation. Over the following years, the base would continue to be debated in Reykjavík as a source of risk and revenue,[12] a symbol of interconnection and empire. But the everyday effects of the Naval Air Station Keflavík would be concentrated on the Reykjanes Peninsula.[13]

I have yet to meet a single Reykjanes resident not related to someone who worked on the base (that is, if they did not once work there, themselves). Icelanders were hired to construct base buildings, service machinery, serve food, and administer payroll. Some, already living in Reykjanes, chose these career paths over the region's traditional fishing industry; others moved to the peninsula specifically to pursue these opportunities. In 1954, a contracting company, *Islenskir Aðalverktakar*, was founded expressly to service the base. Every day, then, hundreds climbed the hill, crossed the highway, and passed through one of the perfunctory armed checkpoints separating Reykjanesbær from NASKEF. Even more depended on a base paycheck or worked in a service industry increasingly bent toward the interests of enlisted men. If the ocean had once been the engine of Reykjanes's economy (like so many others on the island), the

Figure 7. The GIUK (Greenland-Iceland-United Kingdom) Gap, as represented by the CIA during the Cold War. Image reproduced from CIA.gov.

arrival of NASKEF created a new center of gravity that quickly captured the surrounding small towns in its orbit.

The military's conspicuous presence also brought about new connections. Many middle-aged residents of the region fondly recalled to me their early access to American beer, blue jeans, and candy bars—amenities, they liked to remind me, not available in Reykjavík at the time. Meanwhile, NASKEF broadcast Armed Forces Radio at a range that only reached Reykjanes, meaning that the peninsula enjoyed selective access to

Figure 8. Expanding the NASKEF base on Reykjanes, with Icelandic coastal settlements just visible in the background (1954).

"real" rock and roll and radio dramas, a legacy still perceptible in some older residents' Western drawls.

Arnar, a voluble middle-aged mechanic who worked on NASKEF for decades, was quick to tell me about his warm rapport with Americans, his friends who would break the base's strict rules against gift giving to share a turkey with him on Thanksgiving Day. His own invitation for me to spend a weekend at his family's summer house was a direct extension of such hospitalities, and over dinner, tucked away at the cozy wood cabin, he, his wife Margrét, and his son Tómas all regaled me with stories of American characters they had known over the years. But later, sipping beers while the fog rolled in around us, and after Tómas had withdrawn into his iPhone for the night, Arnar also told me about the time his son, at ten years old, had a gun drawn on him by an inexperienced soldier while playing on the fence surrounding the base. For Arnar and his family, intimacy was possible with the military, but it also always came with an edge.

Kolbrún, a warm woman who had worked in the accounting office, also remembered her time working for NASKEF in fond terms. "It was a nice family place" is a phrase she tended back toward over the course of our conversations. But unlike Arnar, who made American friends freely and easily, Kolbrún knew her possibilities were more constrained. When she got the job on base as a young woman, her parents made her promise that she wouldn't run off with an American soldier. At the time Kolbrún laughed at their dramatics, but she told me she took their warning seriously, too. Icelandic women who got involved with Americans got a "bad stamp," she told me. "It didn't matter if it was one or one hundred." If sexual surveillance during World War II had been a matter of state policy, once the American occupation shifted to Reykjanes, the policing of women took on a more intimate guise. It operated through whispers shared between concerned relatives, as well as slurs hurled at girls on sidewalks. So Kolbrún was careful to keep her distance, meticulously managing expectations and appearances over the course of her decades-long base career.

Lilja, an office manager who grew up in Reykjanes, a few years younger than Arnar and Kolbrún, described her own relationship with NASKEF as more explicitly charged. As a young woman, she told me she drove to the base daily to pick up her husband, a painter, from work. At the gate she made a point of speaking Icelandic to the uncomprehending American guards—even though her now-fluent English was already excellent. "We were on Icelandic soil, after all!" she said, laughing at her bold younger self. Lilja nodded when I asked, "So you were against the base politically?" Then she stopped nodding and continued, more subdued, "But you couldn't be political about it. Not when everyone you know worked there, not when they had all this stuff that you want. You can't be against TV." Lilja's principles, then, found a place to live alongside her pragmatism, in a context of uneven economic power.

In its everyday operation, then, the base created ambivalent entanglements across Reykjanes; cultural, commercial, and interpersonal ties were routinely forged and severed, uniquely incentivized and policed. Over time this relationship, however rough-edged, between the military and the peninsula would come to be viewed by outsiders as too close. NASKEF was seen by many Icelanders as a necessary evil and by many others as an imperial abomination. As such, Reykjanes residents' engagement with it marked them as dependent or even disloyal. As Kolbrún put it, "They [Icelanders outside Reykjanes] would say, 'You're in with the Americans' and look down on you." Work on the base was sometimes called *kanavinna* ("Yankee work"), presumed to lack the inherent dignity of Icelandic employment. But on Reykjanes, the base became a lively part of the landscape, a site where relationships of different kinds and qualities troubled attempts to fix its meaning and impact. A source of steady paychecks, a range of relationships, and affective attachments ranging from desire to contempt, the base became an organizing force for possibilities on the peninsula during the Cold War.

The drawdown of NASKEF, then, marked a monumental uncoupling. Arnar, when he described it, mimed grasping something growing and pulling it out, forcefully, by the root. Margrét, who also worked on base in the public works department, described the ensuing period as a "depression, not just economic but emotional." The municipal government set up emergency reemployment programs, which quickly filled in the veritable flood of applicants. But it was not only a matter of losing one's salary, Margrét specified: "The same people who built the base were being forced to tear it down." Icelanders' participation in the foreclosure of their own future (at least the one that had been made most readily available) was, in her view, a particularly painful exercise.

The base closure also drew into sharp relief the ways in which Icelanders' options had been narrowing all along. Education rates, for example, were lower on Reykjanes than they were anywhere else on the island, because well-paying jobs that did not require schooling had been plentifully available on the base for fifty years. Icelanders who held those jobs had been expertly trained in the standards and practices of the US military, but found that their skills did not necessarily translate to off-base work. Meanwhile, American investments in infrastructure and development meant that Reykjanes had been consistently deprioritized for government funds. The peninsula was made multiply vulnerable, then, by its long-term occupation, and the drawdown was only compounded by the international financial crash two years after (described locally as the "double-dip depression"). As the churning rhythms—both productive and disruptive—of base life slowed, then stopped on the peninsula, they created an absence widely felt on Reykjanes and still resonant ten years after the fact.

And yet, for all that NASKEF took with it, it also left quite a lot behind—specifically, a plateau full of facilities ranging from control stations and runways to community centers and secret cables under the sea,[14] all "in the condition existing at the time of their return." These remainders were the loose ends that Reykjanes residents had to work with and have weaved together following the closure of the base.

A BRIDGE TO THE GODS

KADECO, the company specified in the drawdown agreement and asked to "systematically convert the area for profitable civilian uses," was founded in October of 2006, one month after NASKEF officially closed. Named for the Keflavík Airport Development Company, KADECO was and remains responsible for managing Reykjanes's inherited infrastructures. Its original board members were appointed, two from Reykjavík government and one from Reykjanes, and their first daunting task was deciding what to do with all of the leftover space and stuff. One of those board members described the experience to me as "being handed a bag of keys and told to 'do something.'" Early proposals on the table ranged wildly, from luxury resort to international prison, from waste processing plant to rescue squad training facility. But within the first year, the board settled broadly on the idea of "Ásbrú: The Center of Innovation in Iceland."

Ásbrú is an enterprise park with a focus on technology. Today, it includes a "university bridge" program called Keilir, designed to prepare returning students for secondary education; two "incubators," or low-rent office parks for entrepreneurs; a handful of businesses, including car rentals, a hostel, and a gas station; and three large-scale international data centers. The data centers' high-tech image plays well into Ásbrú's promotional material, decidedly forward-looking in tone. Ásbrú's focus on "innovation" is posed as a promise: "The possibilities of the Ásbrú area are endless," its website says. But the name *Ásbrú*, like many place names in Iceland, hearkens back to Norse mythology; Ásbrú is the land bridge (also referred to as Bifrost) that connects the world of gods to the world of men.

The name, as I found in my time there, is fitting: like its mythical name-sake, this Ásbrú is aspirational infrastructure, too. A plot of land, a pile of buildings, and a marketing strategy, nine years in Ásbrú was still coming to be.

I moved to Reykjanes in the spring of 2015, into an apartment building recently and rapidly converted from military housing. Only a few days after my arrival, I was invited up to Keilir, the university bridge program on Ásbrú, to meet one of its administrators, Geir. Wiry and energetic, Geir still looked every inch a teacher, which he was for years before accepting his current position—a new angle from which to influence education, albeit in a context thoroughly saturated with the politics of reoccupying previously occupied space. Geir had been welcoming and warmly supportive of my research; when I first asked about renting an apartment at Ásbrú, he laughed and said, "Sure, we have two thousand apartments, all built from your money!" This was the first time an interlocutor had placed me so squarely within the "you" and "yours" of American militarism, and I felt briefly thrown back on my heels. But while some others' use of the second person plural would be more pointed, Geir's was a genuine invitation. This was someone who spent his days cheerfully sifting through out-of-place Americana, trying to find a way to put it to use; I had the impression, that day, of being added to his pile.

Geir was proud of his part in transforming Reykjanes and eagerly offered to show me around. He was also keenly aware that *someone* had to show me; progress here was not always readily evident, and he wanted me to learn to read it through his well-trained and optimistic eyes. So when I found Geir in the Keilir offices, ribbing receptionists and greeting students by name, he suggested we go for a drive and quickly whisked me out the door. Before getting far, we stopped briefly under an awning for Geir to point across the parking lot at "Iceland's only baseball field," a rusting diamond looking ragged in the rain. I asked if anyone ever used it and Geir laughed at what he clearly considered a good joke.

Geir ushered me into his well-appointed SUV and we set out across the vast plateau. As he drove, he swiveled in his seat to gesture out the windows, illustrating the scope of what he saw as opportunity. We passed the restaurant where he ate his first hamburger (under new management) and the old officers' club, "Top of the Rock" (for sale). We drove by a rather dilapidated church building, its peeling white paint being power-washed off, which Geir informed me had recently been purchased by a Catholic group. But we also drove by a renovated airplane hangar, used since 2013 to host the annual All Tomorrow's Parties music festival, which has drawn the likes of Neil Young, Nick Cave, and Iggy Pop (along with thousands of their fans) to Ásbrú.

On wide, paved roads, past ample landscaped lawns, we drove through blocks of dormitories-turned-apartments, striated with parking lots, picnic tables, and swing sets. Mark Gillem has described these familiar configurations as "simulacra of suburbia" (2007, 74), base place-making designed for American ease. Each street sign, I noticed, was marked in both English and Icelandic; sometimes the terms translated directly, and sometimes they did not. Geir noted here, "You can tell the military took care of its people." Later on, our route would draw a neat line around the particular people the military took care of when we passed the much less comfortable-looking quarters built for Icelandic contractors. But with the neat dormitories multiplying out toward the horizon, Geir explained that only half of these buildings were currently being rented out. For one thing, they all required renovations, and not only aesthetic updates. American outlets run on 110 volts of electricity, while Icelandic appliances require 220 volts. Converting the outlets had turned out to be a tedious and time-consuming process of unbuilding American difference. Furthermore, Geir explained, KADECO didn't want to flood the Reykjanes housing market by releasing hundreds of apartments all at once. Instead, it has been a gradual process, first of making the base livable, and then making the base a place where people actually live.

I felt the subtle intransigence of military-shaped spaces in my own experience of living on Ásbrú. The apartment that Geir's office arranged for me was on the ground floor of a concrete walk-up that was once a single's housing block—an inheritance evident, for example, in the gear lockers located at the end of every hall. This sense of unfinished business was also apparent in the appliances inside our apartments, all of which were American units, much larger than what most Icelanders used. Because parts for such products were no longer available, they became inconvenient or impossible to repair. When my own refrigerator broke down, a young woman in the housing office added my name to a list, explaining

Figure 9. Military dormitories-turned-apartment-blocks at NASKEF/Ásbrú. Photo by author.

that appliances were gradually being replaced by Icelandic models, but only as the old ones died. Over the course of my time at Ásbrú, a common area on the ground level of our building gradually devolved into a dumping ground for household products, rendered by the passage of time out of place.

Such wayward appliances were not limited to NASKEF; over the years, and particularly around the base's closure, some had also made their way into local Icelanders' homes. Over breakfast at the kitchen table of one interlocutor, a middle-aged Reykjanes resident who had worked on base in IT, I noticed his American oven, a distinction I was learning to make from the more widely available European brands. With a conspiratorial grin, he told me that it had died "the other day" (*um daginn,* an Icelandic expression that spans from two days to maybe five years ago), and of course he needed an American part to fix it. So he and a friend had waited until nightfall, then snuck into some of the old buildings on base. "It was creepy," he told me, "empty, like there had been some kind of disaster." The smoke detectors were beeping in one building because the batteries had gone out. This interlocutor was coy about whether he had found what he needed, only gesturing suggestively toward our pile of pancakes. For some, at least, Ásbrú had proven a still-fruitful site of ongoing exchange.[15]

Geir and I lingered for a moment at a small cement tower, one of two checkpoints that once punctuated the fence line, which once defended the NASKEF base. For decades, Icelandic workers would pass through these daily, showing ID on their way in and out. Until 1987,[16] all Icelanders crossed through them to access their own commercial airport. These checkpoints, unsurprisingly, were a pain point for Icelanders, a site where their own sovereignty was routinely suspended in favor of a foreign military power. And so, in the early days after the base closure, many at KADECO felt that the checkpoints should be torn down. The company went as far as seeking estimates on demolishing, but ultimately, one architect who worked at KADECO then told me, "We decided we wanted to hold on to this history." So today the structures stand as relics, unmanned and unmoored[17] at Ásbrú's edge.

Despite, however, the demilitarization of base boundaries, the question of who was allowed inside Ásbrú was a topic of hushed but heated conversation during the time I spent living there. The relatively low cost of housing, especially compared with the soaring rents in Reykjavík, made the area appealing especially for immigrants, who lacked the family ties (and family properties) many Icelanders rely upon during hard times. Their numbers were growing quickly during the time I did my research, coinciding with the ample airport work offered by Iceland's tourism boom, and reached a peak in 2019 when 26 percent of the total population of Reykjanesbær was foreign-born.[18] My own neighbors in my apartment block were a mix of young Icelanders attending the university bridge program and multigenerational Eastern European families with members working at the airport.

These demographic shifts bred anxiety across the highway; people in town routinely expressed a pointed interest in "creating the right community" at Ásbrú. For example, Kolbrún once confided to me her worry that Ásbrú's inexpensive housing would "attract those who, dare I say it, don't want to work." Others went so far as to tell me they had heard rumors of other municipalities "outsourcing their problems" to Reykjanes, encouraging people who relied on social services to move to Ásbrú, even buying them bus tickets and paying their first month's rent. During my time there, I did not uncover evidence of such conspiracy, but I did experience the unsettling attention directed toward residents of the changing base. With my own dark hair, tan skin, and imperfect Icelandic, in Reykjavík I was always read as a voluntary visitor; in Reykjanes I was sometimes not welcomed as such. Meanwhile, friends I got to know in Reykjanes proper (including the interlocutor who had raided the old base for oven parts) described Ásbrú as "isolated" and issued pointed warnings to me about its rising crime.

Geir drove us past a handful of places that remained, even after decommissioning, inaccessible. The data center campus I call Arctera was one of these. But the old base also abuts a portion of the airport still operated by NATO and a segment of former officers' quarters, now held by the Office of the Prime Minister and administered by the Icelandic Coast Guard.[19] Together, this small, still-military area is referred to (for its shape in aerial view) as "the apron." We did not stop, or even slow down, at these edifices; they fell outside of Ásbrú's purview, and thus Geir's vision of its promise.

These pockets of guarded space stood out to me that day and struck me later as I would pass them on my morning runs. They seemed like ostentatious reminders that the transformation of Ásbrú remained incomplete. But longtime Reykjanes residents situated them differently. Eva, born and raised in Njarðvík and now an employee at KADECO, told me, "The fence has always been there, and the fence has always moved." She explained, "While the military was here, the fence was along the highway. Before the highway was built, the fence was all the way in town. It was in the neighborhoods." Today, it rests against "the apron," that last remaining vestige of military activity. Like the foot of a glacier, then, that fence has long been part of the landscape; it is receding, but at a pace that can be hard to read.

Reykjanes residents don't anticipate the fence, or what's behind it, disappearing anytime soon—not least because, in recent years, the United States has signaled a renewed interest in occupying this space. Amidst the broader geopolitical turn toward the Artic, in 2016 the US Navy requested funds to upgrade an aircraft hangar on NASKEF, for the stated purpose of maritime patrols.[20] In 2019, the US Air Force included in its annual budget a plan to spend $56.2 million on construction projects in Iceland.[21] NATO exercises have continued on Reykjanes, even since NASKEF's official closure. Despite, then, its shifting spatial footprint, for many on Reykjanes, American military activity does not appear to be ending so much as ebbing and flowing—less like a glacier, maybe, and more like a tide.

Geir hung a left to drive us by the business incubator, a two-story building with wide windows and an especially ample parking lot—another sign of American difference Icelanders like to point out. Inside, Geir told me, "all kinds of things" were happening—start-up offices, a design studio, a company that makes supplements out of silica. A few weeks later, I would ask to rent a hot desk at the incubator, making the tentative case that ethnography, too, was a kind of creative enterprise. Having recently finished her own MA in cultural studies, the office manager, Lilja, was welcoming and quick to agree. So I took my place on the top floor, beside a young man developing software, and spent the following months writing and transcribing in what turned out to be a surprisingly quiet space. All the businesses Geir described were, indeed, being incubated here—but each with only a couple of employees, in the office only a couple of days a week. All kinds of things may have been happening, but slowly, still coming together, like the rest of Ásbrú.

In contrast to the start-ups being celebrated on Ásbrú, and still emerging at the time I lived there, the most glaring absence, and a frequent topic of conversation among residents, was a more mundane one: a grocery store. The American military population had been served by its own commissary, decommissioned like the rest of the base in 2006. Since then, the closest grocery store had been in Reykjanesbær, requiring that residents drive down across the highway—or, at their own peril, attempt to cross on foot. Beyond the inconvenience, my neighbors described the lack of a grocery store as a depressing indication that this was not "a real place" or "a real community." When I raised these concerns with employees of KADECO, they tended to respond with practiced sighs. "We've taken too much responsibility for the people here," said Daníel, who managed KADECO's PR. "The core has to be developing something new here. The rest of it, we need to avoid." By "the rest of it," Daníel meant the politics of the Ásbrú project, but also the present more generally; KADECO's charge is with the future, and he wanted to keep his eyes on that prize. Ásbrú's currently existing residents, however, critiqued the holding company for pursuing a vision of the future that overlooked their most pressing needs. Their stalemate was another sticking point in the process of trans-formation and meant more tedious trips across the highway from this as-yet "unreal" place.

The crown jewel of Geir's tour, which he saved for the end of it, drove home his attunement toward cultivating possibility, even in the most unlikely place. As we pulled up to three round-topped, corrugated metal shelters, Geir instructed me to follow him out of the car. Shielding our faces from the now-driving rain, Geir told me that these buildings used to be arsenals and pointed out the weapons depositories at their sides. "Guess what they are today," he goaded, then promptly interrupted before I had the chance to guess: "A ballet school!" "Wow," I said, sharing his smile, and paused a long moment to convey my appreciation—but when I started to turn back toward the shelter of the SUV, Geir raised a hand to hold us there a moment longer. "Isn't that just something," he said, then repeated, smiling and shaking his head.

In this section, I have juxtaposed the view of Ásbrú which Geir gener-ously invited me into, emphasizing the area's potential and possibility, with some of the enduring, obdurate influences of long-term military occupation I observed. In doing so, my aim has been to hold them both in tension, without undercutting either perspective; the fact is that both are true. There *were* remarkable transformations happening at Ásbrú, projects that meaningfully repurposed military remainders in useful and inspiring ways. At the same time, NASKEF was a place built for a purpose, and attempts to do something different there still caught and dragged against that grain. History, habit, and the built environment regularly strained against action and imagination, giving pause to those building their bridge to the gods.

Many Reykjanes residents expressed takes on Ásbrú less optimistic than the one Geir offered up. Rúnar, a writer born and raised in Reykjanes, lamented that his father had had to watch the plateau transform "from a desert into a community, then back to a desert again." Pétur, an older Reykjanes resident, dismissed efforts at repurposing the old base out of hand: "Nothing comes from nothing," he said in bitter summary. These sentiments deserve their due as expressions of the difficulty of truly transforming militarized space. For many people, the plateau at the center of Reykjanes had been effectively and irrevocably ruined. But ruins, as

Figure 10. One of two vestigial checkpoints at NASKEF/Ásbrú, which once controlled traffic onto and off the base. Photo by Bragi Þór Jósefsson.

Figure 11. A stretch of fence line left behind by the NASKEF base in 2006. Photo by Bragi Þór Jósefsson.

scholars of material history have argued, can have their own unexpected afterlives.[22] And there is, as Geir patiently and insistently showed me, something other than nothing here. NASKEF's loose ends may be proving resistant to reclamation as Icelandic living space, but they are not unusable. They have been particularly, and perhaps surprisingly, receptive to the data storage industry.

INFRASTRUCTURAL INHERITANCES

Data centers emerged as a possibility on Reykjanes approximately two years after NASKEF closed. While the majority of the industry-building work described in previous chapters has taken place in Reykjavík, data storage—much like long-term military housing—was always meant to be sited out of town. Large warehouse-like spaces known for noise pollution (the steady drone of thousands of servers running twenty-four hours a day), data centers tend to make poor neighbors. They do best on large tracts of unoccupied land. But at the same time, they also require reliable power and internet connectivity. And while data centers tend to operate with small in-house teams—most functions, today, can be handled remotely—they must be close enough to transportation routes that international clients can have on-demand access. The Miðnesheiði Plateau, abandoned by NASKEF, fit this very specific bill.

In 2009, Arctera, a UK-based start-up company, selected Reykjanes as its data center site.[23] Media coverage of the coming industry over the following months was hopeful; in the local paper, the mayor of Reykjanesbær declared that "this high technology will lead to new professional knowledge in Iceland. While making use of green energy, it will greatly strengthen all industry—not only in Reykjanes but in the whole country."[24] In 2011, construction started on Arctera, and the region's first data center became fully operational in 2012. Two others have since cropped up nearby. But despite the story of trail-blazing innovation often attached to Arctera's development (and put forward by the company itself), by situating Arctera and its eventual cohort within the space of NASKEF/Ásbrú, I came to see the data centers in another light—not as a departure or technological "disruption," but as a meaningful continuation of what came before.

Arctera is housed in a facility until recently known as NASKEF Storage Hangar 868. The long, low, deliberately nondescript building is nestled in between the base's water tower and its accounting office, just across the infrequently traveled street from the housing block where I rented my apartment. The window of the kitchen I shared with my fellow floor-mates (another vestige of Naval frugality and fraternity) looked directly onto the facility. From that vantage point, signs of new purpose were only subtly evident in a metal security fence with a gate operated by intercom. Inside, however, Arctera was abuzz.

On one early visit I made to the data center, I was greeted by Stefán, a softspoken Icelandic engineer, and Aaron, the company's affable British head of marketing—one holding a hard hat and the other a reflective vest. "We're under construction," Aaron said, smiling, as he donned his own protective equipment and handed me mine. That much became immediately evident as they ushered me through Arctera's two operational data halls, then one more being assembled by a team of workers before our eyes. As we walked, the two men rattled off metrics, always following up present numbers with predicted ones: "We're currently running at seven megawatts, but we'll go up to ten soon," Aaron told me. "We're on forty acres, and we're currently doubling our footprint." The data center had recently been approved for a major expansion, and a heady sense of bustling activity was all around—contractors erected towering racks to house computer servers while construction workers carried spools of cabling in and out. But in the weeks and months that followed, as I returned to Arctera and spoke further with Aaron, Stefán, and some of their colleagues, I learned to recognize not just the data center's new developments, but also the materials out of which they were being built.

One day, walking with me through the newest data hall, Stefán casually mentioned that it had been NASKEF that transformed the road to Reykjanes from a gravel track into a major highway. "Well," he clarified, "it was built by US dollars and Icelandic work." He went on to say it had actually been NASKEF that built up the airstrip that became Iceland's international airport, which today allows foreign clients to conveniently drop by. It was NASKEF that extended a cable from the electrical grid to supply the peninsula with ample power. Then, as if on a roll, he told me that NASKEF also had paid for the phone line between Reykjanes and Reykjavík, and hastened already-existing Icelandic plans to build a fiber-optic ring around the island. "We plug into these networks," Stefán told me; it was all these overlapping connections that made Reykjanes attractive to the data center industry. Not much later, I made his point back to him: when I asked who the data center contracted for one piece of Arctera's expansion, Stefán told me that it was *Íslenskir Aðalverktakar*—the same company founded to service the base.

If Stefán introduced me to Arctera's inheritance, Aaron would illustrate another layer of this relationship. In an interview in the company kitchen on one of his visits (the proximity of the local airport and ample housing opportunities on Ásbrú allowed the Brit to live in Iceland only part-time), I asked Aaron how Arctera had selected its current site. I dutifully transcribed as Aaron touted the benefits of climate and renewable energy in Iceland generally, hitting all the points I had long heard Egill make. But then, lifting his gaze out the kitchen window, Aaron added, "And of course, we're on a former NATO site. It's a vast piece of land with a secure perimeter, and no large population nearby."

In the then-eight years since NASKEF's closure, the perimeter of NASKEF/Ásbrú had certainly changed. The fence that once surrounded the base had been demolished (or rather, as Eva put it, pushed back); the checkpoints at its edges had been shut down. The security of that perimeter was no longer enforced by the posting or routine patrol of armed guards. And yet, one did feel a persistent deterrent effect still active around the old base. Lilja, the office manager at the business incubator, told me that after all those years the area still "felt foreign." Others from Reykjanes would give me directions, making reference to a fence that had not existed for years. One friend admitted he still instinctively looked over his shoulder when driving through the long-defunct checkpoint. After so many years of being denied or granted only conditional access, many Icelanders still experience this area as not quite their own. While the base's defense systems are no longer operative, then, its practiced distance from the "local population" across the highway, etched into the landscape by American military investments, persists. It was in this sense that Ásbrú's perimeter could still be described as meaningfully "secured."

Infrastructural layering is a well-documented phenomenon, from the construction of modern hydraulics atop old wells and cisterns (Anand 2015) to the repurposing of telegraph routes for fiber-optic lines (Starosielski 2015). Previous infrastructures create paths, which can create path dependencies, or purposeful concentrations over time. As architectural historian Kazys Varnelis puts it, "new infrastructures do not so much supersede old ones as ride on top of them, forming physical and organizational palimpsests" (2005); or, as Shannon Mattern writes, "infrastructure begets infrastructure" (2017, vii). Such accumulative imagery is appropriate in Reykjanes, where data centers directly extend the connective infrastructures originally built to serve the NASKEF base. But it is not only these additive practices that matter to the data storage industry: as valuable as what the American military built up here is what its occupation simultaneously wore away.

Arctera's "secure perimeter" sheds light on such a process: the American military built the fence that once surrounded the plateau, marking the base as a place apart. But it was not the fence itself that persisted, lending itself to the data center's use. Instead, it was the sense of exclusion that fence once concretized that became an asset for developers interested in keeping their data centers secret and safe. Movement between the town and base was made impractical, sometimes impossible, eventually irrelevant. The same engineered distance that makes it so difficult for today's Ásbrú residents to travel downhill to the grocery store also makes it unlikely that Icelanders living in Reykjanesbær will ever venture uphill and onto the former base. While Stefán, then, emphasized the many ways that NASKEF made Reykjanes a densely networked place, it is both the base's connections *and* its selective disconnections that made it appealing to the server farm. Data centers like Arctera have been attracted to the roads and runways, communications cables, and power lines. But they are equally served by the social and spatial arrangements those infrastructures established there. Infrastructures intended to fuel the base community—but also to separate Americans from Icelanders and meet the needs of the former at the latter's expense—were at once built into the material landscape and insinuated into everyday life. These legacies, enduring and appropriated by industry, mean that people, speeding down the Reykjanes highway, still pass through the peninsula quickly—but data is well supported here, as long as it stays.

In her work on the material afterlife of empire, Ann Laura Stoler gives name to the processes by which imperial formations continue to make themselves felt. Critiquing the neat distinction presumed by the term *post*colonial, Stoler locates the ongoing activity of empire in "the material and social afterlife of structures, sensibilities, and things" (2008, 194). Such "ruins" (2008)—or "imperial debris" (2013)—she argues, refuse to be relegated to history; they continue to do damage, albeit in shifting and sometimes surprising forms.

Few sites may evoke the afterlife of empire more poignantly than a decommissioned military base. At Ásbrú, the work of ruination is obvious, from the visceral degradation of left-behind buildings, to the pollution continually rediscovered in the soil.[25] These remainders illustrate the lasting impacts of American base building, even long after the military has ostensibly left. These lingering harms are important to notice, as they belie the apparent retrenchment of empire suggested by the hundreds of American base closures effected over the past forty years.[26] But for Stoler, a key property of ruins lies in their often-unpredictable liveliness. Ruins, in this reading, are not only sites of abject abandonment, or permanent and inevitable toxicity; they also feed into particular future-making projects, even as they foreclose more. Ruination, then, also invites us to rethink the industry that emerges in the military's wake.

On Reykjanes, as elsewhere, data storage has been figured as innovative, something attractive because it is shiny and new. It slips easily into the "promise" of infrastructure as progress, modernity, positive change (Anand, Gupta, and Appel 2018). When Arctera committed to building in Reykjanes and signed a contract with the national power company, then-company president Friðrík Sophusson proclaimed proudly that

> Today's signing marks a distinct turning point in the nation's commercial history, when information technology and renewable energy form the basis for new employment opportunities in a region where the Keflavík Airport Development Company [KADECO] has progressed from retrenchment and is now gaining ground.

But as we have seen, data storage offers not so much a "turning point" but a right-shaped peg for the prominent hole that NASKEF carved out and left on Reykjanes. KADECO, for its part, is not so much "gaining ground" as finding new ways to repurpose territory whose original purpose has proven too sticky to undo. Situating Arctera, then, within the physical infrastructures, social orders, and spatial politics that NASKEF instantiated allows us to observe these leftovers in ongoing action. In taking seriously the histories that data centers slot into, we can trace ruination as it persists—and is perpetuated—through what is most often touted as progress and gain.

Stefán articulated such an analysis one afternoon over coffee at a new shop, just off the road that separates Reykjanesbær from Ásbrú. Stefán was born and raised on Reykjanes—"a local boy," as he calls himself. "When I was growing up," he told me, "I crawled under fences, snuck onto the base to get to the vending machines. And then I grew up and kept trying to get in for the beer." Trained as an electrical engineer, Stefán moved abroad for work before coming home to join Arctera in 2010. He was excited by the opportunity and viewed his position as a chance to give back to the region where he was raised.

That day, Stefán reminded me of how recently Reykjanes became the peri-urban region it is today: "One hundred and fifty years ago we lived in mud houses—now there's all this luxury here." This development, he said, started with the mechanization of Iceland's fishing fleet, and that was quickly followed by foreign industry: the power plants, the aluminum smelters, the military base. Others' words fresh in my mind about Reykjanes's "double-dip depression," I suggested to Stefán that, ultimately, those industries have not treated this area kindly. He agreed that there has been a history here of consolidating wealth for foreign entities that, when it suits them, move away. "This is the fishing element in Icelanders," he said wistfully:

> We only know how to get raw material and sell it away. Take our fishing industry: we build huge vessels that fish for everything, we do the first processing, we put it into freezers and export it. And then Denmark buys a lot and puts a price tag on it for ten times more than we sold it for. It's the same as aluminum—we use our electricity, we import the raw materials, then we process it in the easiest way and ship it away. Then someone else takes it.

In other words, despite the way Iceland is considered integral to these industrial processes, and considers them integral to its own economy (fish and aluminum are the island's two major exports), it can be hard to get their benefits to stick here. The ongoingness of these extractive dynamics on Reykjanes is more than an inheritance of physical infrastructure; it is a troubling "patterning of social form" (Berlant 2016), the outlines of which Stefán sometimes glimpsed in his own industry.

Despite his genuine and well-informed optimism about Arctera, it is clear to Stefán that data storage came to Reykjanes because it was cost-effective, and if that equation changes in the future it will leave. He is hopeful that the industry-building efforts of Egill and others, alongside his own work to establish Arctera, will be effective enough to keep on making Iceland's case. He is intimately familiar with the infrastructural edge that his company has inherited from the base that came before. But data centers, as Julia Velkova has argued, are "impermanent infrastructures" (2019), known for relocating rapidly in response to the shifting demands of capital, the availability of a profitable power contract or generous tax break.[27] As one former NASKEF construction worker said skeptically when I asked him about the new digital prospects on the plateau, "This is not a business you can build on."

In the wake of the base, Reykjanes has experienced more than its fair share of unbuildable business. First, the fishing industry—once the lifeblood of the peninsula—was transformed by the implementation of an individual transferrable quota system, which privatized national fishing resources and distributed them on the basis of previous years' catch. Reykjanesbær (then known as Njarðvík and Keflavík), however, due to the base's economic influence, was allotted fewer quotas to begin with when the right to fish was commodified. Then, the existing quotas were sold outside the region, leaving it a rich but unfishable sea.[28]

In the years immediately following the base closure, the town of Reykjanesbær experimented with a course of privatization, during which time all major municipal holdings (including, for example, the school and the swimming pool) were placed into a private holding company and sold off—as one resident told me, only slightly exaggerating, "even the sidewalks here are leased." The municipality also made several attempts to secure a new industrial player on the peninsula, for example, building roads and a harbor to accommodate an aluminum smelting plant that never came. A silicon factory was built in nearby Helgúvík but was plagued by production issues and shut down after just a few months. Today, the facility is being sold for parts. The slowly closing cracks of this period are still visible: in 2015, Reykjanesbær's municipal debt ratio was 249 percent, far and away the highest on the island.[29] One man I met who had worked on the base for twenty-six years told me he was on his seventh job since it had closed. Should the data centers, too, prove temporary, they will add to this growing pile of difficulty and detritus, further evidence of a territory rendered resistant to attempts to get something of value to stick.

For now, the data centers are expanding—hiring the engineers, contractors, and electricians working away at construction sites like the one I observed. One of Stefán and Aaron's American Arctera colleagues assured me, "We don't really foresee not having construction . . . we're building and building and building." But again, and as Reykjanes residents remember, NASKEF too was building and building and building until the day that it was not. While local media once predicted local hires in the hundreds,[30] only a handful of Icelanders have actually been employed in these facilities. By the time they arrived, management positions were already filled by foreigners and today most work happens remotely, anyway.

All this is not to say that data center development on Reykjanes is fated, technologically determined to replicate what came before. But dwelling on the imbrication of data storage with already existing infrastructures, as well as the social and spatial orders they sustained, serves as a reminder to ask what falls away from industry discourses of digital media as innovative, always emergent, and essentially different from what it has replaced. On Reykjanes, where what came before is inescapably evident, we see how server farms "plug into" not only existing lines of communication, power, and transport, but also patterns of exclusion, extraction, and impermanence.

CONCLUSION

The idea of "making something from nothing" is a common trope invoked across digital industries. In my research, I heard start-up founders, digital

Figure 12. A data center construction site in Reykjanes, with NASKEF water tower visible in the background. Photo by author.

activists, and government officials use this phrase to index the vast wealth and sweeping change that can, supposedly, be summoned with just a laptop and a good idea. It was, in fact, the ubiquity of this sentiment that caused me to sit up and take notice when Pétur, the older Reykjanes resident quoted earlier in this chapter, proclaimed so decisively that "*nothing comes from nothing.*" He was speaking specifically about the impossibility of remaking NASKEF/Ásbrú into something he would want to use. But his sentiment, more broadly, directs us to pay attention to the many ways in which the past gives traction to industries and infrastructures emerging today.

On Reykjanes, we have seen that the entrenched presence of NASKEF has made it difficult for Icelandic people to repurpose the space and structures the military occupation left behind—areas that still "feel foreign," from their too-wide lawns to their vestigial fence lines. And yet, the remainders of the base have been hospitable to the international data centers developing there today.

These data centers' collective footprint is narrower than NASKEF's. Rather than creating a space for engagement—which, in the case of the base, ranged from work to smuggling to love to violence—the data centers' presence, for most residents, is only audible: the lush hum emitted by their fans and backup generators sometimes wafts its way across the highway, creating just-noticeable noise pollution on otherwise quiet evenings in town. The daily felt impact of data centers on Reykjanes is a far cry from the deeply disruptive (and yet sometimes seductive) problem the military base once posed. What persists, though, is the uneasy and uneven relationship between the two sides of the plateau's "secure perimeter." These terraformed logics of inclusion and exclusion, interpolation and exploitation, which I read as "ruins" or imperial debris, are a key element of what anchors data in Reykjanes, today.

For all these reasons Reykjanes, and Ásbrú more specifically, has been the primary site of data center construction in Iceland. A whole segment of the former base site has been zoned for their development, and the proliferating rows of server farms can now be seen from the highway, a blurred sequence in the peripheral vision of drivers who continue to, by and large, speed right on by. But now that Arctera and its neighbors have established "proof of concept," Reykjanes is no longer the only place data centers are being built. Even where existing infrastructures do not lend themselves quite so easily to the project of data storage, other cases are increasingly being made for its development. The next chapter shifts, then, from the urban and peri-urban Southwest to these somewhat more experimental efforts to develop data centers across the Icelandic countryside. In doing so, it takes up the spatial relations that condition the emplacement of data in Iceland and interrogates the techno-optimistic ideal of "connectivity" that frames digital development here and elsewhere.

4   Data Centers, Data Peripheries

If you have been to Iceland and ventured even briefly outside Reykjavík, you have almost certainly traveled along the Ring Road, or *Hringvegurinn*, an 825-mile two-lane highway that traces an outline around the island, linking most of its towns, ports, and tourist attractions. The Ring Road will take you from Reykjavík to Vík's black sand beaches; from the foot of the Vatnajökull Glacier to the Reyðarfjörður aluminum plant; and from Egilsstaðir, the largest municipality in the East Fjords, to Akureyri, the largest municipality in the North. Completed in 1974 as part of celebrations marking the eleven hundredth anniversary of Iceland's settlement, the Ring Road's construction was explicitly conceived as a nation-building project. With the laying of its last bridge came a call for Icelanders to explore their country through automobility, coming to know, claim, and story the landscape in new ways (Árnason et al. 2015). While once rugged—older Icelanders recall having to "wrestle" with the highway— today the Ring Road enables efficient circulation, albeit still occasionally obstructed by snowstorms and errant sheep. Doing so, it embodies what Penny Harvey and Hannah Knox have described as roads' promise of territorial interconnectivity, their capacity to make contiguous the space of the nation and space of the state (2015).

If the Ring Road is a highly visible emblem of connection, a subtler, subterranean circuit follows along the same track. In 1989, the Icelandic government began laying a fiber-optic ring around the island. It was completed in 1991 with support from NATO, which was invested in quickly connecting the radar stations it had erected in Iceland's four corners: Höfn, Langanes, Látrar, and Straumnes. While that original cable has since been largely duplicated by private networks, the ring still forms a vital backbone for Iceland's internet infrastructure, ensuring connectivity for all its cities, towns, and settlements. As a result, the island benefits from extraordinary broadband coverage, with Wi-Fi often, astoundingly, available to Icelanders even when hiking, camping, or at sea. Míla, the company that operates much of the domestic network, makes the comparison to the Ring Road on its website directly: "Míla's system is like a telecommunications highway for voice telephones, cell phones, data transport, and television and radio broadcasts."[1] Other analogies include the description of the fiber-optic ring as an "artery" (*lífæð*) of society, a vital element of Iceland's cultural, political, and economic life (Bjarnason 2010).

These parallel networks, which many Icelanders use daily, have a cohering effect on the island: they remind you that wherever it is that you've strayed to, the way back is always within reach. But connective infrastructures do not simply level terrain as they traverse it. In Iceland, dynamics of spatial power persist between urban centers and countryside, easily mapped and tangibly felt. And as data centers start cropping up not only in the southwestern cities, but also farther out on the ringed infrastructures' range, they highlight the surprisingly complicated relationship between connectivity and marginality.

This chapter takes up the still-emergent phenomenon of developing data storage in rural Iceland. The attraction of data centers in these more peripheral places is both an economic investment and part of a broader bid for *connectivity*, articulated along multiple lines. Infrastructural connection, in Iceland as elsewhere, is often imagined as overcoming, or rendering irrelevant, spatial marginality. And yet, close attention to data center development—in particular, the perspectives of data center developers—complicates this equation. Considering two recent bids for development in rural Iceland, one in Blönduós in the Northwest and another in Hornafjörður in the Southeast, I suggest that while data centers are often imagined as harbingers of connectivity, they are in fact attracted to, and anchored by, a particular kind of marginality. In creating what I term *on-the-way places*, or locations built into others' infrastructures, they tell a different kind of story about the impacts of digital networks than common-sense and self-congratulatory connective accounts. As such, the project of placing data in the Icelandic countryside sheds light on the limits of digital connectivity and redirects our attention in understanding its effects.

CONNECTING THE COUNTRYSIDE

The name *Blönduós* marks, phonetically as well as physically, a meeting point between *Blanda*, a glacial river, and its *ós*, the river's mouth that opens into the sea. A trading post was built at this confluence in 1876, which very gradually grew up into a small town. On the south side of the river is the "old town," a small collection of nineteenth-century houses in varying states of maintenance and renovation, the Blanda Hotel, and the "old church," a small wooden edifice with stained glass windows and a single narrow bell tower; on the north side are the school, the supermarket, and the "new church," a striking stone building designed to evoke volcanic rock. Inland from either side of the river is farmland, which fills in lush and green in the spring.

Blönduós, a town with fewer than one thousand inhabitants, lies directly on the Ring Road. But on a map, you can see that the road bulges to include it—the route would have been about twenty minutes shorter without Blönduós, and most people I've made the drive with wish that it was. I had, in fact, driven at least a dozen times past Blönduós, on trips between Reykjavík and Akureyri, without so much as stopping for gas. I likely would have continued to do so had Omnitech, a 30 MW data center, not been built there in 2019.[2]

When I met with the town's mayor, Valdimar Hermannsson, shortly after the data center's grand opening, he told me that this project had been in the works for some time. Ten years ago, his predecessor had set the wheels in motion, tagging along to conferences like World Hosting Days and pitching a construction site close to the water. "They were thinking about using sea cooling technology—very innovative stuff," he said. The former mayor's efforts attracted some interest from Chinese and Canadian investors, but negotiations never went far. Then, an Icelandic data center start-up made a commitment to build in Blönduós; shortly after, a majority stake in that company was acquired by a data center developer from Luxembourg; shortly after that, it was sold to a French infrastructure firm. That company broke ground in early 2018 and built straight through an unexpectedly mild winter. The data center went online the following spring.

Valdimar and I met in his mayoral office, a modest suite in a building shared with other town officials, as well as the county sheriff and local police. At the entrance, visitors are met with a taxidermied polar bear, one that Valdimar told me was actually shot in Blönduós some years ago—every once in a while, they float over from Greenland on ice floes, taking farmers by surprise. It was quiet that day as I waited for our interview, with only the voices of two young office workers, idly chatting about the day's news, echoing around the empty space. The rest of the town felt equally peaceful, as I went for a walk later on and ate the sandwich I bought at the gas station alone on the river bank. So when Valdimar excitedly described the difference already made by the data center's construction, the contrasts that he drew hit home:

> From October to April, there were ninety people working in this area. This was so many people that the catering business said they averaged selling ninety-six lunches a day. The guest houses [a small cluster of cabins on one river's edge], plus the hotel, were full. The first contractors were hired from the area, but then they needed even more—specialists, for example. Over ninety people for about six months. So that was, we can say, the big boost.

This "boost," as Valdimar put it, was transformative for Blönduós: in recent years, the conversation about this area had been dominated by businesses closing, services being cut, and young people moving away. "There has been more positive news about Blönduós now in one year than there has been for the last twenty years," he said. But even in Valdimar's celebration that day, there was already a sense of retrospective uncertainty. Now that the Omnitech data center was up and running on the town's outskirts, no longer in need of large construction crews, the open question that hung in the quiet air around us was what exactly would happen next.

Over and over again, at every stage of my research, I was told by the people I approached as interlocutors that if I wanted to get to know the "real Iceland," I should go and live in the countryside. The suggestion has come from academics, engineers, and officials, some of whom even went so far as to mention a distant relative who might be willing to let me work a season on their farm. As quickly as I deferred these offers, excusing myself as not that kind of anthropologist, this impulse to push me out toward the countryside struck me. After all, precious few of these people had ever worked, much less lived on a sheep farm, and they saw themselves as Icelandic enough. But the country (*sveitin*), a somewhat moving target that encompasses most of Iceland outside of the Reykjavík area and a select few larger settlements, is routinely figured as a site of enduring tradition and authentic Icelandic culture (Hastrup 1998). Despite the storied centrality of the countryside, however, rural Iceland has long been understood as at risk.

The decline of the country has been commented on by Icelanders since the rapid urbanization of the early twentieth century. In 1860, only 3 percent of Icelanders lived in urban centers (defined as villages and towns of over 200 people); by 1930, 57.3 percent did. In 1860, Reykjavík had 1,500 inhabitants; in 1930, it had 28,300, or 25.8 percent of the country's population (Magnússon 2010, 174–75). Shifts in economic, and later educational, opportunities drove Icelanders, once distributed in agrarian settlements across the country's coastlines, toward the growing city center in the South. The arrival of the British, then American, military in the 1940s (discussed in chapter 3) only intensified this phenomenon. In 1943, approximately fifty thousand soldiers were stationed in Reykjavík, and their presence created an economic boom in town (Hálfdanarson 2011). What's more, despite having no wartime damage to recover from, Iceland received the highest per capita infusion of Marshall Aid, which fueled industrial and urban development in Reykjavík, especially (Ingimundarson 2011). Trace evidence of Iceland's rapid urbanization is visible in the widespread abandoned house (*eyðibýli*) phenomenon: hundreds of farmhouses, in various states of preservation, stand empty around the island, offering haunting vistas for travelers and temporary shelters for grazing livestock.

Regional development plans proposed as early as the 1950s aimed to strengthen rural industry in order to stem the tide of outmigration. By the 1980s, these plans urged the creation of financial incentives (primarily through the tax or student loan system) to entice young people to settle in areas outside the capital. And still, the steady depletion has gone on: between 1991 and 2000, the number of eighteen- to twenty-five-year-olds living in Iceland's relatively remote East Fjords and West Fjords declined by 23 percent (Seyfrit, Bjarnason, and Ólafsson 2010). Today, almost two-thirds of Iceland's population lives in the capital area, and rural outmigration has created a self-perpetuating spiral, in which dwindling populations result in the shuttering of services, which make rural futures even harder to imagine as viable ones.[3] In Blönduós, for example, midway between Reykjavík and Akureyri (Iceland's first and second largest urban centers by far), the hospital has cut down on services, recommending that residents travel to the city for specialized care. Once there were three doctors on permanent staff in Blönduós; in 2015, the town was down to one.

Amidst these conditions, many of Iceland's small towns have eagerly embraced the turn to tourism in recent years.[4] Along the Ring Road, drivers are now met with signage that directs them to tour a glacier or volcano; to watch whales, seals, and Arctic foxes; and to visit museums of exploration (Húsavík), transportation (Ystafell), the "herring era" (Siglufjörður), witchcraft (Hólmavík), and World War II (Reyðarfjörður). Controversially, some rural landowners have started charging admission fees to visitors admiring natural features on their property—a practice that chafes against a long-standing Icelandic right to access and travel through uncultivated land. These initiatives all aspire to distinguish rural areas on the basis of their unique offerings, and in doing so, tap into circuits of international capital now flowing through Iceland annually. By attracting people and keeping them in place—whether tourists who might be enticed to stay a night, or young people who might be encouraged to raise their children in the town where they themselves were raised—they seek to recapture value for the countryside and create economic opportunities there. Blönduós is no stranger to these efforts, as the home of a lovely handicrafts museum and "sea ice exhibition center"; as Valdimar put it, "the town has struggled to specialize."

Data centers do not fit obviously into this paradigm. Modular and intentionally unmemorable warehouses, supporting processes unknown and inaccessible to passersby, data centers lack the local flair of rural tourism initiatives. They do not, at least on first glance, lift up the particularities of place. But by attracting *data* to the Icelandic countryside and creating the means to keep it there, they have been understood as following some of the same logics and responding to some of the same problems. Data's presence, like tourists', is said to multiply markets and opportunities where it moves. That equation is somewhat less direct here—data itself does not consume souvenirs, spa days, or local delicacies. Instead, it is the work involved in caring for data that is imagined as creating a general kind of activity in Blönduós and the broader countryside. Enough activity, and these towns might reverse the centrifugal force of outmigration, might make it more feasible for people to stay.

Discussing his own hopes for the new development, Valdimar told me, "The Northwest region has been lacking in the past twenty or thirty years. And when you come with a new idea, people are like this"—here, he mimes holding his hands up and backing away. Valdimar knows that data centers alone will not fill the void left behind by fishing and farming. "But," he said, "we look at this as a starting point. We both hope, and are quite sure, that even if it takes ten years to get started, this is a good connection."

By "connection," Valdimar was not just referring to technological infrastructure—broadband coverage had long been impressive in Blönduós by then. Instead, the connections Valdimar meant were manifold, including the potential for expanding the current data center campus onto a neighboring property; the way that one data center can beget more development, once the proof of concept is in place; the fact that Blönduós now had a leg to stand on in the national conversation on industrial development, meaning that its voice might be heard more readily in Reykjavík; the fact that Valdimar had personally taken more than a dozen visitors to tour the new facility; and the fact that an American anthropologist was sitting in his office, eagerly writing down his every word.

As Valdimar rattled off these ever-expanding connections, full of potential pointed in every direction, my mind wandered back to a promotional video made to showcase the Blönduós facility that I had watched in preparation for my trip to town. The video opens with a view of the data center, bathed in bright aurora borealis, mobilizing that strategically coded natural imagery perfected by Egill and his team. Then, the camera zooms out and the video is replaced with a map of Iceland, from which dozens of neon yellow arrows spread steadily out and around the globe. Under the print heading "Delivering services to all major continents," Iceland—and Blönduós by extension—is visually rendered a vital hub at the center of international IT. Like that video, Valdimar's discourse positioned his town of Blönduós, until recently viewed as dangerously marginal, as an emerging center of digital development.

The relationship activated here between connectivity and marginality—specifically, that connection is marginality's opposite and antidote—is a resonant and intuitive one. Communicative connectivity is often imagined as a natural solvent for social boundaries as well as spatial ones. Such an orientation is evidenced, for example, in the United Nations' 2016 resolution on the internet, which positions digital access, in and of itself, as "an important tool for fostering citizen and civil society participation, for the realization of development in every community and for exercising human rights."[5] It is articulated even more unequivocally in a leaked memo written by Facebook vice president Andrew Bosworth in 2016: "The ugly truth is that we believe in connecting people so deeply that anything that allows us to connect more people often is *de facto* good."[6] The abiding promise of such connection at any cost, as Anita Say Chan describes it, is that "regardless of the particularities of individual embodiment or local condition, in other words, once online, *all* users could be granted the same agencies on a single network, all differences could dissolve" (2013, 7).

This formulation, which imbues connective infrastructures with transformative social power, hearkens back to European Enlightenment discourses of free exchange. In this era infrastructures, and communicative networks in particular, which made possible ever-expanding flows of people, ideas, and goods, came to be understood as inherently equalizing, "circulating civilization" (Mattelart 2000, 16) or drawing every place they connected into the expanding fold of modernity. As Brian Larkin writes, "it is difficult to separate an analysis of infrastructures from this sedimented history and our belief that, by promoting circulation infrastructures bring about change, and through change they enact progress, and through progress we gain freedom" (2013, 332).

Figure 13. The "old town" of Blönduós in the foreground, and the rest of the town across the river's mouth. Photo by author.

Figure 14. The Omnitech data center site in 2019. Photo by author.

But of course, technological connection is just one way of understanding the path toward progress or freedom. After all, at the same time that Enlightenment-era leaders were espousing the benefits of global connectivity, they were also carrying out the imperial project of dividing and conquering the very same globe—a project in which communicative infrastructures like the telegraph, described by historian Alex Nalbach as "the hardware of Victorian hegemony" (2003), played an active and vital role. Despite, then—or perhaps because of—its longevity, received wisdom about the relationship between connectivity and marginality calls out for a closer look. I interrogate this nexus next by turning our attention to the perspectives of data center developers. Having spent some time in Blönduós, we can appreciate why Iceland's rural municipalities would be drawn to data center development. To understand what data does in these places, however, we need to ask why data centers are drawn to the countryside.

MARGINAL GAINS

The class of people that I call data center developers held a range of formal positions and on-the-job experiences. These spanned from extended stints in the C-suite at long-established corporate entities, to scraping together business plans and courting start-up funding on nights and weekends free from their very different day jobs. What these men (and they were all men) had in common was their practical stake in the project of getting data centers made. These were the people directly responsible for selling, siting, and building data centers in Iceland in ways that would be worth their while.

When I asked them, in interviews at corporate offices, in data halls, and over drinks at industry conferences, why they decided to build their data centers in Iceland, the developers I met unanimously cited power and climate—the low cost of cooling and corresponding green appeal discussed at length in chapter 1. But when I asked them why they decided to build their data centers in the specific town, industrial park, or open lot where they ultimately landed, developers' reasoning narrowed in.

Siggi is an Icelandic engineer who founded a data center company called Polarice in 2009. A self-described "science guy who does business," Siggi had spent swaths of his career working at the national power production (Landsvirkjun) and power transmission (Landsnet) companies. It was there, and in his later work as an energy consultant, that he came to appreciate the equation that made data storage in Iceland a sound bet. "Just by plugging it into the wall here, your data center produces about 1 percent of the greenhouse gases it would produce in New York City. This is a very strong basis for decision making," he said. So, seeing a potentially lucrative opportunity, he incorporated a company and recruited a couple of colleagues to help him get it off the ground in their collective downtime. The first time I spoke with Siggi was at his day job, in an office tower on the industrial edge of Reykjavík, and he made a point of physically clearing the surface of his desk before we began.

In its early days, Polarice was approached about a partnership with an American bank looking to build a data center in Iceland. The bank, through a joint US-Icelandic front company, would fund the venture and Siggi's team would execute it. As such, the team's first task was securing a construction site. Polarice conducted a survey of suitable regions, considering factors like pricing, power access, and seismic risk. Soon, however, they settled on Hornafjörður, a small historic harbor town near Höfn in the East Fjords. Hornafjörður, Siggi told me, was the perfect place for a data center: "On the southeast coast, you have a society that is quite simple— they just have the fisheries, and of course some tourism. Building in a place like this is free from hassles." Later on, Siggi continued: "We don't want to be very big, but we want to expand nice and easy. Thinking about putting it [the data center] in a small sailor town, it's easier to control."

To date, Polarice has not yet built its data center in Hornafjörður. The company got as far as signing development contracts with the municipality when their American partner abruptly pulled out. But Siggi and his team, confident in the value proposition of their location, continue to renew their contracts annually and make their case on the conference circuit, waiting patiently for the infusion of investment that would allow them to finally break ground.

Magnús is a relatively new member of the Omnitech executive board. For the past year, he has served as the company's chief commercial officer, responsible for business development, marketing, and sales. But in that year, his company underwent an acquisition, as well as a major site expansion. As a result, it took me months to get in touch with Magnús, then more months to pin down a time to meet. When our schedules finally coincided, he invited me to a members-only bar in downtown Reykjavík, a sumptuous space tucked away on the top floor of a building on Laugavegur, the city's main drag. As we made our way through the evening crowd to our reserved meeting room, we were slowed to a snail's pace as men called out to Magnús, shook his hand, clapped his shoulder, and promised to call soon.

Omnitech, as previously mentioned, started out as an Icelandic company, before being sold first to a Luxembourg-based data center group, then sold again to a French infrastructure firm. Magnús, having ridden the waves, told me that Omnitech had come out well: "We are now a very strong company with strong funding. These guys share our vision on sustainability, green energy, and that's the big value that we are putting on the table." In the service of this vision, Omnitech has built two data centers in Iceland: one in Reykjanes and one in Blönduós. The Reykjanes facility was first, joining the already-existing cluster of development in the footprint of the former NASKEF base. But in recent years, that data center has run into issues with electricity access on the peninsula.[7] The Blönduós facility, opened in 2019, has become the company's main focus and investment.

Due to Omnitech's somewhat fraught experience in Reykjanes, Magnús emphasized reliable power access in describing the company's decision to build in Blönduós—the site is just down the road from the Blanda Power Station, the fourth-largest hydropower plant in Iceland, with a 150 MW capacity. But another important factor, he said, was "differentiation." "You know, all the other data centers are in the southwest corner of Iceland. We're not. That makes us stand out," he said. "And," Magnús went on, "they [the Blönduós government] actually had plans and had been working on developing industry in the area for quite a while. To create jobs of course, all of that. So they were quite interested in getting a data center in their site." These factors weighed heavily in Omnitech's selection of Blönduós, even overriding the relative difficulty of finding the "human resources" Magnús said they needed in the Northwest.

Siggi, then, in describing Polarice's site selection process, emphasized the smallness and simplicity of the Hornafjörður area, which would make expansion easier to control. Magnús, in speaking to Omnitech's attraction to Blönduós, pointed to the advantage of differentiation as well as the value of municipal interest. Recall, too, one last articulation of site strategy already elaborated in chapter 3, Aaron's assertion that Arctera's location offered "a vast piece of land with a secure perimeter, and no large population nearby." These assessments each reflect a developer's perspective, opinions on the calculated result of commissioned research, keenly attuned to operational risks and costs. They are also all articulations of marginality.

As Aaron notes the appeal of a small and deliberately distanced population, Siggi stresses the relative ease of making arrangements in what he views as a "simple" society, and Magnús notes the advantage of setting oneself off from the pack with the backing of a local government eager for industry, each makes a case for favoring the (spatially and socially) peripheral over the central. Eschewing the conveniences of the urban metropolis, these developers also avoid its drags and downsides by choosing to push their companies farther afield. In many ways, it is a strategic set of *lacks* that attracts them: the absence of threats, complications, and competitors. And in this, the developers with whom I spent time in Iceland are far from alone.

Graham Pickren, for example, has documented the "adaptive reuse" of banks, bakeries, and printing facilities in Chicago as data centers in the wake of postindustrial decline (2017). As these businesses shut down, data center developers have rushed to replace them, taking advantage of their open floor plans and the power capacity they left on the lines. Jenna Burrell, following the long road to launching a Facebook data center in Prineville, Oregon, after the waning of the timber industry which once sustained the town, concluded that the tax abatement deal with Facebook was a rational choice for Prineville—despite its risks and trade-offs—given the area's severe economic need and "the harsh realities of rural spatial marginality" (2020, 286). Mél Hogan, in her analysis of Facebook data centers across the United States, has argued that "desperation seems to be a locative factor" for development, "mitigated only by the fact that the clusters of storage centers are out of sight and out of mind" (2013, 11).

We might conclude, then, from these accounts in Iceland and outside it, that data centers are *attracted* to marginality. The same features that make it hard for Icelandic country communities to sustain themselves—their distance from population centers and centers of commerce, their relative remoteness and inaccessibility—are, in fact, assets for an industry that prefers to operate under the radar and expand undisturbed. Marginality is key to their value proposition, a built-in part of their business plan.

Data centers are not the only ones drawn to margins; anthropologists have long been attracted to them, too. Euro-American anthropology, as

Sarah Green writes, holds the belief that "shining a spotlight on the discarded, ignored, shifting, semivisible, and perhaps transgressive nooks and crannies . . . might help to make the implicit explicit, might draw out the hidden cogs, wheels, or (cob)webs of what we know to be central, and might provide an antidote to master narratives" (2005, 1–2). Margins are valued as field sites rich with significance, places where power is particularly labile (Tsing 1993; Das and Poole 2004), and innovation happens as a matter of necessity (González 2020; Watts 2019). Margins, in other words, are central to our field. And so, one anthropological response to developers' assumptions would be to show how these supposedly peripheral places are actually teeming with life and energy; to counter industry visions of simplicity, isolation, and absence, showing how Blönduós, for example, is in fact far more important than it initially appears. This is undoubtedly true and may be ethnographically generative. And yet, it is not the move I want to make here. Because developers' views may be incomplete or even inaccurate, but this does not make them any less effective. These are ideas that bring things into being. As developers choose to site data centers in particular places, they both make use of existing conditions and continually remake them in their own interests.

ON BEING ON-THE-WAY

The data center in Blönduós is built across from a horse farm. To get there, you take the main road heading out of town, then take a turn away from the river. As the space between passing buildings grows wider, separated by swaths of green pastureland, the data center comes into view on the left. The facility is comprised of six slim warehouses, laid out in rows parallel to the country road that carried you in. A small office stands at the center of the compound, perpendicular to the data halls around it. Like other data centers in Iceland, Omnitech is ringed by a metal security fence with an intercom and automatic gate. If you look carefully, though, a thick line of recently disturbed soil snakes under the fence line and across the grass of two adjacent farms—trace evidence of fiber-optic cabling tracking back to the Ring Road and power lines running from the data center all the way to the Blanda Power Station inland.

How do we know a margin when we see one? On the one hand, driving out to the data center, wind bending grass and whistling through windows across the quiet countryside, only underscores what an out-of-the-way place the town of Blönduós seems to be. On the other hand, there are all these *connections*—these auspiciously visible networks linking the rural municipality to more central circuits of (figurative and electrical) power.

If we subscribe to the view that connectivity and marginality are antithetical, the connected margin would seem to be a contradiction in terms. Connectivity is often said to overcome marginality through the mobilities, proximities, and simultaneities it facilitates. And yet, at the data center in Blönduós, connectivity and marginality seem quite compatible, densely integrated into infrastructural networks, yet retaining a meaningful experience of social and economic exclusion for the people who try and make their lives there. This is not a prototypical margin, an "out of the way place" (Tsing 1993) defined by sheer remoteness or isolation. Instead, we might think of it as an *on-the-way* place, built up in the interests of others, and fixed fast in both infrastructures and imaginaries as a node, relay, or in-between.

The on-the-way offers an angle on infrastructure that differs from better-documented concerns about access to services. Often, infrastructure is read as a relationship between providers (benevolent, unjust, neglectful) and provided for (resourceful, righteous, complex). For example, the fact that the Vietnamese socialist government used water infrastructures to demonstrate its success means that later this competence was called into question as those waterlines fell into disrepair (Schwenkel 2015). Likewise, insofar as heat in Chicago public housing units is understood as emanating directly from the state, falling temperatures make residents viscerally aware of neoliberal austerity (Fennell 2011). But in deliberately multidirectional digital networks, origins and end points are much less clear. Commercial data centers—business ventures that rent space, power, and bandwidth—are neither producers nor consumers. Rather, they store data, on its way to somewhere else, or process data, on behalf of someone else. Those places that host them are not the intended targets of this kind of technological connection, though they are entangled in its effects nevertheless.

In Blönduós, we need only to return to the Ring Road to appreciate the experience of being on-the-way. It makes a difference that Blönduós is looped into the national highway, whereas Sauðarkrókur, a small town just to the east, is not. The road makes it feasible for town officials to even think about trying to capture tourist traffic, as well as developing an industry that requires bringing in specialists and specialized materials. But far more often than not, people still drive right by it, failing to make the turn in, just after crossing the Blanda *ós*. Reykjanes, too, discussed in the last chapter, might be productively figured as an on-the-way place (Johnson 2019a). The US military, in building up the Naval Air Station Keflavík (NASKEF), built the Miðnesheiði Plateau into the expansive project of American military empire. From the perspective of the Pentagon, Southwest Iceland sat at the very center of Cold War actions, networked into supply chains and sonar surveillance programs. And yet, during these years within Iceland, Reykjanes steadily grew to feel more distant, different, and disparaged than it had been before. Today, data centers perpetuate these social and spatial dynamics, between coastal municipality and inland development, and between Reykjanes and the rest of Iceland.

The on-the-way place, then, as I conceive it, is selectively, strategically connected. Its integration into wider networks (for example, national systems of power provision or international circuits of financial investment) serves a purpose that may intersect with but does not emerge directly from local needs. As such, on-the-way places trouble the persistent techno-utopian ideal of communicative connectivity. While IT is still routinely framed as inherently equalizing, as instantiating progress and expanding potential, at the outposts and waystations of the global internet, it becomes clear that the sheer fact of infrastructural connection does not produce parity or guarantee meaningful inclusion.[8] Instead, it may be organized in such a way as to deliberately leave marginality in place.

As we heard from developers, marginality can be an attractive factor in selecting a data center site.[9] Distance, simplicity, and economic desperation can all come to be seen as boons. But in acting on these characterizations of place, developers entrench them—after all, if data centers are drawn to out-of-the-way places, one might ask what interest they have in undoing the marginality that brought them there. On Reykjanes, for example, Arctera does not wish to see a more active community on Ásbrú, more foot traffic threatening its "secure perimeter." Its continual expansion may employ locals in construction, but it also works against the often-stated need to "densify" the Ásbrú area in order to make it feel more like a thriving community. Likewise, the data center at Blönduós would not benefit from building up the rural population, from business booming in the small town.

In creating connected margins, or on-the-way places, data centers do not instantiate a leveling kind of connectivity, putting rural municipalities on par with urban centers as hubs for this innovative new industry. Instead, they serve as landing strips, launch pads, or processing plants for data not necessarily (and in fact, very rarely) affiliated with the place where they are built. As such, they not only choose marginality, but they continually reinscribe it, both by emphasizing it to clients and by making day-in, day-out decisions to maintain rather than transform spatial relations.

In our sustained attention to margins, anthropologists have forcefully argued that marginality is not a fixed property of places or people; rather, it is made and continually remade through everyday activities as well as extraordinary events (Tsing 1993; Green 2005). The development of digital infrastructure and industry should be understood as part of this margin-making process. While often celebrated abstractly for "dissolving distance" (Cairncross 2001) or "compressing space-time" (Tsatsou 2009), the construction of data centers, in practice, plays into existing dynamics of spatial inequity.

All of this is not to say that data centers will not, or categorically cannot, benefit rural communities. In my conversations with officials as well as developers, the promise of secondary industry loomed large. As Siggi put it, "We see that if you start a data center, there will be something that goes on around it—you never know what, but experience shows that there always has been something." He impressed on me the unexpected difference that any new industrial development in rural Iceland can make. A less optimistic friend who lived for years in Blönduós told me, "A data center is only going to create about three jobs in Blönduós." But then again, she added, "For Blönduós, that's not nothing." In 2021, Magnús estimated that Omnitech had in fact employed ten people. He made a point of telling me about one of those employees, an electrician born in Blönduós who had since moved to Europe, but who was happy to move back with his young family, having finally found a job there that suited his skills.

Data centers, then, may indeed have positive economic effects on some rural municipalities; they may, in some cases, prove to be the best among limited options for advancing regional interests (see Burrell 2020). But the data center in Blönduós was understood not only as an economic opportunity; it was also seen as a bid for spatial equity, a means of instantiating connections of all kinds. These connections, I suggest, deserve to be interrogated, rather than read as inherently fruitful. Blönduós, like Reykjanes, is now well connected: the question is how, to whom, and to what ends.

CONCLUSION

Data centers, as we have seen, are often imagined in terms of their connective capacity, their potential to bring about the circulatory promise of infrastructure in general and IT specifically. And data centers, through their development contracts and fiber-optic cables, employment opportunities and power lines, do indeed instantiate a kind of connection between rural municipalities and centers of power. But these are not the free-flowing, reciprocal, and equitable connections often imagined in celebrations of information technology. Instead, these are strategic, conditional arrangements—ones that count on the quiet of a "small population," a "simple society," or distance from competitors and comparison points. They benefit from, and thus entrench, these features, cementing regional inequities. Connection, then, in this mode, viewed from this vantage point, does not oppose or undo marginality; in the space of the data center across from the horse farm (or, the former military base), the two coexist quite comfortably.

Helgi, the Reykjavík representative I met at World Hosting Days, once told me about his childhood on the tiny island of Flatey. Located midway between the Snæfellsnes Peninsula and the West Fjords, home to a single road and a current full-time population of five, Flatey is an indisputably peripheral place in Iceland. Helgi described it as an idyllic place to grow up. But an ambitious young man, he left home early to pursue his multiple degrees in business, then accept increasingly prestigious positions in the field of economic development. He mused, "We used to think that technology would make it so you could just live anywhere, but that hasn't happened. It's something like physics—it turns out places have mass and gravity."

When Helgi raised the possibility of "living anywhere," he had the application-level outcomes of the internet in mind, products and services that allow us to meet our needs online, from remote work to social media to telehealth. These developments, according to Helgi, transformative as they have been, have not yet rearranged those place-based physics in Iceland, have not yet made it possible for someone like him to make the kind of life he wants on Flatey. But another way of looking at the intersection between IT and a place's "mass and gravity" is through the lens of infrastructure.

Turning to data center development in particular, we see not an erosion of, or escape from, these forces; instead, we see a settling in. Data centers become attractive to—and become attracted to—rural municipalities in a context of long-standing drain and decline. While the country is imbued with cultural value in Iceland, most people prefer (or find themselves forced) to live in the city, leaving rural municipalities struggling to give residents a reason to stay. Fighting against such centrifugal drift, town officials like Valdimar have pursued industrial developments that both promise much-needed municipal revenue (even if they do also obtain generous tax breaks) and seem to instantiate increasing connection, understood as capable of overcoming long-standing exclusions. And yet, I have argued that data centers are unlikely to deliver on those latter expectations. As Jody Berland writes, "To struggle against the ossification of centers and margins, it is necessary to reject a mimetic relationship between technological enhancement and future redemption (progress = progress, etc.), and to acknowledge that such enhancement disguises and impedes as well as precipitates social change" (2009, 24). Or, perhaps, as Tom Boellstorff has put it, "The cloud does not connect, it clumps" (2010). Data centers, then, as they make a home amidst the margins, should shake our inherent faith in connectivity.

What we see in rural Iceland should also nuance our calls for digital equity. Here, it is not exclusion, breakdown, or failure (the usual culprits in discussions of infrastructural politics)[10] that foster unequal difference between regions in Iceland. Instead, it is precisely the expansion of functioning infrastructure that sediments spatial inequalities, that creates on-the-way places strung into networks not their own. These uneasy coin-cidences and seeming contradictions call into question not only the effects but the *ideals* of infrastructural expansion—a necessary effort when tech-nological connection is often imagined as a self-evident good. They remind us that the project of building equitable systems cannot be limited to nur-turing "digital deserts" and overcoming "digital divides." Instead, efforts to seek spatial justice across digital networks should also consider the instru-mental inclusion of those most densely networked, those places that are built in because of the ways they have been, and can continue to be, left out.

We have now traced the processes of selling, siting, contracting, and constructing data centers in Iceland—the projects of articulating a rela-tionship between Iceland and industry, and of anchoring that industry in particular locales. Next, the closing chapter finally moves inside the server farm (or rather, it tries to). Turning from anticipatory efforts to everyday operations, this last chapter takes up the practice of data center security, the project of keeping data in and everything else out. Doing so, it makes a case for questioning the threshold (physical, conceptual, and ethno-graphic) between the data center's inside and outside.

PART III Excess

5   Inside Out

When I drove to the data center on a slushy spring morning, the ten-foot-tall metal security fence around it offered the first and only sign that I was in the right place. Technically, the building behind it had an address, but not one that meant much to the GPS system I relied upon to navigate there. No signage marked the data center with the name of a company or indicated any kind of visitor's office. Instead, after driving back and forth past it a few times, I found the gate, entered the range of its surveillance cameras, and pressed the button to trigger the intercom. After giving my name and the name of the representative I was scheduled to meet inside, the gate opened and I was directed around back to the parking lot, where I parked amid a scant handful of other cars. There again, no signs oriented the visitor, so this time on foot I again found and followed the only point of potential ingress, an unmarked door into a beige-colored building that opened onto a cramped and windowless foyer. As I walked in, a young security guard sitting behind a desk turned away from the dozen video feeds running behind him to check my ID and hand me a visitor's badge. He instructed me to wait on a lone plastic chair near the entrance, then swiveled back to his multiplex view of the data center's domain.

.   .   .   .   .

The words above could describe several of my first forays into data centers, highlighting as they do industry-wide security strictures, and the industry-wide hassle of getting inside. Every facility I visited in Iceland employed a majority of these tactics, and several facilities employed them all. In actual fact, my entrée into these spaces started even before I got in my car and started driving, a dubious address plugged into the GPS app on my phone. I set about trying to get access to data centers immediately upon arriving in Iceland but struggled to do so from the start. Company websites included contact information for clients, but none for media, much less curious anthropologists. Unsurprisingly, my inquiries to corporate head-quarters went ignored. Getting past the gates ultimately required a trip to Germany, where I fought the crowds at the World Hosting Days confer-ence and wrangled "face-time" with representatives of some of Iceland's data centers, who rewarded me with their elevator pitches and business cards. A few weeks and email volleys later, I was finally invited inside.

I am not alone in this experience of being held at arm's length. Data storage is known for being a discreet industry, one in which the privacy concerns of clients intersect with data centers' own intellectual property. Oftentimes, data centers do not publish their locations, they do not publi-cize their technology, and colocation centers rarely release the names of their clients, who rent space and infrastructure inside. These norms and policies circumscribed my research. Quickly, I realized that my access to data centers would be limited, occasional, and closely supervised. While I was able to arrange multiple visits to multiple data centers in Iceland (including return trips with the same, and different, interlocutors), my time inside would always be a guided experience that would allow me to see, but not immerse myself meaningfully in, everyday life inside.

In some ways, this vantage point is a distinct limitation. Certainly, other ethnographies will be conducted by industry insiders, which will offer analyses of the inner workings of the server farm this account cannot provide: the labor practices of data center technicians, their embodied relationships to infrastructure and technology, the corporate culture of the data center as a workplace. But my own research set out to ask how data is being placed in Iceland. And in this, the data center's outside is just

Figure 15. The securitized entrance of one data center in Reykjanes. Photo by author.

as important as its inside—the edge between them, and the efforts that go into policing it, perhaps most informative of all.[1]

In this chapter, I relay my own efforts to gain access to data centers, alongside the story of a high-profile server theft in Iceland known as the "Big Bitcoin Heist." Through these breaches, I explore data centers' attempts to prevent them, and the imaginaries they imply about what constitutes a threat here—as well as what is worth protecting. By attending to everyday practices of data center security, as well as a moment when they were rather spectacularly undone, this chapter delves into the data center only to open back outward; ultimately, it contends that the data center meaningfully and materially exceeds itself. In this account, then, I am less interested in revealing data centers' hidden insides. In fact, I suggest that an emphasis on "getting in" misses the point. The inside/outside distinction is intuitive, and emic in the data center industry, but it does not wholly reflect how data centers operate in relation to their surrounds. The "secret" of the server farm, I argue, does not speak to the data protected in the depths of it, but rather to its entanglements right on the surface of the earth.

SECURITY THROUGH OBSCURITY

Shifting from the shared to the specific, I return now to one particular visit, my first time inside Arctera on Reykjanes. After I had sat for a few minutes on the lone office chair in what passed for the data center's waiting room, Aaron, the head of marketing, emerged through a door at the back. The two of us exchanged a few jet-set pleasantries—Aaron had just arrived on a delayed flight from the United States but had gotten lucky with the tailwind and made up time—and then, making sure my visitor's pass was clipped on and clearly visible, he scanned his employee badge to open the door behind us. We stepped into a bright white corridor, with a neatly caged thicket of cables running above our heads. Security cameras, also overhead, followed our progress down it, until Aaron stopped us at the door to one of the server rooms and again scanned his badge to allow us inside.

I followed Aaron over a dust trap, designed to peel dirt from the soles of our shoes, and into the data hall where motion sensors anticipated our arrival. Rising lights revealed rows of steadily blinking computer servers, stacked behind locked and gleaming glass doors. Each contained aisle comprised its own little weather system, with hot air being drawn out at the top of it and cool air filtered in from below. Unlocking one and stepping inside it, where we were enveloped by a soft but steadily droning hum, Aaron told me about some of the clients who rented space in this room: a well-known car manufacturer, for example, had recently moved its high-performance computing needs to Arctera; a lesser-known, but still nameable, insurance company had, too. But not all clients give Arctera permission to divulge their patronage, so Aaron, a chatty guy who kept his data center's secrets out of duty rather than temperament, also hinted provocatively to me about hedge funds and financial services companies based in the United States and England—"of course I can't tell you which ones"—and about future clients whose names I would know, but never will. One of these, Aaron told me, was so concerned about their data that they bought a whole room and installed their own security system on top of the data center's. When I expressed my surprise that Arctera would allow this, Aaron shrugged: "It's like a high-tech hotel. Whatever happens in the room . . ."

On that first tour, I was struck by the data center's aesthetics,[2] its white walls, clean lines, and strangely proportioned spaces, designed to just barely—and certainly not comfortably—accommodate human activity. I asked Aaron if I could take photos using my cell phone camera. He told me that I could take pictures of the racks but nothing outside them, drawing a precise but invisible line between the data center's indistinguishable servers and its particular, proprietary cooling technology. He watched over my shoulder as I anxiously snapped a few bad shots framed by his spatial constraints. Later, after walking with me through two more data halls, answering my questions along the way, Aaron said—by way of conclusion on a tour he'd clearly given before—"Security is a major focus for us. There are twelve security challenge points between you and the data stored here." Straining my memory, I counted up eight of them, and Aaron cheerfully declined to identify the rest.

The many and varied security measures on display during my first visit to Arctera reflect industry standards of practice favoring "layered" or "interlocking" systems. These include physical deterrents like the gate and security guard, RFID tagging of valuable assets, and authentication at multiple checkpoints, as well as less visible protocols surrounding software, communications, and social interaction. Together, they work to create the experience of a highly securitized environment, efforts at protection that are meant to be palpable as one passes through the data center space. I rubbed up against another layer a couple of weeks later, when I interviewed Ingó, Arctera's head of security.

After I passed through the gate, checked in with the security guard, and visibly installed my visitor's badge, Ingó came to collect me and brought us back to Arctera's meeting room, a surprisingly cozy space equipped with a boardroom table and kitchenette, and decorated with several digitally enhanced images of Icelandic nature on the walls. There was also a whiteboard with some residual writing, which Ingó erased rather deliberately upon our entry. Ingó, who looked more youthful than his experience and steady demeanor suggested, had been working at Arctera for four years. Prior to that, he had worked at the Icelandic Defense Agency, a government organization founded after the closure of NASKEF to take over Iceland's responsibilities as a NATO member state (which include operating the radar defense system installed on the island and hosting the occasional military exercise). When he was hired at Arctera, Ingó knew very little about data centers, but he told me, "Right from the get-go, I realized that this would be something beneficial for Iceland. Iceland seemed to have all the ingredients to make this work." So Ingó learned quickly, on the job.

When I asked Ingó what security at a data center looked like, he told me,

> Security on a day-to-day basis is just making sure that everything works. Writing access procedures, making sure that, in terms of both the technical guys and the customers, both in the construction areas that we're constantly building and on the operational side, everything works and is how it's supposed to be.

"What specific threats would you be thinking about?" I asked him, and Ingó gently deferred. "I would say there's not that many specific data center type threats we're thinking of," he said. "The main concern is that nobody gets into the data center unless we know who he is, that he's been approved by someone we trust, and that we know what he's about to do." "And what would you be worried about him doing?" I ventured. Ingó laughed and clicked his tongue.

> You never—I mean—it's a new industry. We haven't really had any incidents or problems. We learn from, we follow other countries closely, we make sure we're up-to-date on what's happening around us, what risks and threats data centers in other countries are concerned about. But I would say we haven't really had any threats.

My conversation with Ingó, which continued for an hour in this vein of friendly stalemate, is of course another site where the Arctera data center's security played out. In declining even to name the impetus for his security system, Ingó built another layer of insulation around it, ensuring that I would not—could not—contribute to any breach. I didn't take it personally: the Uptime Institute, an advisory agency that issues industry standards for data centers, warns that "authorized staff, vendors or visitors" are often overlooked in data centers' security plans, but these trusted outsiders can pose the greatest risk of all[3]—thus necessitating security measures that assume worst intentions. I doubt very much that Ingó suspected me of tampering or corporate espionage, but as he put it, his work was establishing procedures and making sure they were followed by everyone, every day. His tactic of downplaying, even explicitly denying, the risk that surely justified his job, was both a practical act and a performance of security. In treating me as a potential infiltrator, Ingó showed me more than he would explicitly tell.

If Ingó was an airtight cog in the machine of data center security, he admitted that getting everyone on board with these procedures had, at times, been challenging: "From an Icelandic standpoint, there are things we need to overcome." As Ingó explained:

> Iceland has typically been very safe. The crime rate is low, people are in most cases pretty trusting. Reykjavík has maybe a little bit changed, but outside the city, in regular houses, most people don't lock their doors. So for most people, when they come to Arctera, it is a learning process of getting adjusted to how we do things, our strict rules, our access procedures.

I had heard these proud references to Iceland's safety and witnessed for myself (even in Reykjavík) people leaving the house with unlocked doors. "I imagine there aren't a lot of other places like this in Iceland," I said, and Ingó laughed heartily, "No, I imagine prison would probably be the closest thing."

My time at other data centers confirmed Ingó's impressions that industry standard security could feel out of place in Iceland. At another facility, Nordicom, access protocols were no less rigorous—I was greeted by a guard, equipped with an ID badge, and accompanied through the facilities at all times—but there, my interlocutors spoke wearily and joked openly about the data center's stringent rules. "We keep track of everyone who comes into the building," a technician named Jón told me one day, "but it's really just the same guys, again and again." Later, when my visitor's badge fell off in a server room, and I had to spend several mortified minutes searching for it on the floor, Jón smiled indulgently and reassured me, "We're in the middle of nowhere, I don't think we're really a target." For Jón, Iceland's relative marginality served a protective purpose. But later, when I asked him the same question I'd posed to Ingó—*What kind of threat might a data center be worried about?*—Jón gave me the same tight-lipped smile and shrug, saying, "You never know."

"Security through obscurity" is an information security concept most often invoked in order to be dismissed. It has long been understood that secrecy alone is a poor defense: a key hidden under the doormat deters most would-be burglars, but once an intruder figures out the secret, he is able to walk right into the house. Likewise, concealing an information system's vulnerabilities is considered inferior to shoring them up. Still, information security professionals acknowledge that secrecy can form a valid layer of an otherwise robust security complex, like the camouflage painted on an armored tank. The data centers I studied had multiple security systems—visible and invisible, unique to the industry and shared across facilities management more generally—but obscurity was the one I interfaced with most often, and most obviously, in my time inside (and trying to get there). Obscurity shaped my every interaction, not as a blanket prohibition or total barrier, but as a first principle to be negotiated in every visit or interview.

It is not my task here, nor is it within my capacity, to analyze the efficacy of data center security and the obscurity through which it proceeds. Instead, as an anthropologist, an erstwhile interloper, and someone who has bumped up against it for years now, my own interest is in what *else* data center secrecy does.

THE DATA CENTER'S SECRETS

One of secrecy's many ironies is its need to be performed publicly. As Michael Herzfeld writes, "If privacy is so total as to be invisible, it has no semiotic force at all"[4] (2009, 145). Data centers enact this sharp edge of secrecy in their interfaces with "the public." Staying entirely under the radar—for example, refusing all requests for contact—would have been its own kind of obscurity, but the industry, in recent years, has been pushed to open up. So Google and Apple have published aesthetically pleasing photos of their data centers' interiors[5] (which tell the viewer nothing about how they operate), and the Icelandic data centers I encountered in my research invited a professional question-asker inside to politely decline to answer my questions. These are understandable compromises in the face of conflicting interests, but they are also performances of secrecy.

When Ingó answered my questions with a comfortable "no comment," he was not only withholding information, he was also drawing attention to this omission and controlling the terms on which it played out. It was an act that generated "semiotic force" by pointing back to itself, without giving anything else away.

Such performances call attention to the textured borders between what is secret and what is not (see: Ingó erasing the meeting notes on a dry-erase board, right in front of me), and in doing so, they draw a definitive line between the data center's outside and inside. In my interview with Ingó, a word he kept returning to was *access*: who has it, who doesn't, under what conditions it gets dispensed. *Access* was typically deployed around the edges of the data center ("access to the facility"), but it also signaled a progressive series of checkpoints the visitor/intruder could pass through ("access to the server room," "access to the data"). With it, Ingó set up a nested system of insides and outsides, a way of conceptualizing the data center as a fortress or bunker,[6] oriented around a guarded interior space. At the same time, he signaled a distinction between insid*ers* and outsiders. Those in the know had access to the data center, and those with access could come to know that which the data center concealed.[7]

Perhaps, the invocation of "access" struck my ear with particular intensity given how it echoed my training as an anthropologist. "Getting access" is the first rite of the ethnographer, a term that covers a range of indices of inclusion, from getting clearance to spend time in a foreign country, to building real and trusting relationships with interlocutors. Though increasingly subject to critique, in particular by feminist ethnographers,[8] "access" remains a widely accepted prerequisite to ethnography. What it signals, beyond the feasibility of research ("access" is often raised as a concern by granting agencies, too) is that the ethnographer can achieve the kind of immersion needed to claim authority on the basis of intimacy. Ingó's success, then, as Arctera's head of security, seemed at odds with my own as an ethnographer, in a way that piqued both my interest and anxiety.

A second side effect of secrecy is conferring value onto its object: secrecy is a matter of property, as Georg Simmel argued (1906). At the data center, this formulation is not immediately intuitive—in fact, it is precisely the inverse of how Ingó would probably describe his job. Isn't it the valuable property itself that occasions the need for secrecy around it?

But in a data center, the question of property can be hard to pin down. Is the valuable thing the servers running inside it? The infrastructure that sustains them? The actions enabled by access to the facility itself? Ingó steadfastly refused to answer this question, or rather, he answered with a cryptic smile and an all-inclusive "yes." But when I asked Aaron, on one of my visits, what exactly was being protected here, he told me matter-of-factly, "Well, the data in this facility represents billions of dollars."

It is not clear to me how Aaron made this calculation: Was the data stored and processed here integral to generating billions of dollars of profit for Arctera's clients? Would billions of dollars be lost if this data was compromised? Or would the data here be worth billions of dollars to these companies' competitors if offered on a black market or in some back room? However he arrived at his estimate, though, Aaron's assessment suggested that the *data* is the locus of value, maintained via exclusive access. The well-known car company he told me about, for example, relies on Arctera to keep from disclosing its exclusive designs; a film production company that rents server space to render visual effects at Arctera depends on the data center not to leak the season finale of its show. The data center, then, appears as a physical architecture erected around intellectual property, with rings of secrecy enshrouding the data at its core.

At the same time, this mode of secrecy also generates value for the data center, which represents itself as storing and processing data so important the public can't know about it. Take, for example, Aaron's invocation of "companies I would know" in our visit to the server room. This show of secrecy created the impression that Arctera was trusted (even as I was not). As this performance is repeated in promotional materials and at industry conferences, it signals to potential clients the kind of operation Arctera is—one *worthy* of housing "billions of dollars" worth of data within its well-defended walls.

Finally, as secrecy differentiates insides from outsides, and as it endows its object with perceived, and thus practical, value, it also creates an inclination or "incitement" (Dean 2002) toward its own uncovering. I felt this drive at work in my own tortured efforts to get at the data center's always-deferred inside. In my first months of fieldwork, I struggled to get past the data center's gates and guards; once I did, I was presented with another series of locked doors and off-limits zones; then, even admitted (albeit for brief and supervised periods) into those inner sanctums, I found myself confronted by Ingó and Aaron's practiced reticence. I felt alternately tempted and thwarted in these moments, convinced that what must matter most for my research was what lay just out of my reach. But as I progressed farther into the data center's inside, I also began to question my own enrollment in the logics of data center secrecy.

While security practices oriented around "access," and padded with secrecy at their contact points, figure the data center as a closed, contained place and the data stored inside as the locus of value, I have come to feel in my many crossings in and out of them that these are not the most useful frameworks for understanding what data centers do, or what difference they make. Because even viewed from all the way on the inside, introduced by those most in-the-know, the data center stays frustratingly opaque. Shining white walls reflect your own face back to you; towering rows of computer servers blink blind.

Instead, then, of pushing and progressing ever inward, of attempting to expose what lies at the data center's core, I suggest a kind of "infrastructural inversion." A term first proposed by Geoffrey Bowker (1994), and later developed with Susan Leigh Star (2000), inversion describes a kind of figure-ground reversal, a practice of deliberately attending to the aspects of infrastructure that tend to "fade into the woodwork" (2000, 34). These include, among other lines of investigation, bureaucratic labor, industrial standards, technical networks, and regulations. But where infrastructural inversion is often described as a project of turning infrastructures "upside down" (Edwards 2010), I set out to study the data center "inside out." Data centers' insides have been overwhelmingly figured—by industry actors and critics alike—as the primary space of action and site for inquiry. Instead, I suggest we need to trace the vital interconnections between the data center and the world outside.

To make this case, I turn next to a much more dramatic breach than my own entry into Icelandic data centers—a series of server thefts known as the "Big Bitcoin Heist." When a band of thieves succeeded in breaking into several Icelandic data centers, they thoroughly upended the assumptions described here (as well as my own already-tenuous "access") and forced an alternate understanding of data centers' place in the Icelandic landscape.

THE BIG BITCOIN HEIST

After Aaron showed me around the sleek data hall, where secret clients' servers were locked behind glass doors, he led me to the back of the main building, then pushed open the door into the cold, wet air. We crossed a short path to a second, identical building, which Aaron jokingly referred to as "the low-rent zone": Arctera's Tier-1 facility. Data centers are classi-fied by a tier system, with a data center's "tier" referring to the level of security, management, and maintenance it receives. A Tier-1 data center offers basic power, cooling, and connection; a Tier-4 facility provides fully redundant systems, with backup network links as well as fault-resistant and dual-powered sources of cooling, storage, and power.[9] Historically, a tier classification has typically been applied to an entire data center; Arctera, however, then at the forefront of an industry-wide shift toward modularity, contains both a Tier-1 facility and a Tier-3 facility (which we visited earlier) within its compound. This means that at Arctera, a client can easily split their data, for example, storing more sensitive operations in the Tier-3 hall while moving their backups to the Tier-1, thereby maxi-mizing efficiency and cutting costs. Or, alternatively, a client can decide that the "low-rent zone" is exactly what they need.

If that first Tier-3 room had the somber air of a bank vault, the Tier-1 facility was a wall of sound; Aaron had to shout to be heard over the dron-ing hum of hundreds of servers, and the air circulated between them by hundreds of fans. Before us stood rows of floor-to-ceiling metallic scaf-folding, with server clusters out in the open, evenly staggered on the racks. To our left was a wall of power suppliers, with one transformer feeding each aisle. To our right was a forest of soft white filters mediating between the data hall and the fresh air outside. These thin panels were hung verti-cally in the open windows, designed to capture dust on its way in, and they undulated anemone-like in the light breeze, which made narrow beams of fluorescent lighting overhead sway somewhat precariously. When we got closer, I could read the manufacturer labels on the servers; names like Cointerra and Terraminer were subtly stuck on. These Tier-1 inhabitants stacked all around me were machines specifically made for mining Bitcoin.

Bitcoin is a digital cryptocurrency whose value has fluctuated, between the time of this research and this writing, from $227 (August 2015) to

$58,735 (March 2021). It is produced through a computational process called "mining,"[10] or the solving of complex cryptographic puzzles. Solving these problems both verifies Bitcoin transactions (recorded on a public record known as the blockchain) and, in the process, produces more Bitcoins. This system, based on public key cryptography and "proof-of-work" (a system of evidencing computational effort), was designed to decentralize control over the currency: if users' own efforts maintain the blockchain, it eliminates the need for trust in the financial system, as well as the oversight of a central bank.

In the early days, following its release in 2009 by an anonymous entity known only as Satoshi Nakamoto, anyone could partake in this process—and many did, for example, using the central processing units of their personal computers to mine hundreds of Bitcoins a week. But Bitcoin was designed to be a finite resource, with only twenty-one million total Bitcoins available. So fewer Bitcoins are being released now than were ten years ago, and the computational problems required to release and record them have gotten progressively harder to solve. Today, they are so difficult that it takes a pool of specifically engineered servers[11] to participate and make a profit; it is this type of machine I recognized in the Tier-1 data hall.

Bitcoin is not the only cryptocurrency, and Arctera is not the only facility in Iceland playing host to mining operations. In fact, just down the hill from Arctera but still within the footprint of the former NASKEF base is another sprawling operation entirely dedicated to Bitcoin mining. Its six buildings stand like sentinels looking out over the highway. Not far away is a facility built for mining Ether (linked to a blockchain called Etherium), the most actively used cryptocurrency today. There are more, smaller "mines" on Reykjanes and outside it, both known and operating under the radar; the Icelandic government does not currently collect statistics specific to this industry. But it is known that cryptocurrency mining has come to make up the majority of data center operations in Iceland and consume the lion's share of the sector's energy.[12]

The reason cryptocurrency mining has boomed in Iceland traces back to the opportunities and constraints offered on the island, as discussed in chapter 1. Miners, like other kinds of data center developers, are drawn to Iceland for its abundant and inexpensive electricity—especially vital given the power-intensive nature of continuously solving cryptographic problems. In 2018, the energy use of Bitcoin alone was estimated at around thirty-five terawatt hours, or roughly on par with the country of Denmark.[13] Meanwhile, unlike more client-facing operations, miners are less concerned with issues of latency—the fact that Iceland is 750 miles, and therefore twenty to forty milliseconds, away from nearest land. The churning, whirring forms of cryptocurrency mining, then, articulate with the strengths and limitations of the infrastructures supporting data storage in Iceland. Just like there are places in the world that are "good" for mining ore and minerals, Iceland appears to be a place that is "good" for mining cryptocurrency—an equation that has fueled a migration described in the media as a "modern day gold-rush."[14] But also like those other zones of geological extraction, Iceland is not just a reservoir of natural resources ripe for the taking; these are rendered available through structuring assemblages of political power, labor, infrastructure, and capital.[15]

On December 5, 2017, 104 Bitcoin servers went missing from a data center on Reykjanes. A few days later, a nearby facility was targeted, but its security system scared the intruders away. The following week, a data center in Borgarnes, an hour and a half northwest of the capital, was successfully robbed of twenty-eight computers. The next few midwinter weeks passed without incident, during which time the thieves went underground. Then, on the quiet day after Christmas, another aborted attempt was made on Reykjanes. On January 16, a fourth and final burglary on the peninsula[16] brought the total of stolen servers to nearly six hundred and made the series—quickly dubbed the "Big Bitcoin Heist" by the media—the largest theft in the history of Iceland.

The exact value of the heist has been hard to estimate, because of the nature of the loot itself. The thieves did not just steal cash or hardware (the price of which was estimated around two million US dollars); they stole the servers engineered to produce Bitcoins in perpetuity. What this means is that they stole not just a valuable object, but the very means of value production. They didn't just try and break into a few data centers—they effectively tried to commandeer a mint.

It was not long before the culprits of the heist were apprehended; in fact, two had already been detained and questioned after being caught speeding away from the site of the second burglary on the surveillance camera of the Hvalfjörður tunnel. The last big break-in on Reykjanes had been aided and abetted by a data center security guard, who was first extorted, then physically threatened, by the thieves. This man confessed quickly under questioning and pointed the police toward Sindri Þór Stefánsson, an Icelander with a long record of petty crimes. Sindri Þór was arrested, along with four associates who had helped him execute the burglaries, implicated via car rental records and messages extracted from Sindri Þór's phone.

If the international media had already started sniffing around the story of a massive Bitcoin heist, the case became a caper when Sindri Þór left Sogni, the low-security prison in Southern Iceland where he was being held. While Sindri Þór's departure was depicted salaciously as a "prison break," in fact his initial custody had simply expired. Informed by prison staff that he was technically free to leave, but would be arrested again imminently, Sindri Þór chose to climb out a window, hitchhike the sixty miles to the airport, and board a plane bound for Sweden (as it happened, the same plane that was transporting Prime Minister Katrín Jakobsdóttir). From Sweden he traveled by land to Denmark, then Germany, then Amsterdam, where he met up with two of his alleged coconspirators, one of whom posted a picture of the trio to Instagram, hashtagged #TeamSindri. They were apprehended shortly thereafter and extradited to Iceland. In January of 2019, Sindri Þór was sentenced to four-and-a-half years in prison; his fellow defendants were sentenced to two-and-a-half years, twenty months, and eighteen months, respectively.

The servers stolen in the so-called "Big Bitcoin Heist," to this day, have not been found. Under questioning, and later in a strangely indulgent interview with *Vanity Fair* magazine,[17] Sindri Þór insisted that he was not the brains behind the operation. He claimed instead to be taking direction from a mysterious investor called "Mr. X," who purportedly pressured Sindri Þór into carrying out the series of robberies, promising him 15 percent of the mine's future profits in return. "You don't say no to this guy," Sindri Þór told his interviewer. The involvement, or existence, of a Mr. X has not been proven. But the disappearance of six hundred Bitcoin miners into thin air remains perplexing, and speculations about where they wound up abound—most recently, a whiff was caught in Tianjin, China.[18]

In some ways, the story of Iceland's "Big Bitcoin Heist" simply punctures the veneer of data center security I have described: at least a handful of data centers proved themselves permeable, so long as you didn't ask permission to get inside. The data centers successfully breached in the break-ins were Tier-1 facilities, those so-called "low-rent zones" that looked and functioned like any other warehouse—a far cry from Arctera's sleek Tier-3 data hall, full of secret clients' servers kept behind locked doors. And since the burglaries, I am told, their security has been tightened (unsurprisingly, in ways that no one will detail). But I want to suggest that this string of robberies, and especially what happened after them, also unsettles data center security in a deeper way: specifically, it calls into question the very notion of the data center as a physical fortress protecting valuable and vulnerable data from threats. From the vantage point of someone who has just stolen six hundred Bitcoin servers, the data center looks much less like a prison (from which, after all, Sindri Þór "escaped" handily) and more like its servers' metaphorical namesake—a mine.

EXTRACTIVE ENTANGLEMENTS

In the days following the heist, the police tasked with solving the string of data center break-ins employed all the traditional methods at their disposal: wiretapping the suspects apprehended after the Borgarnes burglary, tracing their telephone records and bank accounts. But briefed about the purpose of the stolen bounty, the authorities also monitored the national grid for unusual surges in electricity usage, the telltale sign of six hundred servers plugged in. In the process, they found more than one marijuana grow house,[19] but not the missing miners, which the thieves were savvy enough to keep off the grid. Despite, then, stealing "machines that make money,"[20] the architects (or, following the Mr. X theory of the case, the errand boys) of Iceland's "Big Bitcoin Heist" were left sitting on a shutdown mine.

Their conundrum offers a different perspective on the question of value posed by the data center. While Aaron suggested that data was the locus of value, and thus the object of protection, data was not the target here. The nature of the blockchain means the Bitcoin ledger is public—there was no data on these particular servers that could not be accessed from anywhere else. Hacking that blockchain, in order to move already-mined digital currency from one account to another, would not have required physically accessing the servers themselves. But these Bitcoin thieves glued security sensors, clambered through open windows, and hustled a compromised security guard in order to smuggle the servers out. Are the servers, then, the valuable thing? Not quite. Sure, the stolen servers could be sold on the black market, provided the thieves could off-load them without getting caught. But using these machines to produce Bitcoins as intended would require reliable access to large amounts of electricity; it would require racks to house them and fans to cool them down. As such, it would require making a contract with the power company, engineering at least a rudimentary cooling system, and buying or leasing a large enough facility. The value, then, at play in the "Big Bitcoin Heist" inhered not only in the coding, nor in the computers—it lay primarily in the social and material means to plug them in. Put differently, the value of the mines was not situated in the depths of the data center's insides; instead, it was distributed across an interconnected network of variously positioned people and things. Viewed from this angle, the data center did not so much function to protect the data stored inside it; it functioned to protect the value-generating potential of a select few.

Thinking about the data center in this way links, along with the obvious metaphor, cryptocurrency "mining" to other extractive industries. Extraction, stripped down to its most basic logic, evokes the image of drawing something from the depths to the surface, most paradigmatically, minerals and oil. But in Iceland what is drawn up from tectonic rifts and rivers is *power*, in the form of geothermal and hydroelectric energy. Iceland, teeming with geological activity and generously blanketed by glaciers that melt into mountain streams, produces an abundance of electricity: 55,000 kWh per person annually, as compared to the European Union average of 6,000 kWh.[21] One-fifth of this energy is consumed domestically on the island in houses, hospitals, small businesses, and schools; the rest is directed toward power-intensive industry.

Historically, the most significant of these industries has been aluminum smelting, the process of extracting the oxide alumina from bauxite and using electrolysis to produce aluminum. There are currently three major aluminum plants in Iceland, owned by American, British, and Australian companies; they account for around 30 percent of the island's national exports. This power-hungry industry is what first expanded Iceland's now-impressive electrical grid, primarily through the damming of rivers to feed into hydroelectric power plants (Guðmundsdóttir et al. 2018). It is also what sparked an environmental movement around the turn of the twenty-first century. Spurred to action by the proposed Kárahnjúkar power plant, designed to direct 4,600 gigawatt hours annually to an aluminum smelter in the East Fjords, Icelandic and international activists drew attention to the damaging ecological impacts of damming rivers upstream—including the loss of vegetation and displacement of animal life. In 2003, the Kárahnjúkar project was rejected by the National Planning Agency on the basis of these ecological dangers, but the minister of the environment overruled its decree. The rivers Jökulsá á Dal and Jökulsá í Fljótsdal were dammed in 2008, submerging 440,000 acres of highland, and the Kárahnjúkar hydropower plant opened in 2009—in concert with an Alcoa aluminum smelter in the northeastern town of Reyðarfjörður.

More than the specific ecological harms of damming rivers (and also drilling geothermal boreholes),[22] it is the broader dynamic of seemingly endless expansion at which Icelandic environmentalists take aim. Government and aluminum representatives alike have claimed that Iceland has more than enough energy to go around, citing 30 TWh as the island's annual hydropower capacity.[23] But author and environmentalist Andri Snær Magnason, on researching this figure for his book *Dreamland: A Self-Help Manual for a Frightened Nation* (2006), discovered that this level of production could only be achieved by damming every major river on the island. Projections, Andri Snær has argued, of Iceland's capacity monomaniacally privilege economic growth.

At the same time, Iceland's trajectory of twinned development—power plants developed to serve smelters, specifically—has linked the island indelibly, and sometimes uncomfortably, to the interests of multinational aluminum corporations. In addition to the dubious social responsibility records of these companies—Alcoa, Rio Tinto, Century Aluminum[24]—many Icelanders have critiqued the undue influence of foreign corporations, especially in light of the island's postcolonial history and lingering questions about just what kind of place ("First" or "Third" World, hot commodity or overexploited terrain) Iceland is. As author Guðbergur Bergsson puts it in the documentary Magnason's *Dreamland* was turned into, "Iceland was a colony of Norway, then Denmark, then the US, and now American industry."[25] A friend of mine, long active in environmental politics, conceptualizes aluminum's entanglements in slightly different terms. "Iceland doesn't have a military," she told me. "So Iceland doesn't go to war. But Alcoa makes the aluminum that goes into weapons, and they do that in Iceland, with Icelandic energy. Is there not something about that . . . is that not the same thing?" The question, then, raised by environmental activists is not *Does Iceland have enough energy for aluminum smelting?* but rather *Is aluminum smelting worth sacrificing whichever pieces of the Icelandic environment it consumes? Is it worth compromising whatever part of Icelandic politics it captures or bends in the direction of its will?* Today, these same questions have started to surface in relation to cryptocurrency mining and the broader data center boom.

When data centers first started cropping up in Iceland, the response I heard most often was "They're better than smelters, at least."[26] That is, while data centers were power-hungry, their perceptible externalities were few—a little noise pollution was the worst that neighbors had to contend with, compared with aluminum plants' excretion of dangerous fluoride waste.[27] In the years since, however, concerns have accumulated about the fundamentally extractive nature of the cryptomining enterprise. As more than one person put it over the course of my research—some eagerly and others with apprehension—data centers essentially "export Icelandic power."

Snæbjörn, a geologist who works at Iceland's Natural History Museum, has been one of those critical voices. In 2019, Snæbjörn published an editorial called "Hvalá River for Bitcoin?"[28] (*Hvalá Fyrir Bitcoin?*), in which he critiqued the proposed development of the Hvalárvirkjun hydropower plant in Iceland's West Fjords. The Hvalárvirkjun project sets out to dam Hvalá, an almost impossibly blue river that runs through the mountainous inlands of the West Fjords, creating a cascading series of waterfalls along the way. It would also dam the nearby rivers Rjúkandi and Eyvindarfjarðará, channeling all three into a power station at Ófeigsfjörður, one of the small and sparsely populated places where ocean carves out land from the region's scenic shore. While Hvalárvirkjun has been publicly positioned as solving the problem of energy insecurity in the remote West Fjords,

Snæbjörn notes that, if this were in fact the ambition, a cable would need to be extended westward across the Ísafjarðardjúp fjord. Instead, energy cables are planned to run southward, where power will be extracted from the West Fjords and feed into the grid of HS Orka, a private energy company based in Reykjanes. HS Orka's interests—and more specifically, those of its foreign owners and investors—are not, Snæbjörn suspects, in meeting the energy needs of West Fjords residents; they are in satisfying the growing demand of data centers in the south.

After reading his article, I met with Snæbjörn in the Natural History Museum offices. There, he told me that when he first heard about them, data centers seemed like a good enough idea—"and I'm still not against them outright." But when he learned how dominant cryptomining was becoming in the sector, and how much energy it consumed, this is when he started worrying about Iceland's emerging niche. "It's wasteful," he said simply, to direct these kinds of resources toward a few people's big payday. As we talked through the Hvalárvirkjun proposal and Snæbjörn's organizing against it (focused primarily on a plan to promote the region as a potential tourism site),[29] Snæbjörn repeatedly got up to grab maps and photographs, making sure I could clearly see exactly which fjords and rivers we were talking about—what exactly was on the table as a suggested sacrifice. "Can it be worth this?" he asked. Or, as he put it in his writing, "What is the justification for sacrificing the most significant wilderness in Europe for Bitcoin mining and slightly more profit in the ledgers of foreign investment funds?"[30]

This point about the fundamental elsewhereness of this industry has been made by others in Iceland. Journalist Jón Bjarki Magnússon observed in a 2015 article that one data center then under construction in Reykjanes was "backed by Georgia's Prime Minister, who has been linked to corruption cases. The profits are in the billions, but it is unclear where they will go."[31] Magnússon's assessment referred to money being made in real time, but it might equally be applied to the future of the notoriously volatile industry: hundreds of cryptocurrencies, by the time of his writing, had been launched, failed on the market, and disappeared, taking any infrastructural investments down with them. Smári McCarthy, by that time an MP for Iceland's Pirate Party, declared on Twitter that "Cryptocurrency mining requires almost no staff, very little capital in investments, and mostly leaves no taxes either. The value to Iceland . . . is virtually zero."[32] And yet, the industry's impact in Iceland has been great.

The energy consumption of data centers in Iceland doubled every year between 2013 and 2016, then doubled again in 2018.[33] In 2019, the Icelandic National Energy Authority predicted another doubling by 2022.[34] Data centers now consume more power than all households on the island combined.[35] And in 2020, 37 percent more electricity sales were made to data centers than homes, hospitals, churches, daycares, schools, and ports.[36] While their usage still lags behind the aluminum smelters, data centers have quickly emerged as a major player on the energy scene. In a 2019 report, Landsnet, the national energy distributor, cautioned against potential energy shortages in the coming years, and cited the growth of the data storage industry as a key factor.[37] Of course, the very idea of an "energy shortage" is debatable in a country that produces more energy per capita than anyplace else in the world—orders of magnitude more than its own citizens could ever use. But insofar as energy here is envisioned as an export product,[38] Iceland's landforms and earth processes will continue to be remade in the interests of power-intensive industry.

As Zac Zimmer writes, in a provocative historical comparison between Bitcoin mining and colonial Spanish silver mining at Potosí, "mining is always an act of terraforming, of remaking the earth itself on a geological scale" (2017, 326). "Mining" for cryptocurrency may be one step abstracted from driving pickaxes into the ground, but it remakes the material world around it nevertheless. Deciding what role it should play, then, in Iceland, is not just a practical, solvable problem of energy supply versus energy demand; these are the kinds of questions that Dominic Boyer has called *energopolitical* (2019), which is to say about how power operates over and through energy, and about what kinds of life and thriving would justify expanding the island's already massive energy-making machine. These questions are not new in Iceland—they have been an active site of debate since at least the 1960s, when the first aluminum company, Alusuisse, surveyed Iceland as a smelting site.[39] But they have become increasingly urgent as Icelanders, like all of us, confront the climate crisis and its unfolding effects.

The energy that makes Iceland attractive to industry comes in part from geothermal (approximately 27% of national production) but predominantly from hydroelectric power (approximately 73%). Hydropower, in turn, depends upon the flow of rivers, harnessed by dams and routed through turbines that spin the rotor shafts of generators, converting kinetic to electrical energy. The continual replenishment of this system, the water rushing continually through, is what makes hydropower "renewable" or "sustainable," a resource that can be used without being used up. But rivers ultimately come from somewhere—in Iceland, they originate in a system of glaciers spanning the uninhabited highlands. Today, Iceland is losing eleven billion tons of ice annually; in 2014, Okjökull became the first Icelandic glacier to officially lose its glacial status, having melted until it grew too thin to move.[40] To call hydropower "sustainable," then, is to take a somewhat short view—this form of energy will only be sustainable as long as the glaciers can be sustained.

Iceland's other natural asset that attracts the data center industry is its consistently cool climate, with average temperatures ranging from around 34 degrees in winter to 54 in the summer months. These temperate conditions make it especially easy to provide the kind of ambient cooling we observed in Arctera's facility. But these calculations, too, are liable to change as global average temperatures climb higher—in the Arctic region, especially. In the far North, low temperatures make evaporation impossible as a route for releasing excess heat. Meanwhile, the fact that melting ice and snow reveal darker landmass means that more and more of its territory comes to absorb energy more readily from the sun. Together, these phenomena are known as "Arctic amplification," a cycle that makes climate change in the Arctic especially intense, with temperatures rising twice as fast as the global average since the year 2000.[41] Iceland's very cold, then, convincingly packaged as "the coolest location for data centers,"[42] may also be a less reliable, "renewable" feature of this place than is routinely assumed.

Questions of energy usage, then, take on new meaning in the face of widespread climate disruption. The rationing of power in a place that produces such abundant energy may seem a strange calculation,[43] but life in the Anthropocene has forced such a reckoning, such a reorientation toward space and time scale. Icelanders like Snæbjörn have responded by persistently posing the questions *What should we do with the resources we now recognize as limited? What values do we want our choices to convey?* Such

Figure 16. A stretch of the Hvalá River in the West Fjords, proposed site of hydropower development. Photo by author.

challenges recall the often-asked question *What kind of place is Iceland?* but push it forward—*What kind of place can and should Iceland be?*

It was in the context of these conversations that the "Big Bitcoin Heist" took place. The theft and its thwarted aftermath shed light on the sheer number of cryptocurrency mines working away across the island, as well as the power that each of these consumed—a quantity so great it would register as a visible spike on the national grid. And knowing this, or coming to appreciate it for the first time, most Icelanders I spoke with (outside the industry) regarded the heist with an attitude I would describe as bemusement. No one was saying these were noble actions, exactly. Few positioned the Bitcoin Bandits as Robin Hood types. But wasn't this, I was sometimes asked, an almost victimless crime? After all, what did it really mean for a foreign company to have mining rights in someone else's country? What were Bitcoin mines doing for Iceland, anyway?

The Bitcoin thieves, however inadvertently, drew the extractive and interconnected nature of the data center out into the open—showing how such facilities in Iceland are situated in relation to power plants and pipelines (themselves dependent on particular riverine reserves), showing how they are situated in political processes that figure Icelandic energy as either an abundant commodity or a limited resource whose extraction comes at a cost. They recalled the same inequitable relations raised by US occupation and aluminum companies' multinational encroachment. They also, for just a moment, disrupted those predictable pathways in a way that at least some found pleasurable. As Alla Ámundadóttir, the reporter who covered the case for the newspaper *Fréttablaðið*, admitted, "It's difficult not to root for them."[44]

CONCLUSION

Another day, another data center. On a sunny summer morning in 2019, I drove down a country road to tour a new data center that had gone online just months earlier. Like Arctera, this facility was built to anticipate expansion, and its outskirts were still an active construction site. In fact, it was the site manager, Óskar, who came out to meet me and showed me around the work his team had recently done. Óskar was eager to talk about architecture, about the impressive speed with which these facilities went up. "The most important thing to me," he said, "is that nobody got hurt and that everybody got along in the process." But like Ingó, Aaron, and other representatives, he was tight-lipped about what the servers inside contained and did. He could tell me that this data center was built for high-performance computing, but quickly reminded me there are many things high-performance computing can do: "running simulations, the internet of things, doing data analysis, cryptocurrency mining . . ." (conspicuously listed last).[45] "But *there is no secret*," Óskar said matter-of-factly, and he gestured with open hands at the data center around us, as if I could verify as much by looking around.

"There is no secret" is a line that sticks with me, one that refuses to be cleanly resolved. It is, on the one hand, the kind of thing you would think to say only if there really was a secret. On the other hand, I think that

Óskar got it right. The combined gesture of saying "There is no secret" (meaning: I won't tell you what's on the inside, but this omission is not the kind of concealment you might think) and the invitation to look around me, to direct my curiosity toward the data center's surface rather than pursue access to its hidden depths, reflects both the pride and province of the site manager, and a certain kind of truth.

This chapter has taken up two breaches, or entries into guarded data center space: my own time spent (trying to get) inside a number of data halls, and the series of thefts known as the "Big Bitcoin Heist." My own efforts to access the ever-receding inside of the data center were shaped by practices of secrecy, or "security through obscurity." These efforts framed the data center as a closed and contained space, in which valuable data was protected from a threatening outside. But the series of server thefts that took place in 2017 and 2018 invite us to see the data center in another way. Drawing our attention to the cryptocurrency mining operations that currently make up the majority of the sector in Iceland, the heist shifted attention to the data center's implication in broader extractive dynamics and energopolitics.

You don't have to get to the heart of the data center to learn these "secrets": these are right out in the open. You can follow them in the national energy statistics, published annually for anyone to see. You can read them in the reports of Data Centers Iceland[46] (*Samtök Gagnavera*), an interest group within the Federation of Icelandic Industries, which document steady progress in lobbying the government to meet its needs. You can trace them in the sales contracts of the national power company, Landsvirkjun,[47] which increased to the data center industry from 350 GWh in 2018 to 520 GWh in 2019. Or, if you live in a place like Reykjanes, you can simply count the growing number of unmarked warehouses proliferating on the horizon line. Of course, there are always hidden details— for example, the exact energy prices paid by data centers (discounted from the price offered to citizens) is one of the better-kept secrets outside the industry. But this chapter has argued that we do not, of necessity, need to keep on seeking the secret; we don't need to delve continually further into the data center's depths. Instead, we might practice reading the data center inside out, focusing on its infrastructural, often extractive interconnections with the wider world.

This approach, which situates itself at the data center's interfaces rather than its insides, allows us to understand the object of data centers' security differently—not only the vulnerable data located at the shielded heart of the fortress (within the gate, within the walls, within the server, within the software), but also as the rights to turn energy into currency, to "mine" not only for digital resources, but also, and more indirectly, natural ones. "There is no secret"—or rather, what is secret is not central to engaging with the urgent questions that data storage in Iceland has raised.

Turning the data center inside out also unsettles the borders and boundaries of the server farm. While these edges are fortified through practices of data center security, "challenge points" and mantraps and access protocols, the "Big Bitcoin Heist" demanded that we consider them differently—not as constituting a self-evident and airtight threshold, but rather a strategic demarcation, reproduced alongside an unsettling status quo. In actual fact, the data center exceeds itself, meaningfully and materially. In Reykjanes, it wafts across the highway in the form of a low but disquieting hum. It insinuates itself in Reykjavík, the seat of government, where proposals are considered to expand Iceland's already massive energy infrastructure. It also makes its presence felt at Hvalá, a river that originates in the glacial highlands and spills into the sea over two hundred miles away. It takes turning away from the guarded gates of the data center, and out toward these sites where the cloud becomes ground, to apprehend the data center's excess and thus account for its actual operations and impacts.

Conclusion

In March of 2021, a volcanic eruption began in Geldingadalir, a valley in the Fagradalsfjall volcanic system on the Reykjanes Peninsula. The event, a fissure eruption in which red-hot lava seeped then spewed up from a vent in the ground, had been anticipated for over a month, during which time earthquakes shook Southern Iceland thousands of times a day. Those of us in Reykjavík grew fatigued from waking up to rattling cabinets and the questions "Was that one? Did you feel it too?" Those in Grindavík, the closest town to the eventual eruption, endured the unrelenting calamity of earthquakes of up to 5.7 magnitude, making their multistory buildings sway. And so, when the lava finally started flowing (into a lowland far from homes and critical infrastructure), it felt like a social, as well as a seismic, release.

First, Icelanders flocked to visit the volcano. I set out to see it on the second day of the eruption, following my father-in-law, an experienced hiker, and his GPS. Starting our three-hour trek before sunrise, we passed just a handful of others on a path that cut first along the southern coast-line, then inland toward the source of some faintly yellow smoke. By the time we walked down just a few hours later, we were swept up in a sea of hundreds and a heady air of still-socially distanced camaraderie.

Thousands more would come in the days and weeks later, and all this before Iceland reopened its borders to tourism for the first time since the start of the COVID-19 pandemic, which would again multiply the numbers making the pilgrimage. The government, the search and rescue squad, and the municipality of Grindavík all scrambled to build paths, parking lots, and other infrastructure that could keep pace with the growing deluge.

That spring marked the first time in almost ten years that I had come to Iceland with no plans for conducting research. Having secured a semester-long leave from teaching, I'd moved back to Reykjavík to spend time with friends and family. But taking part in the pageantry around that volcano, there was no escaping the light it shed back on this work. As soon as people reached Geldingadalir, images of it were everywhere. Social media feeds clogged with eruption photos; countless drones were lost flying too close to the flow. A popular rock band recorded a music video at the eruption site, and the national broadcasting service set up a twenty-four-hour livestream. When I made a second trip to Fagradalsfjall at nighttime, eager to see the lava glowing against a dark sky, the sides of the valley were dotted with smartphone lights like a stadium concert, as all of us photographed, filmed, and FaceTimed our friends.

As we now know, most of those photos and videos would not be saved on users' devices, but stored in data centers via cloud services. Posted to sites like Instagram and Facebook, they would be repeatedly accessed as feeds would refresh and reload. And even after the initial frenzy of volcano content died down, the majority of those files would continue to be stored in perpetuity, as pressing reasons for culling one's file collections dwindle and "*keeping* becomes the default way to handle one's data" (Dow Schüll 2017, 46). Participating in this mediatizing moment felt like watching the completion of the condensation cycle that produces the rain clouds we see in the sky: the dramatically splitting land is transformed into data, just as that data works to shape and shift that same terrain. At the same time, the [digital] cloud retreats into the background, unquestioned infrastructure to our experience.

The 2021 volcano proved a particularly striking meeting point of these processes. But of course, and as this book has argued, the cloud also becomes ground here in less spectacular ways. We have observed, for example, how those who stand to benefit from data center development craft convincing narratives linking computational projects to Icelandic landforms, earth processes, and climatic conditions. We have traced how racialized ideals of liberal modernity and postcolonial hierarchies of rank drive anxieties—and aspirations—around data management. Equally, we have seen how sedimented histories of military occupation and rural marginalization draw the development of data centers to particular municipalities, then condition differential access to these sites. Finally, we have followed the ways that social and material landscapes are transformed by expansive construction projects, highly securitized spaces, and the great quantities of power this growing industry consumes. Across these many and varied intra-actions (Barad 2010) between cloud and ground in Iceland, we see how place is made in relation to data, and how data is made in relation to place.

The cloud, then, far from hovering somewhere off in the distance, is densely enmeshed with the world all around us. "Our data," as John Durham Peters has argued, "have won just as much of a planet-steering role as have more basic nature-engineering media such as burning, farming, herding, or building" (2015, 8–9). This is more, then, than a matter of IT's "impacts," a formulation that sets the field of technology too comfortably apart. Instead, it is a question of how data's forms and fixities are produced, noted or naturalized, and ultimately acted upon. These are pressing problems that implicate all of us.

What to do, however, with this information, is a tricky question to answer convincingly. After all, I type these words on software I use as a service (accessed over the internet rather than owned on my hard drive). I will save my draft on Dropbox, share it using Google Drive, and announce its eventual release over social media. You yourself may have downloaded this text as a file for an e-book reader, or perhaps as a pdf from a file-sharing site. The system we have built for managing digital data may be flawed and costly, but it is also so vital it has become all but impossible to meaningfully opt out.

Some efforts at addressing the cloud's externalities are already underway. In the years since I began work on this project, the data storage industry has moved to cut its consumption—from the consolidation of computational effort (in fewer servers as well as "hyperscale" data centers that use energy more efficiently), to advances in cooling technology, to a push toward the use of renewable power. Today, tech companies routinely feature environmental impact statements on their websites; they employ chief sustainability officers and VPs of environment, policy and social initiatives. In 2021, the Climate Neutral Data Center Pact, an outgrowth of the European Green Deal, was signed by seventeen industry bodies committing to reaching carbon neutrality by the year 2030 (AWS and Google were among the signatories; Facebook and Microsoft were conspicuously absent). These changes, emphasized with increasing fervor and frequency by developers I have spoken to over the years, are important and have kept growth in the sector's energy consumption slower than some early estimates.[1] And yet, they will not neatly undo the earthly impacts of data storage this ethnography has explored.

For one thing, many industry analysts anticipate that IT's greening efforts will be outpaced by demand from power-intensive sectors like cryptomining and AI.[2] We have already seen the massive cost of maintaining cryptocurrency networks; meanwhile, training a single large natural language processing model (which enables a computer to parse and respond to speech or text) may consume as much electricity as a car over its entire lifespan.[3] These fast-growing fields will set the pace for data production, much more than the everyday activities (searching, scrolling, swiping, saving) over which most of us have direct control. While power usage effectiveness (PUE), the standard measure of energy efficiency, varies greatly between data centers, on global average it has stayed roughly stagnant for seven years.[4]

We might also question the depth of tech companies' commitment to transformation within the context of their profit-making mandates. As Mél Hogan writes, "Big Tech upholds the idea of shifting its mode of energy production to alternative, sustainable, and renewable sources without implementing radical changes at the level of labour, resource ownership, or conceptions of the environment, which have become more pressing matters at this time of global climactic transformations but remain at odds with capitalist endeavours" (2018, 634). As with other fields pushed by public opinion to address their environmental impacts, we might appreciate the data storage sector's advancements, while also asking after the limits of its self-regulatory initiatives. A case in point: the

IT industry is increasingly recognized as a leader in sustainable development but remains the fastest-growing consumer of water and electricity in the United States (ibid.).

Finally, what we have watched unfold in Iceland further calls into question the viability of these strategies. The island, eminently and long since "sustainable" by the metrics now being pursued by Big Tech, has been figured as an enclave, offshore, and even escape hatch for the data storage industry. Yet even here, we have traced the disruptions of data, the sometimes-surprising ways its accommodation is felt. In fact, toward the final days of drafting this manuscript, signs emerged that an end to the industry's rapid expansion may be in sight. Responding to pressures described in the preceding chapters, in 2021 the national power producer, Landsvirkjun, announced that it would no longer extend new contracts to data centers (later, it specified cryptomining operations). When asked, its representatives stated definitively that it had no plans to build new power plants to support server farms.[5] Later that year, when faced with a short-term energy shortage (brought about by low hydro reserves and a power plant malfunction), Landsvirkjun temporarily cut supply to industrial operations, causing some data centers to briefly shut down. None of this means the industry, so far successful, is immediately or existentially threatened. But if Iceland is viewed as the future of data storage, then we may all be running out of runway.

There is no escape, then; there is no easy answer to the "what now" question often asked of ethnographies. This because data storage is not just a technical problem but an inescapably social one, too (Kirschenbaum 2012). If the cloud in fact occupies space as we allow it, shaped by our existing orders and systemic inequities, then we need to address it just as capaciously and flexibly—not only in the form of targeted industry takedowns, or techno-solutionist attempts to engineer our way out. The association, after all, of data management, and the rights and privileges attendant to it, with the wealthy and white-dominant "First World" is not a technological problem. Neither is the US military's, or offshore industries', enduring and ongoing terraforming of overseas space. And neither is the widespread and shortsighted notion of nature as a resource for capitalist consumption. All of these are grounds well worth troubling, sites where we might situate the politics of data more squarely within our multiple and intersecting struggles in the direction of a more just society. Asking the kinds of questions already being raised in Iceland—at what cost, to what ends, and for whose benefit—does not lead to easy consensus or pat best practices. It does not guarantee a way through. But it does reflect the unequally shared reality we have to contend with, and it allows us to see the cloud with clear eyes—not as ubiquitous, ethereal, or ephemeral, but deliberately placed and resolutely part of this world.

Notes

INTRODUCTION: PUTTING DATA IN ITS PLACE

1. All interlocutors are referred to by pseudonyms in this text, with the exception of public figures speaking in their official capacity and published writers discussing their (cited) writing. The choice to pseudonymize is not self-evident in Iceland, where a small population and even smaller industry make truly airtight anonymity near impossible. I have chosen to try here, to the best of my abilities, to create strategic frictions in the places where they might matter, which has also included omitting and obscuring some identifying details.

2. Data centers are also referred to by pseudonyms in this text.

3. Precision Reports. 2021. "Global Data Storage Units Market Report, History and Forecast 2016–2027, Breakdown Data by Companies, Key Regions, Types and Application." June 22, 2021. https://www.precisionreports.co/global-data-storage-units-market-18626626.

4. Patrizio, Andy. 2018. "IDC: Expect 175 Zettabytes of Data Worldwide by 2025." *Network World,* December 3, 2018. https://www.networkworld.com/article/3325397/idc-expect-175-zettabytes-of-data-worldwide-by-2025.html.

5. Bawden, Tom. 2016. "Global Warming: Data Centres to Consume Three Times as Much Energy in the Next Decade, Experts Warn." *Independent,* January 23, 2016. https://www.independent.co.uk/climate-change/news/global-warming-data-centres-to-consume-three-times-as-much-energy-in-next-decade-experts-warn-a6830086.html.

6. Greenpeace. 2014. *Clicking Clean: How Companies Are Creating the Green Internet*. Amsterdam: Greenpeace International.

7. IBM announced in 2017 its transition from a technology company to a "cognitive solutions and cloud platform company," while Microsoft reorganized itself in March 2018 to prioritize its cloud services sector. The same year, Microsoft stated its plans to develop between fifty and one hundred new data centers a year.

8. See, for example, Derrida's (1996) identification of location, or "place of consignation," as central to the operation of archontic power, one of three essential prerequisites (with "technique of repetition" and "exteriority") for the exercise of this form of authority.

9. In the space of media studies, this move risks sounding like a step backward—the content/form distinction was a foundational fiction of mathematical communications, which media theorists have since richly critiqued (see Halpern 2015). My own intention is not to reinscribe it, but rather show how data's "forms" can be fruitfully conceptualized more broadly than is often done, not only in the medium of storage itself but also extending to the social and spatial arrangements the project of storage precipitates.

10. See Gabrys (2011), Akese and Little (2018), Reading and Notley (2015), Parikka (2015), Cubitt, Hassan, and Volkmer (2011), and Glanz (2012). This work on digital materiality itself draws on a longer tradition of media materialism, developed in different directions by the intellectual lineages of Harold Innis, Marshall McLuhan, and Friedrich Kittler.

11. See Amoore (2018) for an extended discussion on the limitations of taking the *location* of data centers as coterminous with their *geography*.

12. At the same time, historian of science Skúli Sigurðsson has argued that the role of technology is often overlooked in Icelandic historiography: "One of the paradoxes of late Icelandic twentieth-century history is that a society which is primarily the product of technology looks back a thousand years to Leifur Eiríksson's 'discovery' of America in its quest for an identity" (2000, 484). This section, in reading settlement-era history through the lens of technology, aims to draw a through line across these tendencies.

13. Prime Minister's Office. 2003. "Iceland and the Information Society." https://www.stjornarradid.is/gogn/rit-og-skyrslur/stakt-rit/2004/02/02/Islenska-upplysingasamfelagid-2003-Ensk-thyding/.

14. Prime Minister's Office. 1996. "Vision of the Information Society." https://www.stjornarradid.is/efst-a-baugi/frettir/stok-frett/1996/10/01/Vision-of-the-Information-Society/.

15. Icelandic national narrative, which I was taught as a matter of course when I first started studying the island, has long held that the Norse settlers and the captives they brought with them arrived to an uninhabited island around the year 870 CE. In recent years, however, that consensus has been upturned by ongoing

archaeological research. Cross-shaped carvings found in caves in the Seljaland region, dated back to approximately 800 CE, suggest that Celtic-speaking people from Scotland and Ireland had settled in Iceland before the Vikings did (Ahronson 2015). Raised, ring-shaped boundary walls discovered on the Seltjarnarnes Peninsula further indicate Celtic presence, perhaps overlapping with Norse settlers'. This work, which does not speak to possible interactions between Norse and Celtic populations, complicates long-standing stories about the origins of "the Icelanders" and raises questions about Norse colonization, previously theorized as "only ever-incipient" (Kolodny 2012, 331).

16. A key debate in the manuscript scholarship has revolved around how to read these texts, as historical sources or works of literature. The manuscripts were clearly composed by interested parties, then were copied over the course of the Middle Ages, some centuries after the events described. Moreover, as anthropologist Gísli Pálsson has argued, they were written before the modernist distinction between fact and fiction truly and reliably took hold (1995). At the same time, historians have commented upon the surprisingly scientific style of some manuscript writers (Karlsson 2000). Anthropologist Victor Turner, who advocated for an ethnographic approach to the Icelandic saga, wrote that these documents "read like exceptionally well-filled ethnographic records and diaries" (1971, 371). Historian and archaeologist Jesse Byock has argued that these interpretive tensions themselves follow the political lines this section lays out: Icelandic nationalists strategically claimed the manuscripts as literature (evidence of a distinctive cultural tradition), and the Icelandic school of saga studies has upheld this tradition, delaying other modes of inquiry into these texts (Byock 1992).

17. íris Ellenberger has noted that Icelandic historical scholarship has tended to use the term *hjálenda* ("dependency") over *nýlenda* ("colony"), a reflection of both Iceland's political ambiguity and an ongoing exceptionalist tendency to situate Iceland as unlike any other colonies (2009).

18. See Durrenberger and Pálsson (1989), Oslund (2011), and Ísleifsson (2011).

19. Icelanders also had the distinct advantage of being able to read the medieval texts without translation. While Icelandic, Danish, Swedish, Norwegian, and Faroese all descend from Old Norse, modern Icelandic is much closer, in written form, to its parent language than the continental Scandinavian languages.

20. *Mannedsskrift for Litteratur*, VII, 523–34, Karlsson (1995) trans. 44–45.

21. Verena Höfig quotes one justification for studying Icelandic settlement records given in the prologue to an abridged edition of *Landnámabók*: "we can better meet the criticism of foreigners when they accuse us of being descended from slaves or scoundrels, if we know for certain the truth about our ancestry" (2018; see also Durrenberger and Pálsson 1989).

22. Ethnographies of Iceland richly illustrate the unsettled question of Icelandic representation. For example, Danish anthropologist Kirsten Hastrup's *A Place Apart* opens with an arrival scene that deliberately echoes *Argonauts of the Western Pacific*: "Imagine yourself suddenly set down surrounded by all your gear, alone on a subarctic coast, while the bus which has dropped you drives away on the dirt road out of sight, and you stand there like a misplaced Malinowski" (1998, 3). Her subsequent study of what she calls "the Icelandic world" describes the island as remote, exotic, and tradition-bound, and for this has been critiqued by Icelandic anthropologists (Pálsson 1995). At the same time, another strand of scholarship downplays Icelandic difference. American anthropologist E. Paul Durrenberger writes perhaps most definitively: "Iceland is not exotic. It has electricity and central heating and cars and buses. It has telephones that work and supermarkets and electric milking machines and tractors. People live in high-rise apartment buildings or modern single-family houses. Icelanders have credit cards, money machines, color TV. Except for a couple of letters the alphabet is the same as we use for English. Iceland is a thoroughly modern country" (1992, 3).

23. My research proceeded over two summers in 2012 and 2013, fifteen consecutive months in 2014 and 2015, and follow-up visits of between one and five months each year from 2016 to 2020. I also spent ten months of 2021 living in Reykjavík while writing the first draft of this book.

24. Adalbjörnsson, Tryggvi. 2019. "Iceland's Data Centers Are Booming—Here's Why That May Be a Problem." *MIT Technology Review*, June 18, 2019. https://www.technologyreview.com/2019/06/18/134902/icelands-data-centers-are-booming-heres-why-thats-a-problem/.

1. A NATURAL FIT

1. Bawden, Tom. 2016. "Global Warming: Data Centres to Consume Three Times as Much Energy in the Next Decade, Experts Warn." *Independent*, January 23, 2016. https://www.independent.co.uk/climate-change/news/global-warming-data-centres-to-consume-three-times-as-much-energy-in-next-decade-experts-warn-a6830086.html.

2. Greenpeace. 2012. *How Clean Is Your Cloud?* Amsterdam: Greenpeace International.

3. Greenpeace. 2014. *Clicking Clean: How Companies Are Creating the Green Internet*. Amsterdam: Greenpeace International.

4. Glanz, James. 2012. "Power, Pollution and the Internet. *New York Times*, September 22, 2012. https://www.nytimes.com/2012/09/23/technology/data-centers-waste-vast-amounts-of-energy-belying-industry-image.html.

5. Since Greenpeace released its damning report in 2012, the data storage industry has made significant investments in energy efficiency. For example, Facebook's data center in Prineville, Oregon, was widely acknowledged for its energy innovation and LEED certification. The company's data center in Luleå, Sweden, was likewise celebrated for sustainability, based on the combination of cold climate and green energy discussed here. And yet, analysts differ in their assessments of how far the industry still has to go: Anders Andrae and Tomas Edler, for example, predicted in 2015 that data center electricity use would account for 8 percent of global demand in 2030 (2015). Meanwhile, a 2017 report from the International Energy Agency on *Digitalization and Energy* suggested that efficiency gains could keep energy consumption in check.

6. In actual fact, the *Node Pole* is a trademarked term held by the Swedish equivalent of Egill's organization.

7. BroadGroup. 2014. *Iceland's Competitive Advantages as a Global Data Centre Location.* London: BroadGroup; Price Waterhouse Coopers. 2007. *Benchmarking Study on Iceland as a Location for Data Centre Activity.* London: Price Waterhouse Coopers.

8. McCarthy, Smári, and Elena Saitta. 2012. *Islands of Resilience: Comparative Model for Energy, Connectivity and Jurisdiction.* Reykjavík: International Modern Media Institute.

9. It is worth noting, as my interlocutors did, the newness of Iceland's "green" appeal. One man who worked in business development at the national power company once smirked to me that "suddenly, Greenpeace are our friends." When I asked what he meant, he reminded me that Iceland is one of just nine whaling countries and has been shamed for it by environmentalists over the years. Such a shift signals the impact of the nation-branding narratives put forth by Invest in Iceland and their allies.

10. David Nye develops the concept of the "technological sublime," building on the Kantian formulation. Nye argues that the same sense of awe in the face of the incomparable that Kant attributes to encounters with nature can be generated by infrastructural achievement—for example, the Brooklyn Bridge and Erie Canal (1994). See also Larkin (2008) on this term.

11. See, for example, Hogan (2013) and Taylor (2019).

12. Here I am referring to a capacious concept, rather than a translated word. As Sæþórsdóttir, Hall, and Saarinen (2011) argue, the Icelandic *viðerni* is relatively recent, predated by *óbyggðir* (uninhabited land) and *öræfi* (unutilized, wasteland). The conception of Iceland's environment, however, as untamed, unknowable, and ultimately outside of human control is well established as of the Middle Ages.

13. Because of this, scholars have debated the question of how to classify Iceland's political dependency, with suggestions ranging from Hechter's "internal

colony" (Karlsson 1995) to Herzfeld's "cryptocolony" (Gremaud 2014) to participant in the process Osterhammel has described as "colonialism without colonies" (Oslund 2011).

14. See Hálfdanarson (2006) and Karlsson (2000).

15. Forsætisráðuneytið [Office of the Prime Minister]. 2008. *Ímynd Íslands: Styrkur, Staða og Stefna*. Reykjavík: Forsætisráðuneytið.

16. See Benediktsson, Lund, and Huijbens (2011), Sæþórsdóttir, Hall, and Saarinen (2011), and Oslund (2005).

17. In some ways, this success has been overwhelming: in 2015, 1.39 million tourists visited Iceland, far outnumbering the population of 330,000. While the tourism boom allowed Iceland to recover fast from the 2008 financial crisis, the struggle to develop policy, infrastructure, and industry to support this influx has been a contentious subject. Meanwhile, friends of mine sometimes joked about creating "Uninspired by Iceland," a parallel site that would feature traffic jams along the ring road or lines to witness relatively run-of-the-mill waterfalls.

18. Kenyan flower growers, for example, had to destroy three thousand tons of flowers and lost $3.8 million per day of the disruption.

19. The extremely successful tourism campaign "Inspired by Iceland" (dis-cussed above) was actually launched in response to Eyafjallajökull, an explicit attempt to rehabilitate Iceland's international reputation.

20. In *The Trouble with Wilderness*, William Cronon writes that "wilderness hides its unnaturalness behind a mask that is all the more beguiling because it seems so natural. As we gaze into the mirror it holds up for us, we too easily imagine that what we behold is Nature when in fact we see the reflection of our own unex-amined longings and desires" (1998, 472). Wilderness, Cronon reminds us, is not found but socially constructed, in direct relationship to Western losses and lacks.

2. THE SWITZERLAND OF BITS

1. Among these, the Progressive and Independence parties have a long and storied history in Iceland, tracing their roots back to the early twentieth century. The Social Democrats and Left-Greens each formed around 2000, the former a consolidation of four center-left political parties and the latter a rebuff of that unifying move. Newer, smaller parties routinely come into being, some hanging around for a handful of election cycles and others establishing a more durable foothold. In the 2017 elections, for example, eleven parties were listed on the bal-lot and nine had candidates elected to seats in Parliament.

2. I also draw here on Appel's deployment and extension of Maurer's concept in *The Licit Life of Capitalism: U.S. Oil in Equatorial Guinea* (2019).

3. International Modern Media Institute. 2010. "Icelandic Modern Media Initiative." http://immi.is/Icelandic_Modern_Media_Initiative.

4. Reuters. 2010. "New Legislation to Provide Exemplary Protection for Freedom of Information." June 18, 2010. https://rsf.org/en/news/new-legislation-provide-exemplary-protection-freedom-information.

5. Among these cases, *Microsoft Corp v. United States* offers an instructive flashpoint in cloud-based case law. In 2013, Microsoft was issued a warrant by the FBI for all emails and information associated with a target's account. Microsoft contested the warrant on the basis that the emails, while held by an American company, were stored at a data center in Dublin, Ireland, where the FBI had no jurisdiction. In 2014, a federal magistrate judge ruled in favor of the US government, and Microsoft appealed to the Second Circuit. In 2016, the Second Circuit overturned the lower court's ruling, and the US Department of Justice filed an appeal with the Supreme Court. The Supreme Court heard the case in 2018, but before it ruled, Congress passed the Clarifying Lawful Overseas Use of Data (CLOUD) Act, which updated the 1986 Stored Communications Act to compel US-based technology companies to turn over subpoenaed data, regardless of where that data is stored. The contentious nature and protracted resolution of the Microsoft case illustrate the openness of data sovereignty questions at the time. See Jaeger, Lin, and Grimes (2008) and Daskal (2018) for reviews of the broader legal landscape.

6. Barlow, John Perry. 2008. "On the Right to Know." Address given at the Reykjavík Digital Freedoms Conference, Reykjavík, Iceland, July 5, 2008. https://www.youtube.com/watch?v=snQrNSE1T7Y.

7. These conversations held in the early days of my fieldwork were conducted in English—facilitated by the fact that the majority of Icelanders speak English fairly fluently, and many use it regularly for work or school. If there are indeed any languages that one can simply pick up by osmosis over the course of fifteen months of fieldwork, Icelandic is definitely not one of them. I started learning Icelandic in 2013, with a tutor and university course, continued studying the language while living in Iceland from 2014 to 2015, and continue to study it today—I now speak the language comfortably, but not elegantly. Over the course of my ongoing fieldwork, the balance has shifted from English toward Icelandic, but there has always been some degree of mixture involved. I state this upfront because language matters in Iceland, yet is often downplayed in Icelandic ethnography. It is often said that to be Icelandic is to speak Icelandic, a reference to the pride that many take in their language, and a kind of conditional acceptance granted to the children of immigrants raised on the island. That said, Icelanders "of foreign origin" (*af erlendum uppruna*) have long reported that their language skills alone do not grant automatic inclusion in the polity. My language, then, first limited my access—not so much to interviews, but to the background chatter in social spaces, my sense of evolving news stories, and attunement to ambient sound. Later on, it ceased to hinder my understanding, but continues to mark me in the field.

8. See, for example: Gaedtke, Felix. 2014. "Can Iceland Become the 'Switzer-land of Data'?" *Al Jazeera,* December 30, 2014. https://www.aljazeera.com /features/2014/12/30/can-iceland-become-the-switzerland-of-data.; Khazan, Olga. 2013. "How Iceland Became a Paradise for Whistleblowers, Renegade Chess-Prodigies, and Pirates." *Quartz,* June 11, 2013. https://qz.com/93250 /how-iceland-became-a-paradise-for-whistleblowers-renegade-chess-prodigies -and-pirates.

9. As the WikiLeaks summary puts it, "The largest loans are to, effectively, Kaupthing itself" (WikiLeaks 2009, para. 13).

10. In 2010, a Constitutional Assembly was elected for the purpose of review-ing the constitution, which had largely been inherited from the Danish one. Twenty-five representatives (members of the public, including academics, jour-nalists, physicians, a pastor, and a farmer) were elected, though following com-plaints about the election process, the Supreme Court declared its results null and void. Parliament then voted to appoint the elected candidates to a Constitutional *Council,* instead. The process that followed received widespread international attention and is often termed Iceland's "crowdsourced constitution" for the Coun-cil's use of participatory methods and social media to share work with and solicit feedback from the public. The final document, presented to Parliament in July 2011, included proposals for rebalancing proportional representation in Parlia-ment, instituting a separation of church and state, introducing term limits for the prime minister and president, and declaring Iceland's natural resources public property. In October of 2012, voters voiced approval for the new constitution in a nonbinding referendum. However, blocked by opposition from the Independence and Progressive Parties, the constitution was not voted on in Parliament before the end of its term. In April 2013 these parties won a majority in government, and the constitution was not raised in Parliament again. Today, the constitution remains a point of contention, though is still backed by public support—a 2020 poll conducted by Maskína found 53.5 percent of the population in favor and 21.3 percent opposed. A popular graffiti tag around the city of Reykjavík reads "Where is the new constitution? (*Hvar er nýja stjórnarskráin?*)."

11. See Aliber and Zoega (2011) and Durrenberger and Pálsson (2015) on this history.

12. In 1984, Iceland implemented an individual transferable quota (ITQ) sys-tem for six species of demersal fish—an ecological intervention that had massive socioeconomic effects. According to the new system, each fishing vessel over ten tons was allotted a fixed percentage of the annual catch quota; new fishing ves-sels were also blocked from being licensed unless existing vessels were taken out of the fleet. While, initially, quotas could only be transferred through the sale of the boat they were attached to, in the 1990s ITQs became fully divisible, able to be bought and sold on their own. Following this intervention, the stock of fishing quotas quickly concentrated, bought out by a small number of companies

(Pálsson and Helgason 1995). This resulted in many towns "losing" their quotas and overnight finding their fishing industry shut down or operated by an out-of-town concern. The shift, then, to the ITQ system has drastically restructured fisheries on the island and created a lucrative market from which original quota holders (and early buyers) have profited massively.

13. *Útrás* means something like "outward expansion," denoting (in this case, financial) conquest and takeover.

14. International Monetary Fund. 2008. "IMF Executive Board Approves US$2.1 Billion Stand-By Arrangement for Iceland." Press Release No. 08/296, November 19, 2008. https://www.imf.org/en/News/Articles/2015/09/14/01/49/pr08296.

15. See Loftsdóttir (2012, 2019), Chartier (2011), and Ingimundarson (2010).

16. Jónsdóttir, Birgitta. 2015. "Democracy in the Digital Era." *New Internationalist,* January 1, 2015. https://newint.org/features/2015/01/01/democracy-digital-era-keynote.

17. This group notably included Progressive Party politician Sigmundur Davíð Gunnlaugsson, who parlayed its visibility into a successful run for party chairman in 2009. He would serve as prime minister of Iceland from 2013 to 2016, and in 2017 founded the so-called Center Party (*Miðflokkurinn*), in fact relatively far to Iceland's political right.

18. In June 2009, the government of Iceland reached agreements with the United Kingdom and the Netherlands to repay the money lost by IceSave. After the bill regulating the repayment was passed in Parliament, however, President Ólafur Ragnar Grímsson refused to sign it into law. He instead called for a national referendum, held in April 2011, where 59.7 percent of the population voted not to repay. In response, international discourse quickly turned on the so-called "Business Viking": "If your ancestors were marauders," wrote Roy Hattersley in *The Times,* "you're not likely to have qualms about keeping £3.6 billion of somebody else's money" (Hattersley, Roy. 2010. "May I Introduce the Bloody Minded Icelanders." *The Times,* January 8, 2010. https://www.thetimes.co.uk/article/may-i-introduce-the-bloody-minded-icelanders-lvdqcxwg2s3).

19. International Modern Media Institute. 2010. "Icelandic Modern Media Initiative." http://immi.is/Icelandic_Modern_Media_Initiative.

20. See, for example, Hardt and Negri (2004), Shirky (2008), and Dahlberg (2001).

21. CNN. 1997. "Negroponte: Internet Is Way to World Peace." November 25, 1997. http://edition.cnn.com/TECH/9711/25/internet.peace.reut/.

22. Glanville, Jo. 2008. "The Big Business of Net Censorship." *Guardian,* November 17, 2008. https://www.theguardian.com/commentisfree/2008/nov/17/censorship-internet.

23. Barmé, Geremie, and Sang Ye. 1997. "The Great Firewall of China." *Wired,* June 1, 1997. https://www.wired.com/1997/06/china-3/.

24. See, for example, Griffiths (2019) and Jiang (2012).

25. Rosenberg, Matthew, Nicole Perlroth, and David E. Sanger. 2020. "Chaos Is the Point: Russian Hackers and Trolls Grow Stealthier in 2020." *New York Times*, January 10, 2020. https://www.nytimes.com/2020/01/10/us/politics /russia-hacking-disinformation-election.html.

26. These are also practices in which many Western states are well known to participate. For example, in July 2021, the Biden administration accused the Chinese government of hacking Microsoft, and along with European Union and NATO allies, condemned the PRC for state-sponsored cybercrime around the world. Liu Pengyu, spokesman for the Chinese Embassy, responded that the United States itself regularly engages in "large-scale, organized and indiscriminate cyber-intrusion," citing the NSA's global surveillance network revealed by Edward Snowden (Kanno-Youngs, Zolan, and David E. Sanger. 2021. "U.S. Accuses China of Hacking Microsoft." *New York Times,* August 26, 2021. nytimes.com/2021/07/19/us/politics/microsoft-hacking-china-biden.html).

27. These orientations, while ostentatious in the internet era, in fact far predated this technology. The "free flow" doctrine was first deployed by the United States in the Cold War to oppose nationalist regimes of information management in the Third World and promote markets beneficial to Western media industries.

28. Clinton, Hilary Rodham. 2010. "Remarks on Internet Freedom." The Newseum, Washington, DC. January 21, 2010. https://2009-2017.state.gov /secretary/20092013clinton/rm/2010/01/135519.htm.

29. See Chun (2006), Burrell (2008), and Hawthorne (2019).

30. Cohen, Noam. 2010. "A Vision of Iceland as a Haven for Journalists." *New York Times*, February 21, 2010. https://www.nytimes.com/2010/02/22/business /media/22link.html.

31. Rampoldi, Guido. 2010. "Islanda, il paese senza bavaglio." *La Repubblica,* July 26, 2010. https://www.repubblica.it/esteri/2010/07/26/news/islanda _paese_senza_bavaglio-5830551/.

32. International Modern Media Institute. 2019. "IMMI Finally at the Cusp of Implementation." June 28, 2019. https://en.immi.is/2019/06/28/immi-at -the-cusp-of-implementation/.

33. Þingskjal 1787, 149. löggjafarþing 780. mál: upplýsingalög (útvíkkun gildissviðs o.fl.). Lög nr. 72 24. júní 2019. [Parliamentary Document 1787, 149. Parliament 780. Matter: Freedom of Information Law (expanded scope and other). Law number 72 24. June 2019]. https://www.althingi.is/altext/149/s/1787.html.

34. Þingskjal 1786, 149. löggjafarþing 493. mál: stjórnsýslulög (tjáningarfrelsi og þagnarskylda). Lög nr. 71 25. júní 2019. [Parliamentary Document 1786, 149. Parliament 493. Matter: Administrative Procedures Law (freedom of expression and confidentiality). Law number 71 25. June 2019]. https://www .althingi.is/altext/149/s/1786.html.

35. Though Iceland was technically connected by three cables at the time (one to Blaabjerg, Denmark; one to Dunnet Bay, Scotland; and one to Nuuk, Greenland), engineers often left the Greenland cable out of their assessments due to its minimal bandwidth.

36. See also Loftsdóttir and Jensen (2016).

37. These developments have been eased along by legislative changes, outside IMMI, including the 2016 addendum to Icelandic tax evasion law, specifying that the deployment of servers in Iceland does not constitute "Permanent Establishment" and thus does not require the payment of income or value added tax. An Innovation Bill was also passed in 2016, which granted an increase in tax refund ceiling for research and development, and a three-year, 25 percent tax discount for foreign specialists.

3. SOMETHING FROM NOTHING

1. *White Falcon.* 2006. "NASKEF Leadership Announces Plans for Base Downsizing." March 30, 2006. https://timarit.is/page/5836877#page/n0/mode/2up.

2. U.S. Department of State. 2006. *Agreement between the Government of the United States of America and the Government of the Republic of Iceland Regarding the Withdrawal of U.S. Forces from and the Return to Iceland of Certain Agreed Areas and Facilities in Iceland.* 06–929. September 29, 2006. https://www.state.gov/wp-content/uploads/2019/02/06-929-Iceland-DefenseCS.pdf.

3. Forsætisráðuneytið [Office of the Prime Minister]. 2006. *Declaration by the Government of Iceland Concerning New Tasks of the Icelandic Authorities on the Withdrawal of the Icelandic Defence Force.* September 26, 2006.

4. *White Falcon.* 2006. "AFN Keflavik's Weekly Call In Show 'Icebreaker': Base Leadership Answers Questions from NASKEF." March 30, 2006. https://timarit.is/page/5836880#page/n3/mode/2up.

5. Murray, Ben. 2006. "Naval Air Station Keflavik Will Be Shuttered by October." *Stars and Stripes,* May 22, 2006. https://www.stripes.com/u-s-base-in-iceland-packing-it-in-quickly-1.49314.

6. *White Falcon.* 2006. "AFN Keflavik's Weekly Call In Show 'Icebreaker': Base Leadership Answers Questions from NASKEF." March 30, 2006. https://timarit.is/page/5836880#page/n3/mode/2up.

7. At its peak the United States possessed around one thousand bases on foreign soil, the vast majority built during and after World War II. During the Cold War, the "forward strategy" pursued by the Pentagon specifically concentrated bases in Europe, closer to the USSR (Vine 2009).

8. Some historians suggest this declaration was enabled by the alliance on the table with the United States. Valur Ingimundarson, for example, has

documented how Icelandic politicians negotiated with the United States over the date they would declare a republic—and expect recognition in exchange for continued talks (2011). One of my interlocutors, Arnar, described the situation as Iceland's having declared independence under "the shield of the US."

9. See Baldursdóttir (2000), Björnsdóttir (1989), and Ingimundarson (2004).

10. In 1956, American forces were very nearly ejected following the dissolution of a previous alliance between the Conservative and Progressive Parties, and the passage of a Parliamentary resolution calling for the revision of the defense agreement with the United States. The following election, however, put the issue to bed when the Independence Party, having campaigned on fears of communism, reemerged with a majority (Whitehead 1998).

11. A key point of contention in US-Icelandic negotiations was the use of Iceland as a forward base for nuclear war. The State Department had identified Iceland as a launching station for long-range nuclear bombers as early as 1947, but the Icelandic government had always made clear its opposition to the island being used for offensive purposes. While the prime minister secured a personal assurance that Iceland would not be made a staging ground for nuclear warfare (Whitehead 1998), many Icelanders I met in Reykjanes suspected that such a promise would not be respected; some suspected that nuclear weapons had, indeed, been stored here. The NASKEF base itself was built to withstand a "near miss" but not a direct hit.

12. At the height of the Cold War the base accounted for 20 percent of Iceland's foreign currency receipts (Ingimundarson 2004, 68); from 1951 to 2006, the Iceland Defense Force provided between 2 percent and 5 percent of Iceland's GDP (Thorhallsson, Steinsson, and Kristinsson 2018).

13. In addition to the primary base on Reykjanes, the American military also operated radar stations in Höfn, Langanes, Látrar, and Straumnes, and a fuel and ammunition depot at Hvalfjörður.

14. In 1966, a cable extended to NASKEF built Iceland into the American naval sonar surveillance system SOSUS ("sound surveillance system"). As was the case with other base architecture and equipment, Icelanders were both enrolled in and excluded from this project. As the writer Guðmundur Brynjólfsson describes it, "The listening was so top-secret that it was done with gadgets that didn't exist in houses that didn't exist. At the same time, I knew the people who installed the listening cables and built those buildings, I even grinded the rock that went into the concrete used to build some of them" (Jósefsson 2015).

15. This interlocutor's ongoing engagements with Ásbrú call forth Gastón Gordillo's formulation of rubble—the material afterlife of spatial destruction that nevertheless gets picked up and put to use (2014). A distinctly subaltern category of practice, Gordillo's "rubble" is posited in contradistinction to modernist ruins that reify their histories.

16. Jón Kalman Stefánsson reflects on the experience in his novel *Fish Have No Feet* (*Fiskarnir Hafa Enga Faetur*): "Before the days of Leifur Eiríksson Air

Terminal, America was the first thing that foreign visitors saw after coming to this country, as if Iceland were a sort of 'little America', a colony of the United States. It didn't do much for our pride, our self-esteem; it was already difficult enough to think of foreign visitors having to land on Midnesheidi on a wasteland, surrounded by lava that sometimes resembles the devil's thoughts; as if Iceland were in fact little more than the American military base, jagged lava, inhospitable heaths and Keflavík, the blackest place, the wind's spoils" (2016, 345).

17. In 2016, the NASKEF checkpoints became the focal point for an art installation titled "Kwitcherbellíakin" (a deliberately weird Icelandicization of the English "Quit your belly aching"), conceived by Ásmundur Ásmundsson, Hannes Lárusson, and Tinna Gréttarsdóttir. Reflecting visually on themes of privatization, climate change, and Arctic geopolitical tensions, the artists read the checkpoint as a totem of transition, and thus a springboard for cultural critique.

18. Arnarson, Baldur. 2019. "Fjórföldun erlendra íbúa frá árinu 2011" [Fourfold increase in foreign inhabitants since 2011]. *Morgunblaðið*, July 31, 2019. https://www.mbl.is/frettir/innlent/2019/07/31/fjorfoldun_erlendra_ibua_fra _arinu_2011/.

19. The Coast Guard is Iceland's only defense agency, tasked with defending Iceland's shores and surveilling its air space, but primarily involved in search and rescue.

20. Pettersen, Trude. 2016. "U.S. Military Returns to Iceland." *Barents Observer*, February 10, 2016. https://thebarentsobserver.com/en/security /2016/02/us-military-returns-iceland.

21. Kyzer, Larissa. 2019. "One Step Too Close to Having a Military Base Again." *Iceland Review*, June 23, 2019. https://www.icelandreview.com/news /one-step-too-close-to-having-a-military-base-here-again/.

22. See Stoler (2008, 2013), Edensor (2005), and Navaro-Yashin (2012).

23. Arctera is headquartered in the United Kingdom and backed by British, American, and Icelandic investors.

24. *Víkurfréttir*. 2009. "Framkvæmdir á fullu við fimmtíu milljarða kr. gagnaver." August 29, 2009. http://www.vf.is/frettir/framkvaemdir-a-fullu-vid-fimmtiu-milljarda-kr-gagnaver/41791.

25. In 2017, tar and metal pollution were discovered in the Flugvellir area of Keflavík (a former military waste disposal site), just across the road from the base. In 2021, high levels of lead were discovered in the drinking water of Ásbrú. The same year, PCBs, mercury, lead, and uranium were found at a former US radar station at Heiðarfjall.

26. See Khalili (2018) on how the infrastructural power of the US military endures even through peacetime; see Reno (2019) on the heterogeneous afterlives of military waste.

27. See also Velkova and Brodie (2021) on "cloud ruins," the forms of ruination that digital infrastructure, itself, leaves behind.

28. As Kjartan Már Kjartansson, then mayor of Reykjanesbær described it to me, "When I was a child, there were three things here: the naval station, the airport, and the fishing industry. And that's still the way things are, except for the fish."

29. Gunnarsson, Jónas Atli. 2017. "Skuld Reykjanesbæjar var 249% af eignum" [Reykjanesbær's debt was 249% of assets]. *Kjarninn*, July 21, 2017. https://kjarninn.is/frettir/2017–07–20-skuld-reykjanesbaejar-var-249-af-eignum/.

30. *Víkurfréttir*. 2009. "Framkvæmdir á fullu við fimmtíu milljarða kr. gagnaver." August 29, 2009. http://www.vf.is/frettir/framkvaemdir-a-fullu-vid-fimmtiu-milljarda-kr-gagnaver/41791.

4. DATA CENTERS, DATA PERIPHERIES

1. Míla. "Our History." Accessed December 10, 2022. https://en.mila.is/about-mila/our-history.

2. By 2021, the data center had expanded its capacity to 40 MW and had expansions up to 80 MW planned.

3. It is important to note that the economic struggles of small towns sit uneasily with their disproportionate political power. Because of the way Iceland is divided into voting districts, votes cast in national elections by rural Icelanders effectively count more than those cast by Reykjavík residents. This dynamic heightens strain between city and countryside and complicates neat formulations of centrality and marginality.

4. See Lund and Jóhannesson (2014), and Sæþórsdóttir and Hall (2019).

5. UNGA (United Nations General Assembly). 2016. "The Promotion, Protection and Enjoyment of Human Rights on the Internet." Resolution A/HRC/32/L.20. https://www.article19.org/data/files/Internet Statement Adopted.pdf.

6. Mac, Ryan, Charlie Warzel, and Alex Kantrowitz. 2018. "Growth at Any Cost: Top Facebook Executive Defended Data Collection in 2016 Memo—and Warned That Facebook Could Get People Killed." *Buzzfeed*, March 29, 2018. https://www.buzzfeednews.com/article/ryanmac/growth-at-any-cost-top-facebook-executive-defended-data#.pue941Z6d.

7. Due to a combination of industrial development on the peninsula and power contracts promised to so-far-failed industries, Reykjanes needs to build a new energy cable if it is to keep up with demand. The proposed Suðurnesjalína, however, has become an object of dispute as stakeholders debate where (on whose land) such a line would run through and what form (underground or suspended) it would take. As of this writing, data center development has stalled out on the peninsula until the new cable can be put in place.

8. See Di Nunzio (2017) for a complementary argument focused on the concept of "inclusion." Di Nunzio argues his impoverished interlocutors in Addis Ababa are in fact well integrated into reforms, investments, and initiatives; the problem is that their position within them is fixed. As Di Nunzio writes, "*marginality's* apparent antonyms—integration, inclusion, and participation . . . are not straightforward guarantees of emancipation from poverty or subjugation" (2017, 92); in fact, they might work to reproduce the same.

9. The phenomenon of underwater data storage takes this principle to its logical end point. Not only do underwater sites, such as Microsoft's "Project Natick" experiment sited just off the Orkney Islands, allow data centers to access ambient cooling and wave energy, but they also offer the semblance, similar to that of offshore oil rigs (Appel 2019), of freeing tech companies from social responsibilities and engagement with community interests on-land.

10. See, for example, Anand, Gupta, and Appel (2018), Bennett (2005), Chu (2014), Schwenkel (2015), and Von Schnitzler (2017).

5. INSIDE OUT

1. In her work on Italian Freemasonry (2014), Lilith Mahmud makes a compelling case for ethnography conducted deliberately on the "threshold" of insider and outsider status, complicating the presumed equivalence between depth of access and depth of understanding. The positioning of this research and writing draws on her insights.

2. See A. R. E. Taylor on the "technoaesthetics" of data center white space (2017).

3. Ascierto, Rhonda. 2021. "The Insider Threat: Social Engineering Is Raising Security Risks." Uptime Institute, April 19, 2021. https://journal.uptimeinstitute.com/the-insider-threat-social-engineering-is-raising-security-risks/.

4. See also Jones (2011) on secrecy as a mode of social practice and Mahmud (2014) on the art of "discretion."

5. See Holt and Vonderau (2015) for further discussion of data centers' strategic in/visibilities.

6. Tung-Hui Hu has described the growing tendency to build "data bunkers" as reflecting a desire to materialize a sense of protection against the threat of a racialized digital Other (2015). A. R. E. Taylor, by contrast, theorizes the militarized aesthetic of a data center he calls The Fort as a marketing technique that indexes "future proofing," or the implied security of data in perpetuity (2021).

7. Industry observers have frequently remarked upon the "depeopling" of data center space. By this they typically refer to technological developments that render everyday human intervention unnecessary—"remote hands" monitoring

and management systems, artificial intelligence, and automation are all invoked in the dream of the "lights out data center," or the data center that runs without human help. Despite years of enthusiastic predictions, however, that "future data centers will be human-free," people remain an integral part of data centers' operations, tending bodily to both everyday and emergency needs. In fact, Uptime Institute standards currently dictate the presence of one to two qualified staff on site to certify Tier III and Tier IV facilities. But we might think about data center security as a site where a more practical kind of depeopling takes place. Security measures ensure that only a small number of known bodies inhabit the data center at any given time. They also, as A. R. E Taylor has argued, inherently figure these bodies as anomalies, agents of deliberate or accidental harm (2019).

8. See, for example, Hansen and Richards (2019) and Günel, Varma, and Watanabe (2020).

9. There are, in fact, two competing industry standards, those cited here from the Uptime Institute, and the TIA-492, developed by the Telecommunications Industry Association. Both bodies certify data center operations, and Aaron describes the differences between them as "subtle at best."

10. This term, and the extended metaphor of extraction, was used in Satoshi Nakamoto's introduction to Bitcoin ("Bitcoin: A Peer-to-Peer Electronic Cash System." https://bitcoin.org/bitcoin.pdf).

11. In the early 2010s, as a growing number of Bitcoin miners increased the cryptocurrency's "hashrate" and made mining more competitive, mining shifted from CPUs to GPUs (graphical processing units), which proved both faster and more efficient but still amenable to home-based operations. This phase was short-lived, however, as the first ASIC (application-specific integrated circuit) designed for cryptomining was released in 2012. Two hundred times more powerful than comparable GPU miners, but also significantly more expensive, ASIC miners marked a shift toward scaled-up rigs, running hundreds or thousands of machines in parallel—operations like those found in Icelandic data centers.

12. Mallonee, Laura. 2019. "Inside the Icelandic Facility Where Bitcoin Is Mined." *Wired*, November 3, 2019. https://www.wired.com/story/iceland-bitcoin-mining-gallery/.

13. Huang, Jon, Claire O'Neill, and Haroko Tabuchi. 2021. "Bitcoin Uses More Electricity than Many Countries: How Is That Possible?" *New York Times*, September 3, 2021. https://www.nytimes.com/interactive/2021/09/03/climate/bitcoin-carbon-footprint-electricity.html?referringSource = articleShare.

14. Billing, Mimi. 2019. "Can Iceland Handle the Repeated Boom and Bust of Cryptocurrency Mining?" *Sifted*, July 3, 2019. https://sifted.eu/articles/cryptocurrency-mining-in-iceland/.

15. See Appel (2019) and Gilberthorpe and Rajak (2016).

16. The names of most of the targeted data centers weren't reported on, surely the result of some hard-fought face saving so as not to compromise their

reputation for security. Most of their identities, however, are known or obvious to people working in and around the industry. Because revealing the open secret adds little to my argument, I choose not to name them here.

17. Seal, Mark. 2019. "The Big Bitcoin Heist." *Vanity Fair,* November 4, 2019. https://www.vanityfair.com/news/2019/11/the-big-bitcoin-heist.

18. Helgason, Stígur. 2018. "Spyrjast fyrir um 600 bitcoin-tölvur á Kína" [600 Bitcoin Computers Asked after in China]. *RÚV,* February 5, 2018. https://www.ruv.is/frett/spyrjast-fyrir-um-600-bitcoin-tolvur-i-kina.

19. Sindri Þór actually likened Bitcoin mining to marijuana growing, which he had also done: "I wanted to start Bitcoin mining because it is very similar to growing cannabis. Everything is related: electricity, air, heat, cooling systems" (Seal 2019 [see note 20]).

20. Seal, Mark. 2019. "The Big Bitcoin Heist." *Vanity Fair,* November 4, 2019. https://www.vanityfair.com/news/2019/11/the-big-bitcoin-heist.

21. Government of Iceland, Ministry of Industries and Innovation. n.d. "Energy." Accessed December 10, 2022. https://www.government.is/topics/business-and-industry/energy/#:~:text = Iceland%20is%20the%20world's%20largest,is%20less%20than%206%2C000%20kWh.

22. James Maguire (2020) describes the proliferation of anthropogenic earthquakes in the Hellisheiði region as a by-product of geothermal extraction in the Hengill volcano area.

23. Orkustofnun [National Energy Authority]. 2006. *Energy in Iceland.* Reykjavík: Orkustofnun and the Ministries of Energy and Commerce.

24. Aluminum production is an infamously "dirty" industry, with companies consistently ranking highly on lists of global corporate polluters. The industry's environmental impacts range widely, from the mining of bauxite (done primarily in Australia, Guinea, and China) to the toxic fluorides released in the smelting process.

25. Guðnason, Þorfinnur, and Andri Snær Magnason, dirs. 2009. *Dreamland.* Ground Control Productions.

26. Data center developers also position their enterprise in explicit contrast to smelting and the hold it has had. For example, Henk Wiering, president of Greenstone, a software company then pitching a data center construction project in Iceland, argued in the daily paper *Morgunblaðið,* "Iceland has a somewhat monotonous economy. The largest part of its income comes from fisheries and aluminum. All the power is going to the aluminum plants, but it is possible to use those resources considerably better—and what's more, attract projects looking for renewable energy, like data centers, to the country."

27. Toxic fluorine emissions surrounding smelters in Iceland have been a consistent source of concern. In 2012, following measured emissions exceeding safe limits near the Alcoa smelter in Reyðarfjörður, farmers in the area were warned that their hay might be poisonous. In 2016, following a production

accident at the smelter in Grundartangi, horses in the area fell sick from fluorine pollution.

28. Guðmundsson, Snæbjörn. 2019. "Hvalá fyrir Bitcoin?" [Hvalá River for Bitcoin?]. *Kjarninn,* May 14, 2019. https://kjarninn.is/skodun/2019–05–14- hvala-fyrir-bitcoin/.

29. Snæbjörn's and other's efforts, for now, seem to have been successful— thanks more to bureaucratic error than the turning of political tides. In 2019, antidam advocates discovered that the power plant had been planned using a 2002 land record, which turned out to be incorrect. While the 2002 map showed two municipalities (Ófeigsfjörður and Engjanes) bordering the power plant, there were in actual fact three (Drangavík being the third). While HS Orka had secured approval from residents of Ófeigsfjörður and Engjanes, to proceed it would also need to win the votes of Drangavík residents—the majority of whom were opposed. To avoid negotiating with the hostile municipality, HS Orka would have to reroute its planned reservoirs and conduct a new environmental impact report. At the moment at least, the company has decided this power plant is not worth the work.

30. Guðmundsson, Snæbjörn. 2019. "Hvalá fyrir Bitcoin?" [Hvalá River for Bitcoin?]. *Kjarninn,* May 14, 2019. https://kjarninn.is/skodun/2019–05–14 -hvala-fyrir-bitcoin/.

31. Magnússon, Jón Bjarki. 2015. "Vafasamar Tengingar Stærsta Gagnavers Landsins" [Suspicious Connections of the Country's Largest Data Center]. *Stundinn,* September 6, 2015. https://stundin.is/frett/vafasamar-tengingar-staersta -gagnavers-landsins/.

32. Baraniuk, Chris. 2018. "Bitcoin Energy Use in Iceland Set to Overtake Homes, Says Local Firm." *BBC,* February 12, 2018. https://www.bbc.com/news /technology-43030677.

33. Adalbjörnsson, Tryggvi. 2019. "Iceland's Data Centers Are Booming— Here's Why That May Be a Problem." *MIT Technology Review,* June 18, 2019. https://www.technologyreview.com/2019/06/18/134902/icelands-data-centers- are-booming-heres-why-thats-a-problem/.

34. Iceland Chamber of Commerce. 2019. *The Icelandic Economy: Current State, Recent Developments and Future Outlook.* Reykjavík: Iceland Chamber of Commerce.

35. Ingólfson, Birkir Blæer. 2019. "Gagnaver Nota Jafnmikla Orku og Heimilin" [Data Centers Use as Much Power as Homes]. *RÚV,* July 16, 2019. https:// www.ruv.is/frett/gagnaver-nota-jafnmikla-orku-og-heimilin.

36. Rúnarson, Sigmundur Ernir. 2022. "Ein Versta Orkunýting Heims á Ísland" [One of the Worst Energy Users in the World in Iceland]. Fréttablaðið, April 5, 2022. https://www.frettabladid.is/frettir/ein-versta-orkunyting-heims-a- islandi/.

37. Landsnet. 2019. *Afl-og Orkujöfnuður 2019–2023.* Reykjavík: Landsnet.

38. This vision of energy-as-export takes concrete form in the oft-discussed but so far undeveloped idea of building an energy cable from Iceland to Europe. Proposed by National Grid plc in the United Kingdom, and Landsvirkjun and Landsnet in Iceland, at the time of this writing the project remains in the feasibility stage and is not expected to be approved soon.

39. Skúlason, Jón Björn, and Roger Hayter. 1998. "Industrial Location as a Bargain: Iceland and the Aluminum Multinationals 1962–1994." *Geografiska Annaler, Series B, Human Geography* 80 (1): 29–48.

40. Kim, Allen, and Isabelle Gerretson. 2019. "Scientists Memorialize the First Glacier Lost to Climate Change in Iceland." CNN, July 22, 2019. https://www .cnn.com/2019/07/22/world/iceland-glacier-climage-change-trnd/index.html.

41. Scott, Michon. 2020. "2020 Arctic Air Temperatures Continue a Long-Term Warming Streak." Climate.gov, December 8, 2020. https://www.climate .gov/news-features/featured-images/2020-arctic-air-temperatures-continue-long -term-warming-streak.

42. Pedersen, Niklas Lyng. 2019. "Iceland Is the Coolest Location for Data Centers." IBM, September 23, 2019. https://www.ibm.com/blogs/nordic-msp /iceland-data-centers/.

43. Indeed, the energy debate proceeds in Iceland at an angle to many other countries' politics. Because Iceland produces an abundance of electricity, and that production is so tightly linked to industry, it is typically the more conservative parties that loudly champion the use of green energy. Left-leaning parties, while often practically pursuing very similar policies, tend to emphasize the costs of expanding production. This political nexus is explored in the 2018 film *Woman at War* (*Kona fer í Stríð*), in which a middle-aged choir director takes it upon herself to destroy electricity lines and pylons to disrupt operations at the Rio Tinto aluminum plant. The head of the national energy company, Landsvirkjun, described this perspective in the company's annual address as one of "people who hate electricity."

44. Seal, Mark. 2019. "The Big Bitcoin Heist." *Vanity Fair,* November 4, 2019. https://www.vanityfair.com/news/2019/11/the-big-bitcoin-heist.

45. Óskar's comments reflect a coalescing hierarchy in Icelandic data centers between cryptomining operations and others. Some make the link between cryptocurrency and criminal elements; others simply note the volatility of value here, as compared to the computational workload of, for example, research computing. "It's not a serious business," as one developer said. At the time of this writing, one Icelandic data center has declared its commitment to no longer hosting cryptomines.

46. Annual Report, Data Centers Iceland, 2015; Annual Report, Data Centers Iceland, 2016; Annual Report, Data Centers Iceland, 2017–18. (Documents shared with author.)

47. Landsvirkjun. 2019. *Annual Report 2019.* https://annualreport2019 .landsvirkjun.com/company/customers#Agrowingdatacentercustomerbase.

CONCLUSION

1. Masanet, Eric, Arman Shehabi, Nuoa Lei, Sarah Smith, and Jonathan Koomey. 2020. "Recalibrating Global Data Center Energy-Use Estimates." *Science* 367 (6481): 984–86.

2. See Andrae and Edler (2015). Also see: The Shift Project. 2019. "Lean ICT: Towards Digital Sobriety." March 2019. https://theshiftproject.org/wp-content /uploads/2019/03/Lean-ICT-Report_The-Shift-Project_2019.pdf.

3. Strubell, Emma, Ananya Ganesh, and Andre McCallum. 2019. "Energy and Policy Considerations for Deep Learning in NLP." Presentation at the 57th Annual Meeting of the Association for Computational Linguistics (ACL), Florence, Italy, July 2019.

4. Lawrence, Andy. 2020. "Data Center PUEs Flat Since 2013." *Uptime Institute,* April 27, 2020. https://journal.uptimeinstitute.com/data-center-pues-flat -since-2013/.

5. Guðnason, Kristinn Haukur. 2021. "Ekki áformað að byggja upp virkjanir fyrir gagnaverin" [Not contemplating building power plants for data centers]. *Fréttablaðið,* April 20, 2021. https://www.frettabladid.is/frettir/ekki-aformad -ad-byggja-upp-virkjanir-fyrir-gagnaverin/.

Bibliography

Ahronson, Kristján. 2015. *Into the Ocean: Vikings, Irish, and Environmental Change in Iceland and the North.* Toronto: University of Toronto Press.

Akese, Grace A., and Peter C. Little. 2018. "Electronic Waste and the Environmental Justice Challenge in Agbogbloshie." *Environmental Justice* 11 (2): 77–83.

Aliber, Robert Z., and Gylfi Zoega, eds. 2011. *Preludes to the Icelandic Financial Crisis.* London: Palgrave Macmillan UK.

Amoore, Louise. 2018. "Cloud Geographies: Computing, Data, Sovereignty." *Progress in Human Geography* 42 (1): 4–24.

Anand, Nikhil. 2015. "Accretion." *Fieldsights,* September 24, 2015. https://culanth.org/fieldsights/accretion.

Anand, Nikhil, Akhil Gupta, and Hannah Appel. 2018. *The Promise of Infrastructure.* Durham, NC: Duke University Press.

Andrae, Anders S. G., and Tomas Edler. 2015. "On Global Electricity Usage of Communication Technology: Trends to 2030." *Challenges* 6 (1): 117–57.

Appel, Hannah. 2019. *The Licit Life of Capitalism: U.S. Oil in Equatorial Guinea.* Durham, NC: Duke University Press.

Árnason, Arnar, Sigurjón Baldur Hafsteinsson, Tinna Grétarsdóttir, Kristinn Schramm, and Katla Kjartansdóttir. 2015. "Speeding towards the Future through the Past: Landscape, Movement, and National Identity." *Landscape Research* 40 (1): 23–38.

Assange, Julian. 2010. "The Whistleblower." Address given at the Oslo Freedom Forum, Oslo, Norway, May 18, 2010. https://oslofreedomforum.com/talks/the-whistleblower/.

Baldursdóttir, Bara. 2000. "'This Rot Spreads Like an Epidemic': Policing Adolescent Female Sexuality in Iceland During World War II." Master's thesis, University of Maryland, College Park.

Ballestero, Andrea. 2019. "The Underground as Infrastructure? Water, Figure/Ground Reversals, and Dissolution in Sardinal." In *Infrastructure, Environment, and Life in the Anthropocene*, edited by Kregg Hetherington, 17–44. Durham, NC: Duke University Press.

Barad, Karen. 2010. *Meeting the Universe Halfway: Quantum Physics and the Entanglement of Matter and Meaning*. Durham, NC: Duke University Press.

Benediktsson, Karl, Katrín Anna Lund, and Edward Huijbens. 2011. "Inspired by Eruptions? Eyjafjallajökull and Icelandic Tourism." *Mobilities* 6 (1): 77–84.

Benjamin, Ruha. 2019. *Race After Technology: Abolitionist Tools for the New Jim Code*. Boston: Polity.

Bennett, Jane. 2005. "The Agency of Assemblages and the North American Blackout." *Public Culture* 17 (3): 445–65.

Berland, Jody. 2009. *North of Empire: Essays on the Cultural Technologies of Space*. Durham, NC: Duke University Press.

Berlant, Lauren. 2016. "The Commons: Infrastructures for Troubling Times." *Environment and Planning D: Society and Space* 34 (3): 393–419.

Bernal, Victoria. 2014. *Nation as Network: Diaspora, Cyberspace & Citizenship*. Chicago: University of Chicago Press.

Bernburg, Jon Gunnar. 2015. "Overthrowing the Government: A Case Study in Protest." In *Gambling Debt: Iceland's Rise and Fall in the Global Economy*, edited by E. Paul Durrenberger and Gísli Pálsson, 63–77. Boulder: University Press of Colorado.

Bjarnason, David. 2010. "Island Connections: Icelandic Spatiality in the Wake of Worldly Linkages." *Island Studies Journal* 5 (2): 217–36.

Björnsdóttir, Inga Dóra. 1989. "Public View and Private Voices." In *The Anthropology of Iceland,* edited by Gísli Pálsson and E. Paul Durrenberger, 98–118. Iowa City: University of Iowa Press.

Blanchette, Jean-François. 2011. "A Material History of Bits." *Journal of the American Society for Information Science and Technology* 62 (6): 1042–57.

Boellstorff, Tom. 2010. "Culture of the Cloud." *Journal of Virtual Worlds Research* 2 (5): 4–9.

Bowker, Geoffrey. 1994. *Science on the Run: Information Management and Industrial Geophysics Schlumberger, 1920–1940*. Cambridge, MA: MIT Press.

Bowker, Geoffrey, and Susan Leigh Star. 2000. *Sorting Things Out: Classification and Its Consequences*. Cambridge, MA: MIT Press.

Boyer, Dominic. 2019. *Energopolitics: Wind and Power in the Anthropocene*. Durham, NC: Duke University Press.

Brayne, Sarah. 2020. *Predict and Surveil: Data, Discretion, and the Future of Policing*. Oxford: Oxford University Press.

Burrell, Jenna. 2008. "Problematic Empowerment: West African Internet Scams as Strategic Misrepresentation." *Information Technology and International Development* 4 (4): 15–30.

———. 2020. "On Half-Built Assemblages: Waiting for a Data Center in Prineville, Oregon." *Engaging Science, Technology, and Society* 6:283–305.

Byock, Jesse L. 1992. "History and the Sagas: The Effect of Nationalism." In *Sagas to Society: Comparative Approaches to Early Iceland*, edited by Gísli Pálsson, 43–59. Middlesex, England: Hisarlik Press.

Cairncross, Francis. 2001. *The Death of Distance: How the Communications Revolution Is Changing Our Lives*. Boston: Harvard Business School Press.

Carruth, Allison. 2014. "The Digital Cloud and the Micropolitics of Energy." *Public Culture* 26 (2): 339–64.

Carse, Ashley. 2014. *Beyond the Big Ditch: Politics, Ecology and Infrastructure at the Panama Canal*. Cambridge, MA: MIT Press.

Chaar-López, Iván. 2020. "Sensing Intruders: Race and the Automation of Border Control." *American Quarterly* 71 (2): 495–518.

Chakrabarty, Dipesh. 2000. *Provincializing Europe: Postcolonial Thought and Historical Difference*. Princeton, NJ: Princeton University Press.

Chan, Anita Say. 2013. *Networking Peripheries: Technological Futures and the Myth of Digital Universalism*. Cambridge, MA: MIT Press.

Chartier, Daniel. 2011. *The End of Iceland's Innocence: The Image of Iceland in the Foreign Media during the Financial Crisis*. Ottawa, ON: University of Ottawa Press.

Chu, Julie. 2014. "When Infrastructures Attack." *American Ethnologist* 41 (2): 351–57.

Chun, Wendy Hui Kyong. 2006. *Control and Freedom: Power and Paranoia in the Age of Fiber Optics*. Cambridge, MA: MIT Press.

Coleman, Gabriella. 2004. "The Political Agnosticism of Free and Open Source Software and the Inadvertent Politics of Contrast." *Anthropological Quarterly* 77 (3): 507–19.

Couldry, Nick, and Ulises A. Mejías. 2019. "Data Colonialism: Rethinking Big Data's Relation to the Contemporary Subject." *Television & New Media* 20 (4): 336–49.

Cronon, William. 1998. *The Trouble with Wilderness: Or, Getting Back to the Wrong Nature*. New York: Norton.

Cubitt, Sean, Robert Hassan, and Ingrid Volkmer. 2011. "Does Cloud Computing Have a Silver Lining?" *Media, Culture & Society* 33 (1): 149–58.

Dahlberg, Lincoln. 2001. "Democracy via Cyberspace: Mapping the Rhetorics of Three Prominent Camps." *New Media & Society* 3:187–207.

Das, Veena, and Deborah Poole. 2004. "The State and Its Margins: Comparative Ethnographies." In *Anthropology in the Margins of the State,* edited by Veena Das and Deborah Poole, 3–34. Santa Fe, NM: School for Advanced Research.

Daskal, Jennifer. 2018. "Borders and Bits." *Vanderbilt Law Review* 71 (1): 179–240.

Davidson, Peter. 2005. *The Idea of North.* London: Reaktion Books.

Dean, Jodi. 2002. *Publicity's Secret: How Technoculture Capitalizes on Democracy.* Ithaca, NY: Cornell University Press.

Denecke, Mathias. 2020. "Flows and Streams of Data: Notes on Metaphors in Digital Cultures." In *Explorations in Digital Cultures,* edited by Marcus Berkhardt, Mary Shnayien, and Katja Grashöfer, 5–18. Lüneburg, Germany: Meson Press.

Derrida, Jacques. 1996. *Archive Fever: A Freudian Impression.* Translated by Eric Prenowitz. Chicago: University of Chicago Press.

D'Ignazio, Catherine, and Lauren F. Klein. 2020. *Data Feminism.* Cambridge, MA: MIT Press.

Di Nunzio, Marco. 2017. "Marginality as a Politics of Limited Entitlements: Street Life and the Dilemma of Inclusion in Urban Ethiopia." *American Ethnologist* 44 (1): 91–103.

Donner, Jonathan. 2008. "Research Approaches to Mobile Use in the Developing World: A Review of the Literature." *Information Society* 24:140–59.

Douglas-Jones, Rachel, Antonia Walford, and Nick Seaver. 2021. "Introduction: Towards an Anthropology of Data." *Journal of the Royal Anthropological Institute* 27 (1): 9–25.

Dourish, Paul. 2017. *The Stuff of Bits: An Essay on the Materialities of Information.* Cambridge, MA: MIT Press.

Dow Schüll, Natasha. 2017. "Digital Containment and Its Discontents." *History and Anthropology* 29 (1): 42–48.

Duarte, Marisa Elena. 2017. *Network Sovereignty: Building the Internet across Indian Country.* Seattle: University of Washington Press.

Durrenberger, E. Paul. 1992. "Epidemiology of Iceland on the Brain." In *Icelandic Essays: Explorations in the Anthropology of Modern Life,* edited by E. Paul Durrenberger, 1–18. Iowa City: University of Iowa Press.

Durrenberger, E. Paul, and Gísli Pálsson. 1989. "Introduction." In *The Anthropology of Iceland,* edited by Gísli Pálsson and E. Paul Durrenberger, ix–xxiv. Iowa City: University of Iowa Press.

———. 2015. "Introduction." In *Gambling Debt: Iceland's Rise and Fall in the Global Economy,* edited by E. Paul Durrenberger and Gísli Pálsson, xiii–xxix. Boulder: University Press of Colorado.

Edensor, Tim. 2005. *Industrial Ruins: Space, Aesthetics, Materiality.* London: Bloomsbury.

Edwards, Paul. 2010. *A Vast Machine.* Cambridge, MA: MIT Press.

Ellenberger, írís. 2009. "Somewhere between 'Self' and 'Other': Colonialism in Icelandic Historical Research." In *Nordic Perspectives on Encountering Foreignness,* edited by Anne Folke Henningsen, 99–114. Turku, Finland: University of Turku Press.

Eubanks, Virginia. 2011. *Digital Dead End: Fighting for Social Justice in the Information Age.* Cambridge, MA: MIT Press.

Fennell, Catherine. 2011. "'Project Heat' and Sensory Politics in Redeveloping Chicago Public Housing." *Ethnography* 12 (1): 40–64.

Gabrys, Jennifer. 2011. *Digital Rubbish: A Natural History of Electronics.* Ann Arbor: University of Michigan Press.

Gilberthorpe, Emma, and Dinah Rajak. 2016. "The Anthropology of Extraction: Critical Perspectives on the Resource Curse." *Journal of Development Studies* 53 (2): 186–204.

Gillem, Mark L. 2007. *America Town: Building the Outposts of Empire.* Minneapolis: University of Minnesota Press.

Gilroy, Paul. 1993. *The Black Atlantic: Modernity and Double-Consciousness.* Brooklyn, NY: Verso.

Gitelman, Lisa, and Virginia Jackson. 2013. "Introduction." In *"Raw Data" Is an Oxymoron,* edited by Lisa Gitelman, 1–14. Cambridge, MA: MIT Press.

Glanz, James. 2012. "Power, Pollution and the Internet." *New York Times,* September 22, 2012. https://www.nytimes.com/2012/09/23/technology/data-centers-waste-vast-amounts-of-energy-belying-industry-image.html.

González, Roberto. 2020. *Connected: How a Mexican Village Built Its Own Cell Phone Network.* Oakland: University of California Press.

Gordillo, Gastón. 2014. *Rubble: The Afterlife of Destruction.* Durham, NC: Duke University Press.

Green, Sarah. 2005. *Notes from the Balkans: Locating Marginality and Ambiguity on the Greek-Albanian Border.* Princeton, NJ: Princeton University Press.

Gremaud, Ann-Sofie Nielsen. 2014. "Iceland as Centre and Periphery: Post-colonial and Crypto-colonial Perspectives." In *The Postcolonial North Atlantic: Iceland, Greenland and the Faroe Islands,* edited by Lill-Ann Körber and Ebbe Volquardsen, 83–104. Berlin: Berliner Beiträge zur Skandinavistik.

Gréttarsdóttir, Tinna, Ásmundur Ásmundsson, and Hannes Lárusson. 2015. "Creativity and Crisis." In *Gambling Debt: Iceland's Rise and Fall in the*

Global Economy, edited by E. Paul Durrenberger and Gísli Pálsson, 93–105. Boulder: University of Colorado Press.

Griffiths, James. 2019. *The Great Firewall of China: How to Build and Control an Alternative Version of the Internet.* London: Zed Books.

Guðmundsdóttir, Hrönn, Wim Carton, Henner Busch, and Vasna Ramasar. 2018. "Modernist Dreams and Green Sagas: The Neoliberal Politics of Iceland's Renewable Energy Economy." *Environment and Planning E: Nature and Space* 1 (4): 579–601.

Günel, Gökçe, Saiba Varma, and Chika Watanabe. 2020. "A Manifesto for Patchwork Ethnography." *Fieldsights,* June 9, 2020. https://culanth.org /fieldsights/a-manifesto-for-patchwork-ethnography.

Hálfdanarson, Guðmundur. 2000. "Iceland: A Peaceful Secession." *Scandinavian Journal of History* 25 (1–2): 87–100.

———. 2006. "Severing the Ties—Iceland's Journey from a Union with Denmark to a Nation-State." *Scandinavian Journal of History* 31 (3–4): 237–54.

———. 2011. "'The Beloved War': The Second World War and the Icelandic National Narrative." In *Nordic Narratives of the Second World War: National Historiographies Revisited,* edited by Henrik Stenius, Mirja Österberg, and Johan Östling, 79–100. Falun, Sweden: Nordic Academy Press.

Halpern, Orit. 2015. *Beautiful Data: A History of Vision and Reason Since 1945.* Durham, NC: Duke University Press.

Hansen, Rebecca, and Patricia Richards. 2019. *Harassed: Gender, Bodies, and Ethnographic Research.* Oakland: University of California Press.

Hardt, Michael, and Antonio Negri. 2004. *Multitude: Democracy in the Age of Empire.* London: Penguin Books.

Harvey, Penny, and Hannah Knox. 2015. *Roads: An Ethnography of Infrastructure and Expertise.* Ithaca, NY: Cornell University Press.

Hastrup, Kirsten. 1998. *A Place Apart: An Anthropological Study of the Icelandic World.* Oxford: Oxford University Press.

Hawthorne, Camilla A. 2019. "Dangerous Networks: Internet Regulations as Racial Border Control in Italy." In *digitalSTS,* edited by Janet Vertesi and David Ribes, 178–97. Princeton, NJ: Princeton University Press.

Herzfeld, Michael. 2009. "The Performance of Secrecy: Domesticity and Privacy in Public Spaces." *Semiotics* 175:135–62.

Höfig, Verena. 2018. "A Pre-Modern Nation? Icelanders' Ethnogenesis and Its Mythical Foundations." *Scandinavian Studies* 90 (1): 110–32.

Hogan, Mél. 2013. "Facebook Data Storage Centers as the Archive's Underbelly." *Television & New Media* 16 (1): 1–16.

———. 2018. "Big Data Ecologies." *Ephemera* 18 (3): 631–57.

Holt, Jennifer, and Patrick Vonderau. 2015. "'Where the Internet Lives': Data Centers as Cloud Infrastructure." In *Signal Traffic: Critical Studies of Media*

Infrastructures, edited by Lisa Parks and Nicole Starosielski, 71–93. Champaign: University of Illinois Press.

Hu, Tung-Hui. 2015. *A Prehistory of the Cloud.* Cambridge, MA: MIT Press.

Hunt, Dallas, and Shaun A. Stevenson. 2016. "Decolonizing Geographies of Power: Indigenous Digital Counter-Mapping Practices on Turtle Island." *Settler Colonial Studies* 7 (3): 372–92.

Ingimundarson, Valur. 2004. "Immunizing against the American Other: Racism, Nationalism, and Gender in U.S.-Icelandic Military Relations during the Cold War." *Journal of Cold War Studies* 6 (4): 65–88.

———. 2010. "'A Crisis of Affluence': The Politics of an Economic Breakdown in Iceland." *Irish Studies in International Affairs* 21:57–69.

———. 2011. *The Rebellious Ally: Iceland, the United States, and the Politics of Empire 1945–2006.* Dordrecht, The Netherlands: Republic of Letters.

International Energy Agency. 2017. *Digitalisation and Energy.* November 2017. https://www.iea.org/reports/digitalisation-and-energy.

Ísleifsson, Sumarliði, ed. 2011. *Iceland and Images of the North.* Québec City: Presses de l'Université du Québec.

Jaeger, Paul T., Jimmy Lin, and Justin M. Grimes. 2008. "Cloud Computing and Information Policy: Computing in a Policy Cloud?" *Journal of Information Technology & Politics* 5 (3): 269–83.

Jiang, Min. 2012. "Authoritarian Informationalism: China's Approach to Internet Sovereignty." *SAIS Review* 30:71–89.

Johnson, Alix. 2019a. "Data Centers as Infrastructural In-Betweens: Expanding Connections and Enduring Marginalities in Iceland." *American Ethnologist* 46 (1): 75–88.

———. 2019b. "Emplacing Data Within Imperial Histories: Imagining Iceland as Data Centers' 'Natural' Home." *Culture Machine* 18. https://culturemachine.net/vol-18-the-nature-of-data-centers/emplacing-data/.

Jones, Graham. 2011. *Trade of the Tricks: Inside the Magician's Craft.* Oakland: University of California Press.

Jónsdóttir, Sigurveig, and Helga Guðrún Johnson. 2006. *Saga Símans í 100 Ár.* Reykjavík: Síminn.

Jósefsson, Bragi Þór. 2015. *Iceland Defense Force.* Reykjavík: Crymogea.

Karlsson, Gunnar. 1995. "The Emergence of Nationalism in Iceland." In *Ethnicity and Nation Building in the Nordic World,* edited by S. Tägil, 33–62. London: Hurst & Company.

———. 2000. *The History of Iceland.* Minneapolis: University of Minnesota Press.

Kelty, Christopher. 2008. *Two Bits: The Cultural Significance of Free Software.* Durham, NC: Duke University Press.

Khalili, Laleh. 2018. "The Infrastructural Power of the Military: The Geoeconomic Role of the U.S. Army Corps of Engineers in the Arabian Peninsula." *European Journal of International Relations* 24 (4): 911–33.

Kirschenbaum, Matthew G. 2012. *Mechanisms: New Media and the Forensic Imagination*. Cambridge, MA: MIT Press.

Kittler, Friedrich. 1999 [1986]. *Gramophone, Film, Typewriter*. Stanford, CA: Stanford University Press.

Kolodny, Annette. 2012. *In Search of First Contact: The Vikings of Vinland, the Peoples of Dawnland, and the Anglo-American Anxiety of Discovery*. Durham, NC: Duke University Press.

Larkin, Brian. 2008. *Signal and Noise: Media, Infrastructure and Urban Culture in Nigeria*. Durham, NC: Duke University Press.

———. 2013. "The Politics and Poetics of Infrastructure." *Annual Review of Anthropology* 42:327–43.

Latour, Bruno. 1993. *We Have Never Been Modern*. Cambridge, MA: Harvard University Press.

Levine, Caroline. 2015. *Forms: Whole, Rhythm, Hierarchy, Network*. Princeton, NJ: Princeton University Press.

Lewis, Michael. 2011. *Boomerang: Travels in the New Third World*. New York: W. W. Norton.

Loftsdóttir, Kristín. 2011. "Negotiating White Icelandic Identity: Multiculturalism and Colonial Identity Formations." *Social Identities* 17 (1): 11–25.

———. 2012. "Colonialism at the Margins: Politics of Difference in Europe as Seen through Two Icelandic Crises." *Identities: Global Studies in Culture and Power* 19 (5): 597–615.

———. 2015. "The Exotic North: Gender, Nation Branding, and Post-Colonialism in Iceland." *NORA: Nordic Journal of Feminist and Gender Research* 23 (4): 246–60.

———. 2019. *Crisis and Coloniality at Europe's Margins: Creating Exotic Iceland*. New York: Routledge.

Loftsdóttir, Kristín, and Lars Jensen. 2016. *Whiteness and Postcolonialism in the Nordic Region: Exceptionalism, Migrant Others, and National Identities*. Farnham, UK: Ashgate.

Low, Setha. 2017. *Spatializing Culture: The Ethnography of Place and Space*. London: Routledge.

Lowe, Lisa. 2015. *The Intimacies of Four Continents*. Durham, NC: Duke University Press.

Lund, Katrín, and G. T. Jóhannesson. 2014. "Moving Places: Multiple Temporalities of a Peripheral Tourism Destination." *Scandinavian Journal of Hospitality and Tourism* 14 (4): 441–59.

Lund, Katrín Anna, Kristín Loftsdóttir, and Michael Leonard. 2017. "More than a Stopover: Analysing the Postcolonial Image of Iceland as a Gateway Destination." *Tourist Studies* 17 (2): 144–63.

Magnason, Andri Snær. 2008. *Dreamland: A Self-Help Manual for a Frightened Nation*. London: Citizen Press.

Magnússon, Sigurður Gylfi. 2010. *Wasteland with Words: A Social History of Iceland*. London: Reaktion Books.

Maguire, James. 2020. "The Temporal Politics of Anthropogenic Earthquakes: Acceleration, Anticipation, and Energy Extraction in Iceland." *Time & Society* 29 (3): 704–26.

Mahmud, Lilith. 2014. *The Brotherhood of Freemason Sisters: Gender, Secrecy, and Fraternity in Italian Masonic Lodges*. Chicago: University of Chicago Press.

Manovich, Lev. 2001. *The Language of New Media*. Cambridge, MA: MIT Press.

Mattelart, Armand. 2000. *Networking the World, 1794–2000*. Minneapolis: University of Minnesota Press.

Mattern, Shannon. 2017. *Code + Clay, Data + Dirt: Five Thousand Years of Urban Media*. Minneapolis: University of Minnesota Press.

———. 2021. *A City Is Not a Computer: Other Urban Intelligences*. Princeton, NJ: Princeton University Press.

Maurer, Bill. 1997. *Recharting the Caribbean: Land, Law and Citizenship in the British Virgin Islands*. Ann Arbor: University of Michigan Press.

———. 2008. "Re-Regulating Offshore Finance?" *Geography Compass* 2 (1): 155–75.

Mayer, Maximilian. 2019. "China's Authoritarian Internet and Digital Orientalism." In *Redesigning Organizations: Concepts for the Connected Society*, edited by Denise Feldner, 177–92. New York: Springer.

Mixa, Mar. 2009. "Once in Khaki Suits: Socioeconomical Features of the Icelandic Collapse." *Rannsóknir í Félagsvísindum* X:435–47.

Möllers, Norma. 2020. "Making Digital Territory: Cyber-Security, Techno-Nationalism, and the Moral Boundaries of the State." *Science, Technology and Human Values* 6 (1): 112–38.

Nakamura, Lisa. 2014. "'I WILL DO EVERYthing That Am Asked': Scambaiting, Digital Show-Space, and the Racial Violence of Social Media." *Journal of Visual Culture* 13 (3): 257–74.

Nalbach, Alex. 2003. "'The Software of Empire': Telegraphic News Agencies and Imperial Publicity, 1865–1914." In *Imperial Co-Histories: National Identities and the British and Colonial Press*, edited by Julie F. Coddell, 68–94. Cranbury, NJ: Associated University Presses.

Navaro-Yashin, Yael. 2012. *The Make-Believe Space: Affective Geography in a Postwar Polity*. Durham, NC: Duke University Press.

Noble, Safiya Umoja. 2018. *Algorithms of Oppression: How Search Engines Reinforce Racism*. New York: New York University Press.

Nye, David E. 1994. *American Technological Sublime*. Cambridge, MA: MIT Press.

O'Hara, Kieron. 2020. "The Contradictions of Digital Modernity." *AI & Society* 35:197–208.

O'Neil, Cathy. 2016. *Weapons of Math Destruction: How Big Data Increases Inequality and Threatens Democracy*. New York: Crown.

Oslund, Karen. 2005. "'The North Begins Inside': Imagining Iceland as Wilderness and Homeland." *Bulletin of the GHI Washington*, no. 36, 91–99.

———. 2011. *Iceland Imagined: Nature, Culture and Storytelling in the North Atlantic*. Seattle: University of Washington Press.

Pálsson, Gísli. 1995. *The Textual Life of Savants: Ethnography, Iceland, and the Linguistic Turn*. London: Routledge.

Pálsson, Gísli, and Agnar Helgason. 1995. "Figuring Fish and Measuring Men: The Individual Transferable Quota System in the Icelandic Cod Fishery." *Ocean & Coastal Management* 28 (1): 117–46.

Parikka, Jussi. 2015. *A Geology of Media*. Minneapolis: University of Minnesota Press.

Peters, John Durham. 2015. *The Marvelous Clouds: Toward a Philosophy of Environmental Media*. Chicago: University of Chicago Press.

Pickren, Graham. 2017. "The Factories of the Past Are Turning into the Data Centers of the Future." *Imaginations* 8 (2): 22–29.

Povinelli, Elizabeth A. 2006. *The Empire of Love: Toward a Theory of Intimacy, Genealogy, and Carnality*. Durham, NC: Duke University Press.

Reading, Anna, and Tanya Notley. 2015. "The Materiality of Globital Memory: Bringing the Cloud to Earth." *Continuum: Journal of Media and Cultural Studies* 29 (4): 511–21.

Reno, Joshua O. 2019. *Military Waste: The Unexpected Consequences of Permanent War Readiness*. Oakland: University of California Press.

Rheingold, Howard. 1993. *The Virtual Community: Homesteading on the Electronic Frontier*. Boston: Addison-Wesley.

Rofel, Lisa. 1999. *Other Modernities: Gendered Yearnings in China after Socialism*. Oakland: University of California Press.

Sæþórsdóttir, Anna Dóra, and C. Michael Hall. 2019. "Contested Development Paths and Rural Communities: Sustainable Energy or Sustainable Tourism in Iceland?" *Sustainability* 11 (13): 3642.

Sæþórsdóttir, Anna Dóra, C. Michael Hall, and Jarkko Saarinen. 2011. "Making Wilderness: Tourism and the History of the Wilderness Idea in Iceland." *Polar Geography* 34 (4): 249–73.

Schwenkel, Christina. 2015. "Spectacular Infrastructure and Its Breakdown in Socialist Vietnam." *American Ethnologist* 42 (3): 520–34.

Seyfrit, Carole, Thoroddur Bjarnason, and Kjartan Ólafsson. 2010. "Migration Intentions of Rural Youth in Iceland: Can a Large-Scale Development Project Stem the Tide of Out-Migration?" *Society and Natural Resources* 23 (12): 1201–15.

Shirky, Clay. 2008. *Here Comes Everybody: The Power of Organizing without Organizations*. New York: Penguin Press.

Shyrock, Andrew, and Daniel Lord Smail. 2018. "Containers: A Forum—Introduction." *History and Anthropology* 2 (1): 1–6.

Sigurðsson, Skúli. 2000. "The Dome of the World: Iceland, Doomsday Technologies, and the Cold War." In *Aspects of Arctic and Sub-Arctic History: Proceedings of the International Congress on the History of the Arctic and Sub-Arctic Region, Reykjavík, 18–21 June 1998*, edited by Ingi Sigurðsson and Jón Skaptason, 475–85. Reykjavík: University of Iceland Press.

Simmel, Georg. 1906. "The Sociology of Secrecy and of Secret Societies." *American Journal of Sociology* 11 (4): 441–98.

Starosielski, Nicole. 2015. *The Undersea Network*. Durham, NC: Duke University Press.

Stefánsson, Jón Kalman. 2016. *Fish Have No Feet*. Translated from Icelandic by Philip Roughton. London: Hachette.

Stoler, Ann Laura. 2008. "Imperial Debris: Reflections on Ruins and Ruination." *Cultural Anthropology* 23 (2): 191–219.

———. 2013. "'The Rot Remains': From Ruins to Ruination." In *Imperial Debris: On Ruins and Ruination*, edited by Ann Laura Stoler, 1–35. Durham, NC: Duke University Press.

Taylor, A. R. E. 2017. "The Technoaesthetics of Data Centre 'White Space.'" *Imaginations: Journal of Cross-Cultural Image Studies* 8 (2): 42–55. https://doi.org/10.17742/IMAGE.LD.8.2.5.

———. 2019. "The Data Center as Technological Wilderness." *Culture Machine* 18. https://culturemachine.net/vol-18-the-nature-of-data-centers/data-center-as-techno-wilderness/.

———. 2021. "Future-Proof: Bunkered Data Centres and the Selling of Ultra-Secure Cloud Storage." *Journal of the Royal Anthropological Institute* 27 (S1): 76–94.

Thorhallsson, Baldur, Sverrir Steinsson, and Thorsteinn Kristinsson. 2018. "A Theory of Shelter: Iceland's American Period (1941–2006)." *Scandinavian Journal of History* 43 (4): 539–63.

Thórisson, Skarphédinn. 1984. "The History of Reindeer in Iceland and Reindeer Study 1979–1981." *Rangifer* 4 (2): 22–38.

Thylstrup, Nanna Bonde, Daniela Agostinho, Annie Ring, Catherine D'Ignazio, and Kristin Veel. 2021. *Uncertain Archives: Critical Keywords for Big Data*. Cambridge, MA: MIT Press.

Trouillot, Michel-Rolph. 2002. "North Atlantic Universals: Analytical Fictions, 1492–1945." *South Atlantic Quarterly* 101 (4): 839–58.

Tsatsou, Panayiota. 2009. "Reconceptualising 'Time' and 'Space' in the Era of Electronic Media and Communications." *PLATFORM: Journal of Media and Communication* 1:11–32.

Tsing, Anna. 1993. *In the Realm of the Diamond Queen: Marginality in an Out-of-the-Way Place*. Princeton, NJ: Princeton University Press.

Turner, Fred. 2006. *From Counterculture to Cyberculture: Stewart Brand, the Whole Earth Network, and the Rise of Digital Utopianism.* Chicago: University of Chicago Press.

Turner, Victor W. 1971. *An Anthropological Approach to the Icelandic Saga.* London: Tavistock.

Varnelis, Kazys. 2005. "Centripetal City: The Myth of the Network." *Cabinet* 17. https://www.cabinetmagazine.org/issues/17/.

Velkova, Julia. 2019. "Data Centres as Impermanent Infrastructures." *Culture Machine* 18. https://culturemachine.net/vol-18-the-nature-of-data-centers /data-centers-as-impermanent/.

Velkova, Julia, and Patrick Brodie. 2021. "Cloud Ruins: Ericsson's Vaudreuil-Dorion Data Centre and Infrastructural Abandonment." *Information, Communication & Society* 24 (6): 869–85.

Verne, Jules. 1871. *A Journey to the Centre of the Earth.* London: Griffith & Farran.

Vine, David. 2009. *Island of Shame: The Secret History of the U.S. Military Base on Diego Garcia.* Princeton, NJ: Princeton University Press.

von Bargen, Julian, and Adam Fish. 2020. "Technoliberalism in Iceland: The Fog of Information Infrastructure." *Canadian Journal of Communication* 45 (2): 1–14.

Vonderau, Asta. 2017. "Technologies of Imagination: Locating the Cloud in Sweden's North." *Imaginations: Journal of Cross-Cultural Image Studies* 8 (2): 8–21.

Von Schnitzler, Antina. 2017. *Democracy's Infrastructure: Techno-Politics and Protest after Apartheid.* Princeton, NJ: Princeton University Press.

Walford, Antonia. 2020. "Data Aesthetics." In *Lineages and Advancements in Material Culture Studies,* edited by Timothy Carroll, Antonia Walford, and Shireen Walton, 205–17. London: Routledge.

Watts, Laura. 2019. *Energy at the End of the World: An Orkney Islands Saga.* Cambridge, MA: MIT Press.

Whitehead, Thor. 1998. *The Ally Who Came in from the Cold: A Survey of Icelandic Foreign Policy 1946–1956.* Reykjavík: University of Iceland Press.

WikiLeaks. 2009. "Financial Collapse: Confidential Exposure Analysis of 205 Companies Each Owing above EUR45M to Icelandic Bank Kaupthing, 26 Sep 2008." July 30, 2009. https://wikileaks.org/wiki/Financial_collapse: _Confidential_exposure_analysis_of_205_companies_each_owing_ above_EUR45M_to_Icelandic_bank_Kaupthing,_26_Sep_2008.

Zimmer, Zac. 2017. "Bitcoin and Potosí Silver: Historical Perspectives on Cryptocurrency." *Technology & Culture* 58:307–34.

Index

tudes of Icelanders toward, 89–90,
91–94, 106–108, 180nn10,13, 181n25;
decommissioning (2006), 88–89, 94–95;
economic impacts of, 180nn12,14;
employment at, 90–91, 106, 180n14;
history of, 89–90, 118, 179–180nn8,10–
11; and nuclear weapons, 180n11; pollution from, 181n25; repurposing, 86–87;
as ruin, 102, 104, 108, 109, 113,
180n15, 181n25. *See also* Ásbrú: The
Center of Innovation in Iceland (repurposed American military base)
NATO (North Atlantic Treaty Organization):
continued presence after NASKEF
decommissioning, 100; Iceland as member, 90, 141–142; soldiers stationed at
NASKEF, 90
nature: emphasized in promotional material
for data centers in Iceland, 30–31,
36–38, 43, 48–49, 50, 173n10; and ide-
ologies of IT, 8, 39, 43, 48–49; operation-
alized as infrastructure, 51–52; protection for its own sake, 4–5; the tourism
industry and, 42, 44, 156, *159*. *See also*
environmentalism; glaciers; volcanic
eruptions; wilderness
neoliberal reforms: banking deregulation, 64,
65; privatization of fishing industry, 64,
110, 176–177n12; privatization of
municipal holdings, 110–111
Netherlands: and the IceSave crisis, 67,
177n18; place-based pitches for data
center siting in, 32
"new communalists," 39, 43
New York Times, 34, 70–71, 74
Njarðvík, 86, 88. *See also* Reykjanesbær (consolidating the towns of Keflavík, Njarðvík,
and Hafnir)
Nordicom (*pseud.*) data center, 143
Norway: data centers in, 35; Iceland as
dependency of, 13, 40, 173–174n13;
information legislation of, 55, 61; in the
Kalmar Union, 13, 40
NSA (United States), 178n26

Oddsson, Davíð, 12, 17, 64
Okjökull glacier, 158
Omnitech (*pseud.*) data center (Blönduós):
benefits expected by township, 120–121,
131, 132; design of, 127; differentiation
from other data centers, 125; employment at, 117–118, 120, 130; infrastructure of, 125, 127; ownership of, 117,

125; and pattern of impermanence, 117–
118; siting of, 116–117, 125
Omnitech (*pseud.*) data center (Reykjanes/
NASKEF), 125
on-the-way places: overview, 24, 165; defini-
tion of, 116, 128; relationship to connectivity and marginality, 125–127, 128–
131, 132–133, 183n9
Ortelius, map of Iceland (1570), 13, *16*
Oslund, Karen, 17, 40, 41, 42, 66,
173–174n13

Pálsson, Gísli, 21, 40, 66, 171n16,
172n22
Parliament (*Alþingi*): legislative process of,
58; political parties in, 53–54, 174n1;
protests at, 65; tax breaks passed to
encourage data storage industry, 179n37.
See also IMMI (Icelandic Modern Media
Initiative)
Peters, John Durham, 165
Pickren, Graham, 126
place: making of, 15, 172n22; relationship to
data, 1, 5–6, 24–25, 165
Polarice (*pseud.*) data center in development,
123–124, 125
pollution: from aluminum smelting, 185–
186nn24,27; data center noise, 104,
113, 155; left by decommissioned military installations, 108, 181n25; from volcanic eruptions, 44–45. *See also* climate
change; environmentalism
postcolonial, as term, critiqued, 108
postcolonial sovereignty, and the Icelandic
manuscript archive, 17
Povinelli, Elizabeth A., 73
power usage effectiveness (PUE), 166
Prime Minister's Office, nation-branding
projects emphasizing nature and Icelandic character, 42
Progressive Party (*Framsóknarflokkurinn*),
54, 174n1, 176n10, 177n17,
180n10
progress narratives: of information technology (IT) and the Icelandic national narrative, 11–12, 170n12; of infrastructural
connection, 120–123, 129, 130, 132–
133, 183n8
promotional material for Iceland as data
center site: emphasis on nature in,
30–31, 36–38, 43, 48–49, 50, 173n10;
narrative work of, 3–4, 31, 43–49, 50,
51–52; video pitch, 36–37, *38*

Founded in 1893,
UNIVERSITY OF CALIFORNIA PRESS
publishes bold, progressive books and journals
on topics in the arts, humanities, social sciences,
and natural sciences—with a focus on social
justice issues—that inspire thought and action
among readers worldwide.

The UC PRESS FOUNDATION
raises funds to uphold the press's vital role
as an independent, nonprofit publisher, and
receives philanthropic support from a wide
range of individuals and institutions—and from
committed readers like you. To learn more, visit
ucpress.edu/supportus.